RECORDING IN SOCIAL WORK

Not just an administrative task

Liz O'Rourke

This edition published in Great Britain in 2010 by

The Policy Press
University of Bristol
Fourth Floor
Beacon House
Queen's Road
Bristol BS8 1QU
UK

Tel +44 (0)117 331 4054
Fax +44 (0)117 331 4093
e-mail tpp-info@bristol.ac.uk
www.policypress.co.uk

North American office:
The Policy Press
c/o International Specialized Books Services (ISBS)
920 NE 58th Avenue, Suite 300
Portland, OR 97213-3786, USA
Tel +1 503 287 3093
Fax +1 503 280 8832
e-mail info@isbs.com

British Library Cataloguing in Publication Data
A catalogue record for this book is available from the British Library.

Library of Congress Cataloging-in-Publication Data
A catalog record for this book has been requested.

ISBN 978 1 84742 756 4 paperback

Cover design by Janna Broadfoot
Front cover: image kindly supplied by www.istock.com
Printed and bound in Great Britain by Hobbs, Southampton

Contents

To Irene and James Minogue, Mum and Dad,
who are no longer here, but whose influence I better
appreciate the older I become

Acknowledgements

I should like to thank Hazel Grant and Ann Morrison, who have helped develop my own understanding of the issues in relation to recording in social work. Hazel proved an especially stimulating influence during our collaboration on the second training manual, which was written during the period of the research.

My daughters, Kathryn O'Rourke and Kerrie Allen-O'Rourke have provided keen support and much valued practical assistance where my own skills in negotiating information technology have been lacking.

A special debt of gratitude is owed to Nina Curtis who, as my secretary, typed most of the transcripts and also inputted the SPSS data. In addition, she dealt with much of the administrative follow-up during the questionnaire phase of the research. She has been diligent, conscientious and cheerful even with the more tedious aspects of the project.

My partner, Michael Clarke, who himself is a sociologist, has been a constant source of support, helping to develop my ideas at crucial stages of the project, and being available to patiently listen to the inevitable frustrations, doubts and uncertainties I experienced during the five years. I am also appreciative of his forbearance during that time, when the research had to take precedence over many aspects of our lives.

I should especially like to acknowledge the social workers who generously gave of their time to be interviewed and provided me with such rich material. I hope they enjoyed the experience of the interviews as much as I did. I am grateful to the various people in the social services departments who cooperated in this research, and who facilitated the recruitment of both interviewees and questionnaire respondents. I am also grateful to the large number of social workers who completed the questionnaires. Finally, I would like to thank the hundreds of social workers who have attended my training courses on recording over the years, and contributed to the discussions, which highlighted the issues that originally stimulated this research.

Introduction

I have been involved in training social workers in recording skills for over 12 years. This was not a conscious or calculated career decision on my part – social services departments were beginning to identify recording as a training need; there were very few people delivering it; and I was prepared to develop it as a specialist area. The need for training stemmed partly from more staff becoming involved in the recording task who had not previously contributed to client records. This was particularly the case in provider services, those actually providing care, for example, residential and day care services, where once only supervisors had recorded; now hands-on care staff were increasingly being given that responsibility. There was also growing anxiety, with the arrival of data protection (1998 Data Protection Act) and freedom of information (2000 Freedom of Information Act) legislation, that recording could leave departments vulnerable to legal challenge. A similar impetus to recording training had briefly occurred with the introduction of clients' right to access to their records in 1989 (1987 Access to Personal Files Act). The government investigation into recording practice in social services, *Recording with care* (Goldsmith and Beaver,1999a), also raised concerns over standards of practice in recording.

I initially worked with staff in provider services. I was reluctant to work with social workers because, not being qualified myself, I felt not only less credible to be doing such training, but I also doubted my ability to deliver training that would be either appropriate or relevant. Increasingly I found myself under pressure from training officers to deliver courses to social workers. And to my surprise my training was very positively received.

I was aware that, for many staff, recording is a tedious chore and one that is often seen as getting in the way of the real work, that is, the face-to-face work with the client. Indeed many staff will say that they went into caring work because they like working with people, and so they resent the paperwork, which they see as reducing the time they have with clients. I realised that if I was to make any impression with my training, I needed to encourage staff to look at this taken-for-granted activity in a completely different light.

Recording is less about writing ability and more about how we observe and listen, take in information, process it and interpret it. By requiring staff to question their assumptions about how they would describe and interpret different behaviour, I tried to get them to understand that their taken-for-granted view of reality is more problematic than they might have realised. Recording focuses on the most basic questions about how we make sense of our world and how we then describe that process to someone else. Staff are invariably motivated by their concern to act in the best interests of their clients, and they become profoundly discomfited when they consider how their recording may disadvantage those same clients.

> Workers are in a powerful position to define the reality of the caring situation in their terms, to describe it from their perspective and to believe that their professional expertise ensures their objectivity. Service users, by virtue of their very disadvantage in requiring help and support, may find it extremely difficult to put forward any alternative to the way in which their situation has been described and defined by professionals. (O'Rourke, 2002, p 1)

The more training I was doing, the more material I was developing. Eventually this led to my first published training manual, *For the record* (O'Rourke, 2002). This publication helped to establish my reputation as an 'expert' in recording skills training. It was followed in 2005 with *It's all in the record* (O'Rourke and Grant, 2005).

In 2003 social services departments were trying to implement two government initiatives, the *Single assessment process* (DH, 2002a) and *Fair access to care services* (DH, 2002b). 'Single assessment', by encouraging greater sharing of records between social services and health particularly, and 'fair access', by making more explicit the process by which decisions regarding resource allocations were made, raised the profile of recording by social workers. In addition the government was requiring departments to introduce electronic recording. Recording, having been something of a neglected issue in social services, was attracting more attention and moving further up the training agenda.

As I worked with increasing numbers of social workers, I began to identify issues that seemed to go beyond those of staff training. I began to question the assumption made by departments and myself, that problems with recording practice are solely due to skill deficiencies among workers. I found many workers who recognised good practice in recording, but felt it was difficult to always follow those principles in their own work because of the pressures they experienced. These pressures were not solely to do with volume of work or shortage of time. They were more complex and seemed to indicate contradictory tensions in the recording task itself. I began to formulate the idea of a research project investigating social workers' attitudes towards and experience of recording. I wanted to understand how they experienced these dilemmas and how they responded to them.

That research has taken over six years and involved over half the social services departments in England and Wales. This book presents the findings from that research.

Signposting

Chapter One examines the history of recording in social work and the extents to which recording, as an aspect of professional practice, has been neglected over the decades.

In Chapters Two and Three I distinguish the role of social work from the significance of the social work record in order to first establish the context of modern social work, and then locate the record within that context. To that purpose Chapter Two examines the role of the social worker in the context of late modernity, exploring both the preoccupation with risk that has come to dominate the work of social services, and the contradictory demands placed on the role of social worker. For those familiar with this literature, this may be an optional chapter. Chapter Three goes on to specifically focus on the social work record and how the ambiguities and contradictions of the social work role impact on the record. It examines how the record can be understood as a social construction, an organisational product, where it plays an increasingly important part in the ongoing regulation of individuals and organisations within the context of a risk society.

In Chapter Four I set the scene for the substantive chapters which discuss the research findings. This chapter provides a summary of the design and organisation of the research, as well as a description of the sample characteristics of both the interviewees and the questionnaire respondents. It also demonstrates the way recording remains a submerged subject for many social workers.

Chapters Five, Six and Seven present the research findings. Chapter Five introduces the demands inherent in the recording task and identifies the tensions between those demands. Chapter Six discusses the resources/constraints that impact on that task, either facilitating or obstructing the demands. Chapter Seven explores the specific dilemmas that arise as a consequence of the conflicting demands, exacerbated by the constraints.

Chapter Eight summarises the research findings and discusses their implications. It concludes with recommendations for both policy and practice.

ONE

Recording in context

Recording in social services is an everyday activity for social workers. As we shall see, although it takes up a good deal of their time, is essential to ensuring service delivery and critical in demonstrating accountability, yet it remains a curiously neglected topic in terms of research and social work education. This book explores social workers' lived experience of recording, and in so doing tries to answer why recording attracts so little attention other than the periodic castigation of social workers when poor recording is cited as evidence of their failure in another inquiry into yet one more scandal.

This first chapter explores the way in which recording has been seen as a neglected area in social work in spite of an increasing emphasis on accountability. This is followed by a description of the recording task and a discussion of its dilemmas.

In order to ensure clarity it is important to define terms from the outset. All references to 'recording' are concerned with written information concerning clients. The term 'client' was widespread for many years, but the term 'service user' is more commonly used today. Both will therefore be used in the book.

Recording: a neglected area in social work

Attitudes towards case recording are generally negative, a fact that is reflected in the literature (see, for example, *Boring records*, by Prince, 1996). Case recording is neither a topic nor an activity that usually excites great enthusiasm among social workers. Prince (1996, p 1) refers to the 'apparently, unpopular, time consuming practice of social work case recording'. She acknowledges that social workers are concerned with how far their records adequately reflect the content and quality of their communication with clients: 'The status of such "records" ... can be variously described as ephemeral, incomplete, exaggerated, controlling, therapeutic, injurious, protective, important, obligatory, useful ... ie what it actually *is* is "in the eye of the beholder"' (Prince, 1996, p 1). It is seen as a neglected area. Timms (1972, p 5) talked of 'the marked lack of enthusiasm for the topic', and noted the absence of a contemporary British text on the subject which 'seems neither noted nor mourned' (p 1). Thirty years later, Walker and Beckett (2003, p 123) state 'Recording and record keeping are probably the least addressed task faced by social workers in whatever practice context, yet they consistently appear in critical comments from joint inspections and public inquiries into deaths of clients'.

Records highlight the issue of how language is used both by service users to construct their stories and social workers to tell the service user's story. Yet the issue of language in social work literature is concerned mostly with language related to oppressive practice. Certain groups are identified as being disadvantaged in their competence in using the language of professionals, and are then not always understood or are even misrepresented (Pugh, 1996). The concern with language has also extended to a preoccupation with what is recognised as 'political correctness'. Within social services there has been a great sensitivity to the negative associations of certain words, and this has led to what may seem a very prescriptive view of language (Pugh, 1996). Despite the potential for this to extend more generally to the subject of recording, there is little evidence for this – recording remains a neglected issue. 'The conclusion is still that recording is a bureaucratic exercise designed to meet service specifications or agency requirements. In practice case notes can be either so brief and perfunctory or so long and meandering to be both lacking in utility and satisfying no one' (Walker and Beckett, 2003, p 124).

While there is a consistent theme of recording being a neglected subject throughout the literature, it will be helpful to examine the significance of recording during the period in which social work has evolved in the UK.

Development of recording in social work

In the 19th century records were concerned to provide details of charitable activities, involving one-line entries, stating name, problem and help given. The record was seen as incidental – it was important to record what was done, rather than provide an account of how and why a decision was made. Beatrice Webb, in her diary of 1886, writes of a conversation with Octavia Hill, after having argued the wisdom of writing down 'observations so as to be able to give true information, Octavia objected ... "what you wanted was action"' (Webb, 1926, cited in Kinnibrugh, 1984, p 26). Recording was no more than an administrative process.

By the 1920s recording had become part of the professional practice of social work. Sheffield (1920, p 13) argued, 'It is not too much to say that a case work agency that keeps poor records is giving ineffective or superficial treatment to clients'. This underlines the fact that recording is not just crucial as evidence for how an agency may have conducted its work, which may help determine questions of accountability or even liability, but it is also central to enabling an agency to actually function and to provide a service to its clients. Sheffield emphasises the importance of the record for continuity of work and avoiding the client having to repeat information. It is interesting that Bristol (1936) and Hamilton (1946) do not mention accountability as such in their reasons for the importance of recording. Instead, recording is valued as a way of better understanding social problems and social needs, and as a way of improving society.

Hamilton (1946) identified four purposes of recording: practice, administration, training and research. Training and research became a primary focus for recording, particularly in the form of process recording. The influence of psychoanalytic theory and the greater emphasis on personal relationships had underlined the idea of the therapeutic relationship. Recording was seen as a tool for reflecting

–

on this relationship and so the process record became an important part of social work training. According to Heywood, the process record is 'the finest teaching tool we know' (1964, p 128). Recording was undertaken as a means to provide evidence for social workers' reflection and developed practice. Others were more critical of the meandering nature of process recording (Hamilton, 1946). Timms (1972) thought it helped to develop a distorted view of recording among students, which led to long-windedness, which might be useful to the social work student but not to the practitioner. Timms (1972) argued that while social work literature acknowledged the importance of recording, its reliance on exhortation as a means to improve practice among workers was inadequate. He cites three quotations on recording practice made at different times. In 1917 Richmond commented: 'case records often show a well-made investigation and a plan formulated and carried out, but with no discoverable connection between them. Instead, at the right moment, of shutting his eyes and thinking, the worker seems to have shut his eyes and jumped' (p 348).

The Younghusband report (1959, para 606) is equally concerned at the state of social work records:

> We saw a good deal of totally inadequate recording which did not go much beyond names and addresses, as well as some well-kept and informative case papers. Both we and the field investigators frequently noted with regret the lack of an adequate social history, or of information on which to base appraisal of a situation or evaluation of progress, or on which a new worker could plan his [sic] initial approach to an individual or family. The whole concept of providing a social work service by the most appropriate officer or department breaks down if records do not contain basic data and significant facts.

The Younghusband report identified pressure of work and lack of clerical support as partly responsible for these problems, but also argued that poor records resulted from that fact that 'their value is not always recognised' (para 606). Rennison (1962) picks up this question of the value or the point of the record. She questions the actual purpose of the records in social work agencies: 'Social work records tend to amble along, full of descriptive and evaluative material but so verbose and so lacking in point or structure that reading them is tedious and unrewarding' (p 67).

Social work records are held as important and yet they are consistently criticised; it seems there is little discussion of how to improve recording other than to urge practitioners to just do better. At the same time there seems to be a lack of clarity around the purpose of the record, or what it is supposed to achieve. Timms (1972) argued for further research into the uses and potential uses of social work records. He urged that more time be given to:

> ... direct teaching about and around recording.... Records try to tell a story, sometimes of the past, but always of the present interaction

between any agency and particular clients.... Other disciplines have been concerned with how stories are adequately told, in particular history and sociology. Exploring the perspectives offered by these disciplines will help us to see the potentialities of the social work record in a new light. (p 68)

The process record dominated until the 1970s and reinforced the status of the record as a repository for the worker's thoughts and reflections. Case notes were seen as the worker's own personal aide-memoire (Hill, 1978). The Department of Health and Social Security Development Group report also described social workers using case records as private notes of their ongoing relationships with clients (HMSO, 1977), although it should be emphasised that the account of the relationship was purely from the worker's perspective and at times could include 'tendentious or pejorative material' (Kinnibrugh, 1984, p 27).

After the publication of the report into the death of Maria Colwell (HMSO, 1974) and the subsequent stream of inquires that followed the deaths of children in the care of social services during the 1980s, recording became more significant as a consistently criticised factor in many of those inquiries (Prince, 1996). Despite the increased concern of social work accountability, and the importance of the record in demonstrating that accountability, little has changed, and even as recently as the Laming Inquiry into the death of Victoria Climbié in 2003 (House of Commons, 2003), poor and inadequate recording was identified as part of an overall system failure. The relationship between recording and the management of risk will be discussed more fully in Chapter Three.

Kinnibrugh (1984, p 26) argued that there was a more fundamental ambiguity to recording which was inherent in the social work role itself: 'the ... imprecision and unsatisfactory nature of social work records is partly a reflection of the number of different purposes they serve. It may be that this in turn is a reflection of the diverse and sometimes conflicting goals which social work itself serves'. Kinnibrugh identifies the three strands of social work activity as 'casework/therapy, service delivery and social control' (p 26). The tensions between these different strands may then lead to unresolved questions about what to record, and in what detail.

On the one hand, it is recognised that recording can provide a focus for the wider uncertainties and complexities around the social work task, while on the other hand, we keep coming back to recording as basically boring – it is possible to speculate that part of the reason for the neglected status of recording is that it is seen as both complex and boring and so is left to languish. 'It should be added that social workers' general lack of interest in the subject of recording is paralleled by the lack of attention accorded to it in their professional training' (Kinnibrugh, 1984, p 28). Again the point is made that textbooks give little attention to the subject and that few courses in either the UK or the US include it in the social work training curriculum (Pinkus, 1977; Kinnibrugh, 1984). Ames (1999, p 227) states that 'For more than 50 years, social work educators have been criticised for failing to teach recording skills, yet today few texts and curricula on recording exist'.

Recording with care – Summary report (Goldsmith and Beaver, 1999b) examined standards of case recording in seven social services departments and concluded that 'case recording had been given insufficient management attention' (p 1). The report identified inconsistency in standards as one of its main findings. Management 'commitment should be explicit in recruitment, induction, training, performance appraisal, auditing, monitoring and review. In those departments where this happens, backed by random, routine auditing of case records and linked to performance appraisal, standards of recording do improve' (p 5).

Client access to records

One of the most significant concerns in relation to recording has been with the issue of access, that is, the right of service users to have access to their files, which came into force in April 1989 (1987 Access to Personal Files Act). Much of the literature was concerned with the anticipation of access (BASW, 1983; Kinnibrugh, 1984; Øvretveit, 1986), and the experience and consequences of access (Prince, 1996; Pithouse, 1998). During the 1980s there was a growing momentum to give clients the right of access to their case records. In 1983 the British Association of Social Workers (BASW) identified a set of principles for an ethical records system, together with ethical principles in the recording of client information. It recommended greater openness in sharing information with clients.

Øvretveit (1986) conducted an action research project into recording practice prior to the introduction of the right of access in 1989. He called for training on basic recording skills and standards, enabling workers to 'make objective and factual records, to present an evidential and logical basis for assessments, and to formulate objectives and decide action' (p 46). There was a concern that once clients could see their files, there would be increased challenges over what they saw in those files, calling into question the professional standards of recording practice among many social workers. He found that workers struggled to identify what was relevant to record. They had difficulty in making objective records of 'observed behaviour or of physical or material circumstances' (p 44). They were unclear as to the status of different information in their recording and they had 'difficulty in writing down what they were aiming to achieve and why' (p 45).

Although social services was the first of the public services to open its records to its users, anticipating the 1998 Data Protection Act, this later legislation, perhaps because it applied to all information systems, underlined even further to staff the importance of recorded information:

> The Data Protection Act (1998) has concentrated people's attention on how the principles of confidentiality are applied practically in the day to day work of health and social care agencies. Information Governance, arising from the Caldicott Report (1997) into information

handling in the NHS, came into care agencies in 2001. It provides a comprehensive and ethical framework for handling and sharing the highly personal information that such agencies manage. (O'Rourke and Grant, 2005, p 1)

The 2000 Freedom of Information Act has reinforced the sense that recorded information is increasingly an issue of public interest. As more information is computerised, it is leading to a greater public concern about what information is recorded and who has access to it. The spirit of these various pieces of legislation, concerned with the collection and storage of information, has encouraged a more open approach between organisations and their customers. The significance of recorded information is recognised in that social services staff are now required to routinely share certain documentation with their service users. Copies of assessments and care plans are sent to service users, and their signatures are necessary to verify that the documents are accurate accounts. Recording in recent years is being encouraged as a far more collaborative process involving the service user and the worker in a joint activity.

The recording task

Having looked at the development of recording practice and its critical evaluation over the years, we will now look at the recording task and outline the basic paperwork involved in social work recording.

Reference has already been made to the central task of assessment. This would follow a referral that might be made by the service user, someone connected with them or another professional involved in their care, for example, a general practitioner (GP). When people are in hospital there may be a referral to a hospital social worker made by the ward staff in preparation for a patient's discharge, particularly if there are concerns about the individual's capacity to manage at home. Delays in assessing such individuals and processing their discharge may lead to 'bed-blocking', for which social services are financially penalised.

The referral may be in the form of a telephone call, a written statement or much less usual these days, in person. Since the introduction of single assessment or unified assessment (Wales) in 2004 (there was considerable variation in the promptness of implementation by different social services departments) the referral should trigger a 'contact' assessment where basic information is collected and an outline identified of the problem or area of need. This information may be recorded by administrative staff with no social care experience, but who are specifically trained in undertaking 'contact' assessments. If the information collected suggests that the need requires further exploration and the service user is agreeable to being assessed, then the care manager will undertake an assessment. That assessment has to be completed and recorded within a specified time period. A copy of the assessment should be given to the service user.

The assessment is used to evaluate eligibility for services. Since the introduction of 'fair access to care services' around the same time as 'single assessment', workers have had to identify the level of risk to someone's independence each need represents. The levels of risk are: critical, substantial, moderate and low. Departments set the threshold according to their own budgetary situation. Most set their threshold to cover risks which are judged to be critical and substantial. The application of these more explicit criteria was an attempt to introduce a fairer, more consistent and transparent way of making difficult decisions about how resources should be allocated. Decisions about resource allocation depend on a written report, sometimes accompanied by the assessment, which is submitted to a manager or resource allocation panel. Once a decision has been made, the care manager is then able to commission the necessary services and draw up the care plan, which should list what services are being provided and what outcomes they are meant to achieve. Copies of the care plan are sent to both the service user and the agencies providing the services.

In addition to the assessment documentation, workers are also required to record any telephone conversations or meetings in their 'contact' or 'observation' sheets. The contact sheet is that part of the client file where the ongoing record of the various contacts or activities the worker has had are logged. These entries may vary considerably in their length and detail. It is often the contact sheets that cause the greatest problem for recording. Essentially workers know that if they have not recorded something, including an attempted telephone call to the GP, they have no evidence for that action. It may be that attempted telephone call that becomes a significant issue in a subsequent investigation.

Tensions inherent in the recording task

From the discussion so far it can be seen that that social work records have to fulfil a number of different purposes and be appropriate to various readerships. For example,

1 Certain records are routinely shared with service users. Assessments and care plans have to be written in a way the service user can understand and will feel comfortable with.
2 Records are written to ensure continuity. A case may be handled over time by a number of different practitioners, and it is crucial that information necessary to understand what has happened with an individual is clearly recorded. Often these records may be accessed in emergencies when it is vital the information can be quickly and readily understood.
3 The record, in the form of reports making a case for resource allocation, has to persuade managers that this particular service user fits the department's eligibility criteria and, without the input of services, would be at risk. Often these decisions are made by managers at panel meetings where a large number

of requests are processed at the same time. There may well be limited time to consider each individual report.

4 The record has to provide information to the agency and the direct care workers who will be working with the service user. The information should enable the agency to understand the needs of the service user and the most appropriate way to approach and work with that individual.

5 Parts of the record may well be used to provide statistical information for the department in order to provide evidence of its performance to central government. In addition to information linked to performance indicators, recorded information may also be used to help plan the shape of service delivery.

6 Ultimately the record is the evidence of the individual worker's performance. The record may well be the basis on which management identify concerns about a worker's practice. The record is the basis on which a worker may demonstrate that they have taken action when others may be denying that they have. The record provides the evidence about a complex process of decision making, which may involve inherent uncertainties and risks concerning a vulnerable service user. The record is the only evidence that will have any legal significance in the event of a complaint or investigation. The record must therefore always conform to the rules of evidence to protect both the individual worker and the department.

One of the key principles of effective writing is to write for the reader, to be aware of them and their level of understanding in judging how to communicate most appropriately. One of the biggest dilemmas in social work recording is that the record is written for various purposes and for a number of different audiences. Within the overall recording task, certain records are more routinely going to be read by some groups than others, but nevertheless many records are not specifically aimed at one readership. This uncertainty around the focus of the record gives rise to a number of dilemmas; some of these dilemmas were noted by Morrison (2001). While focusing on developing skills in recording, she still conceded:

- sometimes it appears impossible to highlight the positive aspects of a person's life and still obtain the required resources
- it is not easy to present the conflicting views of carers and service users and still respect confidentiality. (p 48)

In my training I have been concerned to emphasise key principles in good recording practice (O'Rourke, 2002; O'Rourke and Grant, 2005). These have included the following.

Person-centred recording: this encourages an approach that puts the service user at the centre of the recording process. The record should always reflect the service user's view of their situation. This does not preclude also stating the worker's view, particularly if there is a discrepancy between service user and worker, but it should be possible to hear the service user's voice in the record, including direct quotes.

Distinguishing fact and opinion: there should be a clear distinction between the status of different information, observable fact, hearsay and interpretations or opinions.

Focused recording: this requires a clear identification of the relevant information in order to understand the background and causes of the service user's areas of need, the aims of the intervention and the objectives necessary to achieve those aims. It is only in this way that there can be any meaningful evaluation of the effectiveness of that intervention.

As I was conducting my training, I was aware that workers were often very aware of these principles, but expressed frustration in that they felt they were being put in a position where it was impossible to follow them. Time pressures and volume of work were predictably the most commonly cited reasons for such frustrations, but there seemed to be other, more complex, reasons. In order to better understand these reasons I began to keep a diary. The idea was already forming of a possible research project, but the issues were still unclear . As I worked with more and more groups, certain themes began to emerge which formed the basis for further questions. An extract may serve to illustrate the rich vein of information that the diary provided. It discusses the issues raised by a group of care managers on one of my standard courses on recording skills.

1   There was a sense that the discouragement to use critical or negative language (in describing service users and their situation) had just been replaced with coded messages. Everyone knew what they meant, but they sounded more polite, even though they carried, for the workers, the same negative implications.

2   The mental health workers raised the problem of being open and honest with service users, sharing what they had recorded, which the service user may resent and then they still have to continue working with that same service user. This was particularly difficult around the decision to section (compulsory admission to psychiatric hospital).

3   The problem of the resource allocation panel came up again. One participant described it very eloquently. First you had to exaggerate all the negatives in relation to the service user in order to make a case for funding. You then had to warn the service user that they would not recognise themselves in the description (they read) and hope this did not have a negative impact on them. And then, having got your funding (and this is particularly relevant regarding a residential placement), you had to persuade a home to take the person, when they would argue that they were not equipped to cope with the level of need, given your description. You then had to persuade the home manager that the person was not as bad as you had described.

4   There were further issues around information sharing between agencies. An example was given of a patient in hospital who had been diagnosed as terminally ill, but not told, and led to believe that he would be treated/cured. He was then pronounced ready for discharge.

> The social worker went along (to the ward) to discuss discharge arrangements and the patient was confused because they thought they were going to receive treatment. The medics continued to avoid the issue and social services was blamed (and charged) for a delayed discharge.
>
> 5 There was also the issue of workers with long experience who had worked in a psychotherapeutic way and felt frustrated and resentful that they were no longer able to work like that and then narrowed their focus more deliberately: "We don't deal with the emotional issues any more. We've blotted that out, because we're not allowed to work like that any more".
>
> 6 One worker said she was uneasy about quoting a client, feeling that sometimes people would say things to you face-to-face that they may not be so comfortable with seeing written down, shared with other people.

This entry identifies the typical issues that were arising again and again in group discussions on the training courses I was delivering. It also indicates the very thoughtful and, at times, poignant examples of dilemmas around recording with which workers were struggling. I was being exposed to these issues on a regular basis. On the one hand, they were becoming very familiar; on the other, they were throwing up intractable but fascinating questions about how practitioners managed to negotiate their way through the complex demands and tensions experienced in the recording task.

Social workers are involved in the complex business of interpreting the service user's narrative, and then constructing their own narrative from that interpretation, within the framework of their understanding of the professional and organisational expectations placed on them. They are required to record using language that is accessible to service users, but which will still be credible to other professionals. Their role is largely concerned with assessing and managing risk, while still respecting the rights of individuals. Their record is the evidence on which decisions regarding resource allocation will be made, while also providing an accurate and holistic picture of the service user. In a society increasingly preoccupied by risk (Giddens, 1990; Beck, 1992), the record also provides the evidence, for audit and legal purposes, on which their own and their department's performance and liability will be judged. It is the often unpredictable and indeterminate audience of the social work record which makes record keeping such a difficult task (Hall et al, 2006).

There were clearly tensions in this task. In writing a record to be shared with the service user there may be information that is sometimes difficult or embarrassing to openly share. This dilemma might take another form, in that sometimes carers or relatives of the service user might give the worker certain key information that they did not want shared with the service user. Unable to share this information with the service user, there may well be real difficulty in explaining a decision in the copy of the assessment shared with the service user.

Another common theme (sometimes raised rather tentatively by participants on my training course) was the pressure, when making resource allocation requests, to describe the service user in the worst possible terms as far as their level of need was concerned. The workers felt that this was a highly competitive situation and that they were more likely to be successful if they emphasised the negatives, although it was acknowledged that this might be upsetting for the service user to read. Although Morrison (2001) also acknowledged this, it still seemed a controversial area to identify as a dilemma, and I found senior managers were reluctant to recognise that this occurred. If it did occur, they felt it was due to workers misunderstanding the process by which resource decisions were made.

Recording was throwing up so many seemingly intractable issues which went way beyond a simple question of skill deficiency that I began to feel it was almost inevitable that my training work should now extend into the area of research. As I became aware of the extent to which recording had been identified as a neglected area over the years, but nevertheless one that people recognised was vital, I was curious as to how far recording did provide a focus for the ambiguities of the social work role itself. While Kinnibrugh (1984) had identified the tensions between the therapeutic, service delivery and social control aspects of the role, I felt that, although these were still relevant, the situation was more complex. Recording, far from being boring, seemed more like a hot potato that people were eager to avoid, or a can of worms that was potentially too messy to explore. Either way successive generations of social work teachers, trainers and managers have been reluctant to address it.

I decided to focus primarily on the tensions inherent in the recording task and specifically on the problems posed by the different readerships of the record as well as examining social workers' more general attitudes towards recording. I wanted to understand why this important, but neglected, issue had proved so difficult for so long. Why was it possible to read decades of comments on poor recording practice and so little understanding of why generations of workers still struggled with this task?

TWO

Social work, risk and modernity

This chapter provides a brief discussion of the characteristics of society in late modernity, the dominance of heightened perceptions of risk and the development of the reflexive self in terms of the expectations that are placed on experts, and how that has shaped our view of social workers. It then looks at the decline of the welfare state and the rise of neoliberalism and the consequences for social work. There is an extended discussion of the introduction of the 1990 NHS and Community Care Act and its consequences, as this had a profound impact on the organisation of adult social services. The chapter concludes by examining the tensions in the role of social workers or, as they are now more often referred to in adult services, care managers, and the extent to which those tensions have increased our tendency to trust or blame social workers in late modernity.

Late modernity and risk

'Late modernity' is the term used to describe the current phase of development of modern institutions in western societies. Giddens (1991) characterises modernity as a period in which reliance on tradition for organising social life has declined and the pace of change has accelerated. Late modernity, it is argued, has reorganised time and space and allowed social relations to be recombined across wide space and time dimensions. Increasingly we live in a world that is more dominated by global influences, but also one in which we are, it is argued, more reflexive as individuals. We are bombarded by vast flows of information and aware of more possibilities in terms of how we might live our lives than previous generations, and so the self is reflexively made in a diversity of choice and uncertainty, where 'the cultural codes used to negotiate these decisions become more and more complex and variegated' (Szerszynski et al, 1996, p 12). That uncertainty arises not only from such a variety of possibilities, but also from the unpredictability that confronts us, despite our dependence on ever-increasing expert knowledge.

Modernist thinking has been dominated with ideas of progress based on the assumption that rationality and scientific and technical knowledge can be relied on to gain ever more control over our environment and our lives (Webb, 2006). The ideas formulated in the Enlightenment heralded growing certainty of understanding of our world, based on secure and accumulated knowledge (Giddens, 1991). While scientific and technical advances have had an enormous impact, there is a growing awareness of their limitations. Indeed science itself, it is argued, is not an orderly process of growing certainty, but one of regular crises and revisions (Kuhn, 1962). The scientific enterprise depends fundamentally on radical doubt (Giddens, 1991). Scientific uncertainty and the tendency for experts to contradict one another, as well as the realisation that progress often has unanticipated costs, has undermined our deference to expert knowledge (Giddens, 1991; Beck, 1992; Lupton, 1999). The more we acquire knowledge, the more uncertain we become (Stalker, 2003).

While it can be argued that we have become more sceptical of expert knowledge, we still turn to it in order to try and manage the uncertainty it has generated. Late modernity has become dominated by preoccupations with risk, the calculation of uncertainty in order to avoid potential hazards (Giddens, 1991; Beck, 1992). While Beck is concerned about increases in actual risks, which he argues has led to a greater awareness of human responsibility for both creating and controlling risk, Giddens believes that it is our reflexivity, our sense of responsibility for constructing ourselves and our world, that has led to a greater focus on risk (Horlicks-Jones, 2005). For Beck, reflexive modernity means self-confrontation with the effects of a risk society. For Beck and Giddens, reflexive modernity is an ongoing process of self-evaluation, in which we are all engaged, trying to anticipate the outcomes of different courses of action, trying to avoid the risks and hazards, which an error of judgement may precipitate.

This leads us to what Giddens refers to as 'life planning', the 'strategic adoption of lifestyle options, organised in terms of the individual's projected lifespan, and normally focused through the notion of risk' (Giddens, 1991, p 243). 'The do-it-yourself biography is always a "risk biography", indeed a "tightrope biography", a state of permanent (partly overt, partly concealed) endangerment ... the do-it-yourself biography can swiftly become the breakdown biography' (Beck and Beck-Gernsheim, 1996, pp 25-6). Life planning is therefore always precarious and may become especially problematic at times of 'fateful moments' (Giddens, 1991), which are critical points in our lives when decisions are made, or actions taken, which may have profound consequences for our subsequent biography. As Webb argues, 'For those who fail new forms of technical planning, calculation and expert mediation, such as social work, are introduced to structure identity and develop systems of competence and efficiency' (2006, p 36).

It is acknowledged that a focus on 'life planning' presents an individualistic theory of the reflexive self that downplays the structural and political causes of the problems experienced by individuals. Social problems become individualised rather than considered as the consequences of relations between individuals and social structures (Kemshall, 2002). It is argued that many clients of welfare services and others subject to structural inequality are unable to exercise such 'choices' because they 'lack the resources and techniques with which to engage in the project of self-reflexivity' (Lupton, 1999, p 114). Lash (1994) points to access to the new information and communication structures, which are generated by expert systems as an important determinant of whether someone becomes a 'reflexive winner' or 'reflexive loser'.

Social work in late modernity

Social work draws on expert knowledge and claims its authority on the basis of that knowledge, but expert knowledge is increasingly contested (Giddens, 1991). We look to experts to provide guidance in the choices we make and yet we are increasingly sceptical of expert opinion. At fateful moments we may turn or be referred to social workers in the expectation that they will provide expert support. As such, social work can be seen as part of the rise of expert mediation, which is concerned to support people in the negotiation of the more complex personal relationships characterising late modernity. Giddens (1991, p 6) talks of the pure relationship as one that depends no longer on the trust established through kinship, social duty or traditional obligation, but one that 'exists solely for whatever rewards that relationship as such can deliver'. The pure relationship, according to Giddens, depends on intimacy, trust and commitment and is part of the reflexive project of the self. The more prevalent the pure relationship, the more we need to become accomplished in understanding ourselves in order to communicate emotionally with others (Giddens, 1992). Webb (2006, p 37) argues that 'the pure relationship has become central to the way people organise their intimate lives and also the way that experts such as social workers attempt to maintain or reconstruct them'.

Furthermore social work has become significant in what Giddens (1991) refers to as the 'sequestration of experience', that is, the separation or concealment from everyday life of existentially troublesome experiences connected with birth, sexuality, madness and death. Ferguson (2001, p 43) argues that these were hidden 'within the walls of institutions such as clinics and hospitals'. He goes on to argue that it is the 'return of the repressed' since the 1970s which has given rise to fundamental moral crises around self-actualisation and life planning and which are now the defining feature of social work. The return of the 'repressed' has also heightened concerns around risk, as those formerly incarcerated in institutions are now living in the community, giving rise to questions about their safety and that of the public.

A further shift discernible in late modernity is the extent to which the process of ageing in late modernity is also being redefined. Retirement is no longer seen as a process of decline and inevitable infirmity. Chronological age is 'discredited as an indicator of inevitable age norms and life styles' (Bury, 1994, p 10). Phillips (1996) argues that social work should take on this more positive view of ageing, and not foster the dependency inherent in more traditional models of practice, although there is an acknowledgement that, as people live longer, with significant increases in those over 85 (Kemshall, 2002), priority will be given to those most at risk, concentrated in what Laslett (1994) has termed the 'fourth age'.

While Giddens discusses 'life planning' as a process involving individuals in making successive choices which result in a certain 'lifestyle', thus suggesting liberation from traditional ways of living, it is also possible to view the seemingly countless possibilities as still bounded by more subtle forms of social control.

Governmentality is the concept developed by Foucault (1991) to explain the form of social regulation and control that began to emerge in 16th-century Europe. Foucault saw power operating at a micro, local and covert level 'rather like a colour dye diffused through the entire social structure and embedded in daily practices' (Turner, 1997, p xii). Governmentality is concerned with the regulation of everyday life, with individuals actively involved in their own self-governance. The choices that people make are regulated through this more insidious form of control, and so the distinction between successful and unsuccessful choices is only made meaningful through this process.

Social work is part of the regulatory framework of modern society. Regulation is a more explicit form of social control in late modernity, concerned with order, standards, conduct, calculation and rule following. Regulation is a response to uncertainty. It attempts to maintain order and manage uncertainty, and is a regime of risk management carried out by expert mediating systems on behalf of the state or some other institution. Beck (1995) has predicted a legitimation crisis, which will be suffered by bureaucracies unable to control the escalation of risks and the resulting loss in public confidence.

Social work is increasingly expected to regulate risk (Parton, 1996; Kemshall, 2002; Stalker, 2003; Webb, 2006). 'Assessment of risk and its management has become a dominant theme in social work in the past decade ... the concern with risk assessment has been a reaction to a wider demand for greater public accountability of professionals in all spheres' (Walker and Beckett, 2003, p 37). The authority of social work may be undermined if it is not seen to be effectively discharging its responsibility to manage risk among the most vulnerable in our society. In this context, it has an explicit authority in terms of its legal powers, but social work also reinforces those more subtle forms of control, which are concerned with what constitutes socially and morally acceptable behaviour. In this sense social work can be seen as one of 'the institutions of normative coercion' (Turner, 1992, p xiv). These institutions exercise a form of surveillance over everyday life and a moral authority by providing explanations and solutions to the problems experienced by individuals. Their 'coercive character is often disguised and masked by their normative involvement in the troubles and problems of individuals. They are coercive, normative, and also voluntary' (Turner, 1997, p xiv). Horlicks-Jones (2005) has argued that the idea of risk itself is used as a set of disciplinary techniques to shape individual behaviour and engender forms of self-discipline. Risk, from a Foucauldian perspective, is a 'moral technology' (Ewald, 1991).

Social work occupies an uneasy space between, on the one hand, a source of expert knowledge and support, which may assist people in making important and potentially empowering decisions about their lives (Phillips, 1996; Ferguson, 2001), while on the other, a means to control and regulate how we are expected to behave in the most personal and intimate aspects of everyday life. At the same time it is charged with the responsibility for managing risk to ensure that people make appropriate decisions that do not expose themselves or others to unacceptable levels of risk. Social work began and continues to exist in a state of ambiguity and tension, expected to exercise both compassion and control, mediating between the state and the individual, the public and the private (Clarke, 1993; Jordan, 1997).

The development of social work in the UK

The establishment in 1869 of the Society for Organising Charitable Relief and Repressing Mendicity was for the purpose of encouraging the impoverished classes to better themselves and their situation by greater self-discipline (Hopkins, 1996). Charitable relief was administered by volunteers according to what they saw as rational and scientifically informed judgements: 'They investigated each case systematically and distinguished between the helpable and those who were not' (Seed, 1973, p 40). Woodroofe (1966) describes the forms and report books issued in which confidential records of each case were written. 'The casework assessment method involved the completion of administrative enquiries, the preparation of proposals based on the evidence of "witnesses interviewed" and the submission of the proposals to the committee for the deployment of charitable funds' (Hopkins, 1996, p 23). It is interesting to note how closely this resembles the care management process today. Similarly, caseworkers also acted as brokers, knowledgeable about sources of charitable funding and the eligibility criteria they operated. Moral support was provided through the development of the 'beneficient relationship' but the main preoccupation was with efficient administration. This early phase in the history of social work was more explicitly concerned with the regulation of socially and morally acceptable behaviour, although its emphasis on self-improvement is redolent of aspects of reflexive modernity's concern with the self as a project.

While social work had originally developed as a philanthropic activity, it became increasingly professionalised during the 20th century and was carried out by the state or by voluntary bodies on the state's behalf. The hardship suffered by many during the 1930s Depressions demonstrated the worst effects of the free market, and led to calls for more state intervention at both the economic and social welfare level. State control, introduced during the Second World War, provided the basis for the Beveridge report (Beveridge, 1948) and the further extension of state powers. The welfare state was created, providing a system of social security which guaranteed a minimum level of health and social services.

The Curtis report (HMSO, 1946) heralded the establishment of local authority children's departments as part of the overall plan for post-war reconstruction. Social work during the 1950s became increasingly dominated by ideas derived from psychoanalytic theory that led to psychodynamic casework (Webb, 2006). The belief was that the emotional and psychological problems of people could be addressed through a therapeutic relationship. Psychosocial well-being was the objective. The emotionally and psychologically well-adjusted individual would be a more effective socially functioning individual. This was concerned with more subtle forms of control and influence that attempted, according to some (Broadie,

1978), to manipulate and pathologise disadvantaged people. Psychodynamic casework was a more active and in-depth engagement with the client, which focused less on practical problems and more on understanding the individual. It was therefore more time consuming and more expensive and, as demand grew for social work services, concerns about rising costs became more pressing.

In 1974 the Seebohm report (HMSO, 1968) led to a fundamental reorganisation of social services. Generic social work departments were introduced, combining children's and adult services under one organisation. This was seen as a more rational way of managing social work. The emphasis was increasingly on effective resource management, bureaucratic efficiency and legislative responsibilities (Webb, 2006). Therapeutic work declined and task-centred, crisis intervention approaches took centre stage. The approach was short-term and focused on changing maladaptive behaviour according to learning theory principles. The 1970s saw a brief rise in radical social work, influenced by materialist socialist ideas, as well as emancipatory politics, which focused on representing and promoting the rights of discriminated groups (Taylor, 1993). This gave rise to community-focused approaches. By the end of the 1970s, however, increasing concerns about rising costs, and doubts over the efficiency of public sector services, together with political suspicion in the case of social services, gave rise to the neoliberal agenda.

The decline of the welfare state, the rise of neoliberalism and the introduction of community care

While the welfare state had its beginnings in the social reforms introduced in the early 20th century, the Keynesian welfare state was introduced at the end of the Second World War in an attempt to protect people from the vagaries of economic instability and the injustice of social inequality. Despite such optimistic ideals, the commitment to central planning and universal provision began to falter with the economic turmoil of the 1970s. The Conservative (Tory) government of 1979 saw curbing inflation rather than full employment as its priority (Hopkins, 1996). As the welfare state was seen to be the fastest growing sector of public expenditure, and was also assumed to be the least efficient, it became a prime target in their strategy. State welfare was also seen to encourage underclass dependency that undermined self-reliance (Marsland, 1996). Market discipline was introduced in the belief that only the market principle could deliver efficiency and effectiveness in public sector provision. Discouraging reliance on the welfare state and thus 'welfare dependency' was seen to promote individual initiative. The criticisms levelled at social services were not that different from other public sector bodies and were as follows:

1   Without the incentive of the market either to maximise efficiency or otherwise go out of business, the delivery of public sector services would never be cost-effective.

2 Social services were dominated by the way its provider services were organised. The services were seen to exist for themselves rather than meet the needs of clients. Clients were expected to fit in with the menu of services on offer.

3 Social services were not close enough to their customers and so did not sufficiently understand their needs. This has always remained a particularly troublesome issue, in that identifying the 'customer' in social services is often problematic. Is it the client or those who may feel responsible for the client? In the case of mental health services more complicated issues of control confuse even further the issue of who is the customer.

4 Social services were seen as not sufficiently accountable for what they did and how they did it.

In adult social services these criticisms led to the Griffiths report in 1988 (DHSS, 1988) and the introduction of the NHS and Community Care Act in 1990, at which point, some would argue, social work began to disappear (Hadley and Clough, 1996; Jones, 1999). The 1990 NHS and Community Care Act fundamentally changed the operation of social services departments, making them enablers rather than providers, coordinating and purchasing care rather than delivering services directly.

A mixed economy of care was created, where providers of services would be from the private and voluntary sector as well as the public sector. The government was concerned to increase the market share of the independent sector and required that 85% of the transition funds transferred to local authorities with the introduction of community care should be spent in the independent sector.

With the introduction of community care social workers became care managers and were now expected to be 'needs-led' rather than 'service-led' in their approach to assessments. Care managers were not necessarily qualified social workers. Rather than fitting clients into particular services, there was supposed to be a more imaginative response, appropriate to the particular individual need. 'Consumer choice replaced equity as the tenet by which service was judged' (Hopkins, 1996, p 30). Care managers were expected to design 'care packages' around the client, while at the same time ensuring the most cost-effective arrangement. Budgets were devolved down to care management teams, and care managers found themselves commissioning and contracting services with a whole range of different service providers. Care managers were not expected to have any involvement with the client beyond assessing and setting up the package of care. This was to be completed as speedily as possible in order to close the case and move on to the next one. Care managers were not expected to hold cases for long periods. Recording therefore became far more focused on recording the identified needs and the process of commissioning services.

Harris (2003) contrasts the rhetoric of community care with the reality, by distinguishing between 'marketisation' and 'managerialism'. Marketisation is concerned with the demand side of the market, where the market rationale is driven by consumer choice. This should ensure 'needs-led' individually tailored services, with the freedom to purchase the most appropriate services. This also presumes choice over the style of service delivery. Indeed 'choice' and promoting 'independence' were key principles behind the introduction of community care. Managerialism, on the other hand, is concerned with the supply side of the market, where the market rationale is driven by state control. That state control is dominated by limited budgets and the pressure to ensure available services for large numbers of clients. This led to set lists of contracted services and laid down specifications for service operation. Harris argued that community care was inevitably going to conform more to the managerialist model.

The experience of care managers was that despite the promise of being able to devise individual care packages, increasing pressure on budgets drove them further into having to work within block contracts, where a limited supply of providers were identified and they were to be used, regardless of whether that was the most appropriate choice for an individual client. The pressure on budgets led to increases in individual workload, redistributing more work to lower-paid workers, raised charges for service users and a greater reliance on stricter eligibility criteria for entrance to service provision. Not much had changed for the client. Care managers found themselves increasingly operating as 'gate-keepers, rationing ever more scarce resources' (Harris, 2003).

The initial focus on cost savings, management by objectives and budgetary controls was followed by increasing attempts to control the processes and outcomes of service through quality control and performance measures. Contractual accountability resulted in 'increased monitoring, regulation and inspection' (Phillips, 1996, p 138). Relying on market mechanisms alone had not brought the results anticipated by the Tory government, although even Margaret Thatcher had established a curious dialectic of regulation. As public sector industries were deregulated or privatised during the 1980s, corresponding agencies of regulation were set up, so allowing 'enterprise to flourish within a structure of due process' (Webb, 2006, p 59).

With the advent of New Labour in 1997, Harris (2003) argues that New Labour's strategy was to modernise the social work business. It exerted ever tighter and more centralised regulation of the work of the public sector through complex inspection and audit mechanisms (Power, 1997), together with pervasive surveillance through performance measures, targets and league tables (Harris, 2003). The work of social services was becoming ever more accountable in terms of efficiency, while its effectiveness was increasingly being measured in terms of its capacity to manage risk.

Risk regulation and neoliberal market economics have been interdependent in shaping management practice in social services, relying on technical rationality, planning and calculation to manage risk (Webb, 2006). Howe (1991) argues that by expanding the scope of rules, routines and procedures, managers have diminished professional discretion. The issue of discretion is nevertheless a complex one and will be explored further in the next chapter. New public sector management is concerned with capturing and controlling knowledge to avoid risk and ensure greater organisational efficiency. That knowledge relies on ever more sophisticated systems for collecting information, including electronic case recording, which will be discussed in the next chapter.

Inevitably reliance on performance measures that can be counted encourages a quantitative rather than a qualitative approach to performance management. So the number of activities can instantly be known, but the quality of work requires further investigation. Even when 'quality standards' are implemented, such as that all service users should receive a copy of their assessment and, where services are arranged, a copy of their care plan, the standards measured are purely in terms of compliance. So the service user may receive the worst possible assessment and care plan, but nevertheless the standard has been met. There is a discrepancy between the rhetoric and the reality in community care and care management leading to ambiguities and tensions in the roles of those involved. These are explored in the next section.

Ambiguities and tensions in the care manager's role

Postle (2002, p 336) indicated that her review of the research on care management revealed 'a picture of a generally demoralized and dissatisfied workforce at practitioner level, with few indications of optimism about their work'. The National Institute for Social Work study identified that role ambiguity, which exposed staff to conflicting demands, was a significant source of dissatisfaction (Balloch et al, 1999).

Practitioners identified a 'honeymoon' period after the 1990 NHS and Community Care Act was introduced, during which they were able to be more 'needs-led' in their approach to assessments and care planning, but this was short-lived as budget cut-backs resulted in reduced resources (Postle, 2002). Increasing pressure of demand has led to faster and more reductionist work processes, resulting in less time to carry out assessments properly. Webb (2006) refers to a 'case closing culture' where workers are under pressure to close cases prematurely in order to demonstrate high volume turnover in order to meet performance targets. 'The disadvantage and resultant incongruity of rapid throughput is that there is a focus on risk and a fear of censure if anything should go wrong while, concurrently, care managers operate in a way in which risk is less likely to be ascertained and managed' (Postle, 2002, p 345). Social workers feel caught in an impossible dilemma, expected to work according to certain principles of practice, such as promoting choice, which are espoused in government policies, but without the resources to implement those same policies. What has 'emerged is not a system characterised by choice and diversity but one dominated by rationality and hierarchy' (Powell, 2001, p 21).

Bourdieu (1998, p 2) comments ruefully on the situation, 'I think that the left hand of the state has the sense that the right hand no longer knows, or worse, no longer really wants to know what the left hand does. In any case it does not want to pay for it'. He regards it as inevitable that social workers will feel undermined and betrayed when they are sent into the front line to try and compensate for the inadequacies of the market without the means to do their job.

Care management devolved budgetary responsibility to cost centres. The argument was that this would empower those making decisions over resource allocations, and ensure those decisions were made closest to the point of service delivery. As Clarke (1996, p 59) has argued, this has only served 'to constrain professional autonomy by having professionals internalise budgetary disciplines'. This is likely to increase the pressure on professionals to couch their decisions in terms of managerial imperatives such as cost and rational efficiency, and discourage a position of advocacy on behalf of service users' needs.

Determining the eligibility of service users for service provision has become a central part of the assessment process. While the rhetoric suggests that this is about ensuring that services are appropriately prioritised to those most in need, 'such prioritization necessitated gatekeeping and targeting … assessment itself became a major tool for rationing access' (Kemshall, 2002, p 78). The Department of Health guidance to practitioners on assessment (HMSO, 1991) emphasised the importance of risk assessment but acknowledged that judgements might vary over prioritising risk to independence and risk to physical well-being. The more recent Department of Health guidance on eligibility (DH, 2002b) has emphasised risk to independence, but when prioritising between someone whose physical well-being is of concern and someone whose independence is jeopardised, scarce resources are likely to be allocated to the former. Richards (2000) has argued that social workers, in order to ensure low-level cases are prioritised, can emphasise possible risks in terms of harm to the individual or the community.

The tension between risk and independence may also have to be balanced in other ways. Mental health work underlies this most obviously. Social services are concerned with the care of vulnerable adults, who may be at risk as a consequence of their disability or their infirmity. Decisions over how to manage the element of risk have also to be weighed against client choice and the concern to promote and maintain independence.

Work within adult services may be made even more difficult by virtue of the calculation of the risk being made quite differently by the service users and those who either care for them or who have some responsibility or concern for them. It was acknowledged in the Department of Health guidance *Independence, choice and risk* that:

> The possibility of risk is an inevitable consequence of empowered people taking decisions about their own lives. But the issues around choice and risk are complex, and when things go wrong people often look for someone to blame, not wanting to take responsibility for themselves. (DH, 2007, p 8)

Typically workers may find themselves having to make decisions regarding the appropriate response to an older person who is no longer able to care for themselves, perhaps with a degree of cognitive impairment in relation to certain decisions, but who is still adamant that they wish to remain living independently. The family, not to mention neighbours, on the other hand, may have very different ideas, motivated by anxiety and a concern to protect. The social services record may be vital in detailing how the risks are calculated in that situation.

Individuals have the right not to have their independence unnecessarily restricted due to other people's anxieties about them: imposing restrictions may well compromise their quality of life (Lawson, 1996). Kemshall (2002) argues that community care and the calculation of risk are inextricably intertwined as community provision, compared with residential provision, inevitably entails higher levels of risk. 'In an era of increased litigation and accountability for risk decisions, it is perhaps not surprising that the subsequent development of community care has resulted in a growing emphasis upon formalized risk policies and frameworks for the assessment of risk' (Kemshall, 2002, p 79). Risk in care management can therefore be seen as a monitoring tool and as a mechanism for accountability, as well as a rationing device.

Douglas (1992) identifies the term 'risk' as a 'forensic resource' used to investigate what has gone wrong and to allocate blame and liability. Kemshall (2002) underlines this forensic function in social services, arguing that the avoidance of litigation, public blame and vilification has become a central preoccupation. This returns us to the issue of trust in experts and the way that a preoccupation with risk has eroded public trust in professionals who work with risk and in the institutions they represent (Giddens, 1994). This has had particular consequences for the practice of social work, where attempts to ensure trust have actually undermined the trusting relationship at the heart of social work and added further tensions to the social work role.

Trust and blame in social work

Trust has a peculiar significance in social work. For clients to engage with social workers they not only have to trust in the professional knowledge and competence of those practitioners, but also in their commitment and concern. Smith (2001) distinguishes between trust and confidence. She argues that while we have confidence or not in expert knowledge and competence, which depends on someone's capacity to do their job according to recognised standards, trust is concerned more with personal and organisational integrity. Smith argues that much of the emphasis on performance measures and audit systems in social services is concerned with confidence. She argues that this overlooks important dimensions of social work in which trust is significant.

Service users depend heavily on what Giddens (1990) refers to as the demeanour of system representatives. As noted by Smith, 'An absence of trust at the point of access may itself impact on confidence and suggest that further contact should be avoided' (2001, p 296). She goes on to suggest that social workers also need to demonstrate that it is safe to trust, particularly to service users who have given up on trust as a consequence of painful and damaging experience. Trust is also crucial in understanding service users' accounts. They 'will not take the risk of giving a truthful account (of events or actions) or an authentic account (of problems, experiences or feelings) if they expect to be disappointed' (Smith, 2001, p 298). While service users may simply require practical support, there is often also a need for interpersonal help in the form of understanding, comfort and guidance. Smith warns of service users who may experience system confidence, but who do not experience the kind of trusting relationship with a social worker, which ensures sensitivity and responsiveness. She argues that confidence has come to predominate as the only means by which government can effectively regulate and control the activities of social work. This has implications for the relationships between managers, frontline practitioners and service users (Webb, 2006). Trust is left as an invisible trade practised at the margins by workers trying to maintain a sense of professional integrity.

We return to the seeming impossibility of the social work role. Franklin and Parton (1991, p 39) describe it as 'essentially and necessarily an ambiguous and messy occupation where the outcomes are rarely clear cut and where the methods of achieving them are variable and likely to be contested'. This is exacerbated by working with a largely vulnerable and marginalised clientele which makes for a weak political constituency. Even when the social work task is being fulfilled as well as might be expected, there is a huge potential for criticism.

Social work struggles to maintain confidence with ever more elaborate systems to account for its work to reassure both the public and government. Its embattled position leads to more defensiveness. Parton (1998) claims that making a defensible decision has become more important than making the right decision (although these are not necessarily different). When things go wrong, courts and official enquiries are increasingly expected to examine decision-making processes in retrospect (Carson, 1995). Steele is not alone in noting that 'social workers are damned if they do and damned if they don't' (1998, p 9). As a consequence, the written accounts of what they do are crucial evidence of the effectiveness or otherwise of their actions. This is the subject of the next chapter.

THREE

The social construction of the 'real' record

Chapter One considered social work records from the perspective of their relative significance in the 'doing of' social work. The discussion was concerned with the historical development of recording in social services, and the extent to which records are a subject of critical scrutiny and at the same time neglected. In this chapter we move on to a more considered discussion of the way social work records are produced and the various influences which shape the way they are written. We begin by exploring social work records as social and organisational products and then move on to look at records within the context of an audit society, where records play an increasingly important part in the ongoing regulation of individuals and organisations within the context of a risk society. This is followed by an examination of the 'paperwork burden' and the extent to which the production of the record is the main social work activity, not only in terms of time, but also in terms of purpose.

Records as professional and organisational constructs

The little research that has been undertaken on social work recording has tended to focus on the construction of the records. The social constructionist tradition in sociology has emphasised the record as an organisational product, designed to present an organisationally acceptable account of an 'approved' reality, rather than one that reflects actual reality. Indeed the notion that you can produce an objective, factual record, or that there is an actual reality which we might be capable of describing, would be seen as problematic within this tradition in sociology. Garfinkel (1967, p 120) pointed to the clinic record as a 'contractual' rather than an 'actuarial' record, a product concerned with portraying a relationship 'in accord with expectations of sanctionable performance by clinicians and patients'. The record was required to demonstrate that a professionally competent service had been appropriately delivered.

Cicourel (1968) was concerned with how records were created by practitioners and how such records provided practitioners with 'correct' depictions of character structure, morality, justice, legality, criminality and illness. The record was used to construct a 'reality' defined by organisational objectives as understood by practitioners. Professional consensus gave the record an authority, or what Zimmerman (1969) saw as its 'plain fact' character, where importantly subjective assessments were turned into objective facts. The record was the means by which the professional judgements and interpretations made by the practitioner were given an authority, which was then independent of the individual who made them. The record had a life of its own, and its influence could continue for many years beyond even the career of the original contributor of a particular record.

According to Prior (2003, p 3), 'every document stands in a dual relation to fields of action'; case records are not just repositories of information, but agents in their own right, giving rise to further action and interpretation. A particular perspective and a particular form of accountability is being established. 'In this sense records are part of a reflexive accounting, a demonstration of "doing all the right actions"' (Hall et al, 2006, p 102). Records have consequences. Records will describe a particular situation in such a way so as to suggest that a certain response is then seen as necessary, and indeed even inevitable. Drawing on Garfinkel, Hall et al (2006, p 103) assert that:

> ... there are constraints of a general nature on self-reporting in the institutional context, mainly because of the uncertainties about how an entry will be interpreted in the future. Moreover, the report is now produced for a particular audience and for a specific purpose, although what constitutes the audience and the purpose will vary across contexts and across time.

So there is a concern that the record should reflect proper professional judgement and competence, not only in the immediate context of the ongoing work with an individual case, but also at some possible later point when it might be read in very different circumstances.

Hall et al (2006) are particularly interested in the categorisation and accounting practices used in social work files – what is included in the record and what is left out, and how that shapes a particular view of the service user and the approach adopted by the worker and agency. They argue that practitioners form a view of a child or a family. Categories such as 'cooperative' or 'uncooperative', 'worthy' or 'unworthy' are formulated, if not explicitly then implicitly, and subsequent events will then be interpreted according to those categorisations. The process becomes self-fulfilling. Once someone has been designated in a certain way then it is all too easy to only see as significant the evidence which supports the original designation. As Cicourel (1983) suggests in relation to medical records, it is often a case of *recoding*, through a process of recontextualisation, rather than *recording*. Again the point is being made that the record is a construction to legitimate and justify the way in which a professional judgement has been made and a certain course of action followed.

In the context of psychiatric institutions, Goffman (1968 [1961]) points to the way in which during the life of a given case, more and more information that supports the professional categorisation is included so as to arrive at a fit. So there is rarely any mention of what the patient is able to do as opposed to what they cannot do, or any references to their past lives, other than those that reinforce the designation of the patient as 'sick': 'this is done by extracting from his whole life course a list of those incidents that have or might have had "symptomatic significance"' (1968, p 144). Clients are described in ways which emphasise their role as needy and requiring support, which both legitimates and justifies the action taken in response to that client.

In addition to underlining the patient as 'sick' or the service user as 'in need', the record is used to demonstrate the competence of the worker. Pithouse (1998) viewed social work records as a 'negotiable resource within an invisible trade'. He researched an area childcare team in the late 1980s and then revisited the team 10 years later. In the first visit, prior to the introduction of access legislation, he identified a 'proprietorial attitude' to records. There was an acceptance that the record constructed an approved reality rather than an actual reality, as the extract from Pithouse below shows:

> Childcare worker to team leader and researcher:
> Look! (holding manila file) I've had this case and I've been able to
> do nothing with them (clients) but I've made it *look* (her emphasis)
> dynamic (laughs). (Pithouse, 1998, p 51)

The suggestion in this particular example is that the worker did not feel any particular sense of professional discomfort in admitting this verbally. Perhaps because she felt the failure was with the family and not with herself, and that social work was a messy business in which it was not always possible to achieve a successful intervention, despite all best efforts. Nevertheless there is an awareness that the record should not reveal this more messy reality, and instead a more acceptable version of the intervention is constructed.

The record was therefore seen as an unreliable source of information. It served the purpose of ensuring that the worker was seen to be doing their job and would therefore be protected from any unnecessary interference. Supervisors did not look to the record to know what was going on in a case, preferring to talk to the worker instead. Pithouse (1998, p 53) describes the general view of the recording task as a 'tedious but unavoidable task that gets in the way of "real" work with the consumers'. There is almost a cynical view of the record as being irrelevant to what really mattered. This was before clients had a right of access and so there was little concern at having to explain the record to them. In addition it was accepted that the record did little other than to present a superficial account that not even supervisors took seriously. It was a means to suggest a competent service was being delivered, which it was, as far as most workers probably were concerned. They simply considered it necessary to ensure that the record provided a more sanitised version of events, which would satisfy those removed from the actual day-to-day reality of professional practice.

Ten years later Pithouse found that workers still saw the paperwork as a 'burden'. Yet there was a greater awareness of its importance, particularly in relation to providing evidence in the form of 'reports ... for court, for reviews, planning meetings, you name it. Recording is key to what we do' (Pithouse, 1998, p 59).

Client access had also concentrated workers' minds, and they were now more careful to record in a way that would stand up to a client's challenge. In addition, Pithouse describes a more prescribed way of working which left individual workers far less discretion: 'This shift to a more self protective and "fact" based approach to recording and monitoring work was far removed from over a decade before.... There were now clear procedures to be followed within specified time periods in respect of different types of referral' (p 63). The record was used as evidence to demonstrate that these procedures had been followed. The overwhelming concern, however, was ensuring that the record would cover workers' backs. '"Your head's on the block if you haven't done it right." "There's great pressure on not getting it wrong. A greater sense of insecurity ... the fear factor is almost tangible – there but for the grace of God"' (quoted in Pithouse, 1998, p 62). This begins to anticipate the concerns around the record as part of the apparatus of risk management. As practitioners feel under greater pressure and are subject to greater regulation in how they work, so the record assumes greater significance as evidence as to how far they have met the required expectations.

As Kagle (1993, p 193) argues, 'like physicians who have learned to practise defensive medicine, social workers have learned to practise and record defensively'. According to Walker et al (2005), 'under-recording' can also serve a defensive purpose in a climate of increasing professional accountability. Harris (1987, p 66) believes that social workers, subject to such pressure, may produce records to protect themselves, 'rather than ones that are in the best interest of their clients'. The record can induce a sense of vulnerability in the practitioner. It is a constructed account which is designed to demonstrate competence, but the more the record is subject to scrutiny the more it may be seen by practitioners as the basis on which their professional reputation may ultimately be decided.

In one of the few studies investigating social workers' experience of recording, Prince (1996) interviewed workers in children's services and found practitioners complaining of the lack of training and procedures in how to record, with the sense that they felt 'abandoned' (p 35). She undertook her research at the same time clients were being given the right to access their files. She was particularly concerned with exploring the impact that sharing files with clients would have on how social workers recorded information, and the dilemmas this might create.

Prince identified confusion over how to write sensitive information, particularly when that was in tension with making a case for resource allocation:

> On the one hand she (SW) needed to convince the education authority that expensive resources were needed, that aspects of the child's background prevented his educational needs being met by ordinary provision, and that the facilities needed were not those of the social services care system. On the other hand, the written contribution had to avoid many things: raising the level of parental defences, guilt or anxiety so that provision was refused; jeopardising future work by damage to SW's relationship with the family; reducing the child's

chances of acceptance by the specialist provision by over-emphasising levels of emotional disturbance or social problems. The SW was constantly wrestling with words to make a good case for resources in a way which parents could tolerate, without loss of trust in her ability to help them in the future. (Prince, 1996, p 133).

In the above extract Prince captures the dilemma of the record being read by different audiences. In children's services, although the client is the child, it is often the parents who will read the file, and they may react adversely to information which the practitioner has to record in order to ensure the required organisational response. Burnham (1989) identifies similar tensions in writing medical records. Anxieties over the reaction of clients to reading their records underline the sense of the record as evidence of the practitioner's observation and surveillance of the client. This leads on to the next section where we look more specifically at the record as the product of a process of surveillance.

The record as surveillance

The introduction of client access brought into sharp relief the record as a process of monitoring which then had to be explained to the service users. Records are inevitably a form of surveillance, but it is the increasing expectation through freedom of information legislation that records should be open to scrutiny that makes that surveillance more explicit and more apparent to both practitioner and client, with consequences for the relationship between them.

Prince (1996) confronts the issue of the power of the record as a form of surveillance and sees it as a system of 'intense registration and documentary accumulation', described by Foucault (1975, p 189). Clients 'referred' become 'cases' to be interviewed during which a history as well as a considerable amount of personal detail will be taken and retained. 'Foucault's concepts of the "discourse of power", "disciplinary techniques to manage bodies", "hierarchical surveillance" and "the examination" are useful and vivid ways to consider what such diligent information gathering was actually doing to the balance of power between worker and client' (Prince, 1996, p 119). Prince argues that by using a Foucauldian approach in studying the 'micro' transactions in the recording process, case recording is elevated from 'a "boring chore"' to one in which 'power is exercised rather than possessed; it is not attached to agents and interests, but is incorporated in numerous practices' (Barrett, 1991, p 135, cited in Prince, 1996, p 119).

The very exercise of observation and interpretation of clients' behaviour, and the recording of those observations and interpretations, is an exercise in power, which is the prerogative of the practitioner. The record, even now, is largely written by the practitioner. The spotlight is on the client, much less so on the practitioner. The record is concerned to present an account of the client, to analyse their actions rather than consider the interaction between client and practitioner, with the practitioner's behaviour subject to the same level of scrutiny and questioning.

In any case the practitioner is the one who tells the story and so is able to tell it in their terms.

As the scope of social work extends so too does the surveillance net. Clarke (1996, p 46) argues that as social services rely increasingly on informal provision, namely family carers, and assess not only service users but also carers and their needs, this 'creates new forms of discipline and surveillance over family life'. So the surveillance net may extend beyond the service user as social work shifts its focus to include carers, both family and other informal support networks.

So far we have considered the content of the record but the issue of surveillance leads us to also explore the means by which records are made. Social work records are now largely made and stored electronically, and this raises further questions as to the power of recorded information. Anxieties over breaches in confidentiality and unauthorised access to records seem to be greater with the introduction of electronic files (Gould, 2003). The closer links between health and social services, as well as increased working with voluntary and private sector agencies in providing adult care, inevitably drive all towards 'greater integration, dissemination and sharing of data' (Gould, 2003, p 42). Although legal restrictions proscribe the sharing of personal information between agencies without the service user's informed consent, this may cause conflicts with delivering timely and effective intervention.

> There will always be significant numbers of people in need of services, often urgently in need, who have not gone through a process of consenting to the use of personal information. What should be the reaction of practitioners? Respect the absence of consent and not give the best service? This would put them in breach of their common law duty of care. Ignore the absence of consent and get on with the job (common practice for many)? There is an information dilemma in need of resolution. (Glastonbury, 2001, pp 9–10)

Practitioners often remain confused as to what information can and cannot be shared and with whom, as so many inquiries would suggest. The more different agencies are required to work collaboratively, the more the issues and dilemmas around information sharing will arise.

The concern around electronic recording arises from the ease with which information can be shared between agencies, despite the protocols. Social work records are just part of the huge amount of information that is stored about us by many organisations. As far back as 1974, James Rule concluded that 'databases enable the detailed reconstitution of the daily activities of any individual' (p 273). Poster (1990, pp 97–8) goes further and argues that databases can be seen as 'the multiplication of the individual, the constitution of an additional self, one that may be acted upon to the detriment of the "real" self without that "real" self ever being aware of what is happening'. The 'virtual' self may assume greater significance in the decisions that are being made in respect of the 'real' self. It is the vision many dread that wrong information about us may be held electronically, of which we are blissfully unaware, and yet that same information may be repeatedly used by others in making decisions that may have profound and lasting consequences for us.

The power of databases to enable information about us to be shared by others in ways over which we have no control raises the spectre of Foucault's Panopticon, an idea he borrowed from Bentham. The all-seeing Panopticon was a means to observe, control and discipline behaviour. For Bentham this was a rationalist, humanist way of reforming criminal behaviour, whereas for Foucault (1975), it was a system of domination. The ideal form of surveillance is the totally observed individual, who becomes a self-observing and self-disciplining agent (Miller and O'Leary, 1987). Systematic record keeping was integral to the success of the regime of total surveillance. Poster (1990, p 93) argues that 'today's circuits of communication and the databases they generate constitute a Superpanopticon'. The essential feature of this form of surveillance is that it induces a form of self-regulation. It relies on clear expectations around what is required in order to be seen to conform, and the extent to which people then feel they are being scrutinised encourages that conformity.

The social work record may be seen as part of the Superpanopticon which is scrutinising the service user, but at the same time it may also be a means to scrutinise the practitioner. Harris (2003, p 69) points to the impact of the growing business approach in social services and social work, involving both 'the intensification of work and an increase in the scrutiny of work'. More and more departments are using computerised systems for case recording, which has 'subjected social workers' recordings to standardised procedures for information processing, codifying professional knowledge and giving it to managers' (p 69). From this statistical information is produced which is crucial in central government's evaluation of departmental effectiveness and efficiency.

The workplace for increasing numbers of social workers is a networked space in which not just their output but also the processes followed to achieve that output can be constantly monitored. 'Any lacuna is filled by a power of accountability, or what might be called the governance of visibility through the lens of technology' (Webb, 2003, p 167). Workers are aware that team managers can instantly check on their progress and any lapses in efficiency can be promptly addressed.

The monitoring process is one of infinite regression in a situation where accountability is established through documentary evidence of efficient and effective performance. Management focus is on capturing and controlling knowledge (Gould, 2003; Webb, 2003). This preoccupation with documentary evidence has led to what Power (1997) has called the 'audit society', which promises control through organisational transparency. This is seen as a technical response to risk and regulatory failure, but he warns against the audit process becoming little more than 'shallow rituals of verification' (1997, p 123). Braithwaite (1984, p 139) argues that audit inspections 'ensure the quality of your records, not the quality of your deeds'. Power (1997, p 140) argues that the audit process 'necessarily insulates itself from organisational complexity in order to make things auditable'. Perhaps this is not so far removed from the unreliable record identified by Pithouse in his first investigation of the children's social work office in the late 1980s as it might initially seem.

Social work is a complex, ambiguous and often uncertain business and audit is increasingly being used to hold individual practitioners and their agencies to account (Parton, 1996). 'Notions of risk are becoming increasingly endemic in an organisational culture that needs a common forensic vocabulary with which to hold individuals accountable, and to allocate scarce resources' (Kemshall et al, 1997, p 224). Yet reliable predictions are difficult and risk assessments are inevitably individualised. 'Emphasis is then placed on documentation of risk, step-by-step procedures that can be audited and the creation of processes that can demonstrate "defensibility" and withstand hindsight scrutiny in the light of things going wrong' (Kemshall, 2002, p 84). In social work, when things go wrong, there are often tragic consequences.

Recording and risk management

The need for accurate information and good recording practice has been identified in inquiries into deaths of children ever since the 1970s: 'Over the last 25 years, inadequate case records have often been cited as a factor in cases, with tragic outcomes' (Goldsmith and Beaver, 1999a). Records have been criticised for being incomplete, inaccurate and failing to distinguish fact from opinion. In the case of Maria Colwell, 'inaccuracies and deficiencies in the recording of visits and telephone messages played a part in the tragedy' (Prince, 1996, p 15). Recording has become more and more associated with concerns around accountability: 'The 1980s was a decade of inquiries into and reports on the many aspects of social work practice which helped to create a beleaguered context to the profession' (Cochrane, 1993, p 82). Kinnibrugh (1984) describes social workers as recording more information than other professionals because they felt more vulnerable than those working in other agencies such as health. It is ironic that in the case of Maria Colwell social workers were subject to greater criticism because their more detailed recording provided the damning evidence of their failures (Kinnibrugh, 1984).

Social workers practising in the field of childcare, and in the developing area of child protection, where it was assumed the record would be an important part of the evidence on which decisions were made, were becoming more aware of the scrutiny to which their records could be subjected. Despite this awareness, problems around recording and the sharing of information continue to be an issue of concern, and were identified as recently as 2003 by Lord Laming (House of Commons, 2003) as contributory factors in the death of Victoria Climbié. In discussing the Laming Report, Cowan (2003, p 272) states that, 'It is rare for an inquiry into adverse healthcare events not to discuss record keeping in some context'. While the most recent case of 'Baby P' focused more on the issue of the individual professional competence of practitioners, concerns around the quality of evidence gathering as well as the efficiency of information sharing still featured.

Laming urged for a more sceptical approach in the processes of observation and analysis which are integral to the recording task. He also recommended that multiagency staff should 'create a shared language and understanding of local referral procedures, assessment and information sharing and decision-making' (House of Commons, 2009, p 89). Once again it is argued that the quality of information in case records and the appropriate sharing of that information are crucial in the effective delivery of social work.

Shepherd (2006), examining the report from the Bichard Inquiry (2004) following the Ian Huntley case, although concerned with police records, states that 'four of Bichard's 31 recommendations were specifically related to records management systems and a further three to the quality and timeliness of data input' (Shepherd, 2006, p 7). Records and their management are attracting increasing attention, with a specific journal dedicated to the topic, *Records Management Journal*, first published in 1989. In a society increasingly concerned with the effective management of risk, the record is ultimately the lasting evidence of the process that has been followed.

Records are the means by which social services, as well as other organisations, may well be found wanting in the management of risk, and so the recorded risk assessment is crucial in demonstrating competent professional and organisational practice. The assessment of risk is increasingly based on technical and rational calculations. Castel (1991) argues that the focus is no longer on the individual, but on a combination of risk factors. As a result, the 'operative on the ground now becomes a simple auxiliary to a (case) manager whom he or she supplies with information derived from the activity of diagnostic expertise. These items of information are then stockpiled, processed and distributed along channels completely disconnected from those of professional practice, using in particular the medium of computerised data handling' (Castel, 1991, p 293). Risk assessment is increasingly approached by the use of checklists, which are seen as crude and blunt instruments (Froggett and Sapey, 1997).

Kemshall (2000, p 52) argues that this results in a dissonance between managers and professionals, with the former valuing 'actuarially based knowledge for its consistency and accountability, and practitioners valuing professional, individualised judgement for its flexibility and responsiveness to individual factors'. This suggests a fundamental dilemma for professional practice. The concern to evidence a rational process in the identification and management of risk leads to a greater reliance on a rather simple calculation of risk factors. The subtle interplay between factors, which may be more evident to the practitioner on the ground, is seen as irrelevant in this preoccupation with systems that leave little room for individual judgement. Individual judgement is seen as fundamentally subjective and therefore more unreliable and prone to error – and ultimately less defensible.

It could be argued that the concern with accountability is leading to the record assuming a greater significance to the service user than the actual intervention. Increasingly social workers are concerned with producing information rather than services. Prince (1996, p 47) quotes a social worker from her research: 'the irony is, files now assume a great value; the family can have a file but not a service'. Huntingdon and Sapey (2003, p 68) argue that the 'outputs of social work are measured in terms of information known about social services' clients, rather than the material services provided to them'. Increasingly social workers are required to meet performance criteria through the demonstration of completed assessments and reviews (Huntingdon, 2000). So the relationship is curiously reversed, and clients now provide information to workers to ensure targets are met, rather than workers providing services to clients. The assessment is undertaken and duly recorded and the client, who may then be considered ineligible for a service, becomes the 'virtual' subject of the 'real' record (Huntingdon and Sapey, 2003).

Huntingdon and Sapey (2003) believe that the focus on risk is the inevitable consequence of trying to reconcile a needs-led rhetoric within a resource-led service. They note that:

> There is an inherent contradiction in policies that demand more time to be spent on the gathering and recording of data, when service provision is declining, at least in relation to demand. In this situation recording as a system of accountability takes on a new meaning. Whilst the government might appreciate the limitations of focusing on risk, its analysis nevertheless places the responsibility for assessing and managing risk on professionals and managers. (2003, p 73)

The problem of trying to reconcile the rhetoric and the reality lies with the professionals and their managers, while the record is the means by which government is able to hold those same practitioners to account, without having to manage the inherent contradictions it has created.

The paper burden

It would seem the record has become an end in itself: 'Social workers spend more and more time writing records and reports to the point where the written word may be assuming more social significance than the events described' (Davies, 1991, p 11). The record represents the collection of information or knowledge, and whether that is produced and distributed in hard copy or electronic form, it is seen as 'paper', and as a burden (Ericson and Haggerty, 1997). Increasingly practitioners' time is taken with producing records rather than in face-to-face work with clients. At the time of her study, conducted in the late 1980s, Prince (1996) found that clinic social workers estimated 20% of their time was spent on recording. The 'real' work was beginning to lose out to paperwork (Camilleri, 1996). At one time recording was a secondary activity that could be delayed, but now it has to be completed before a social services intervention can be implemented (Postle, 2002). Pithouse (1998) found that by the late 1990s social workers spent far more time recording than 10 years previously. Jones (2001) found that practitioners felt increasingly governed by paperwork and procedures.

More recent research revealed that 75% of 1,000 social workers said that they spent more than 40% of their time on paperwork, and it was the most significant factor in causing one in four of them to seriously question their future in the profession. This research also saw social workers bemoaning the lack of time with service users, arguing that the time they did spend in face-to-face contact was taken up with the bureaucratic processing of assessments, rather than support and counselling (Revans, 2007). The production of the record has become the central task as far as many social workers are concerned. It consumes more time and it is more significant as a measure of their professional effectiveness. It is not surprising that a Department of Health consultation document in 2000 speculated that the British personal social services might feel that they are being 'swamped' by an information agenda. This is a picture replicated in many parts of public sector services.

A recent study by the American Hospital Association (2001) revealed that in the emergency department every hour of patient care generates an hour of paperwork. 'The 1990s were characterised by a major shift from administrative hospital information systems to clinical information systems' (Sermeus, 2003, p 152). Ericson (1993), looking at the experience of the Canadian police, reported that they spent more time recording investigative activities than doing actual investigative work. In a later study by Ericson and Haggerty (1997), patrol officers estimated 60-80% of their time was spent on paperwork as opposed to 'real' policework which was crimework, 'the briefcases were as fully loaded as the shotguns. Unlike the shotguns, which most officers had never used, the briefcases were opened repeatedly during the shift' (p 297).

The study argued that the concern to produce knowledge in order to manage risk had generated the paper burden. Often the knowledge was demanded from the police by other organisations as part of their own strategies in managing risk. The evolution of the 'occurrence report' form from a single side of A4 paper to 12 electronic pages of fixed classifications is an illustration of how the demand for more information is ever increasing. As one officer said, 'the more information you have, the more information people want, so you gather more, so they want more, and so you just keep going and going and going' (quoted in Ericson and Haggerty, 1997, p 375). In England and Wales, just one task, the requirement that all audiotaped interviews with suspects should be summarised on a standard form, is estimated to require the full-time efforts of 1,400 police officers, the equivalent of 1% of the entire constabulary (RCCJ, 1993).

Records, rhetoric and reality

In addition to the time spent on recording, concern has arisen as to the quality of information produced. With greater reliance on prescribed schedules for information collection, which has been reinforced by computerisation, there is a fear that quality is losing out to quantity – the priority is producing statistics. Poster (1990, p 38) argues that computerised information collection encourages a reliance on fixed-choice tick boxes that suggests a spurious certainty, 'the power of bureaucracy derives in good part from the linguistic form instituted by computerized databases, the code which generates a form of language without ambiguity'.

Social services assessments are seen as increasingly reductionist, with a reliance on tick boxes instead of narrative analysis (Phillips, 1996; Middleton, 1999; Postle, 2002). Assessment is no longer an exercise in professional skill but instead one of procedural administration. Standardised forms 'it is argued ensure fairness and even-handedness. Unfortunately, they also mitigate against highly individualized assessments which take into account particular needs and wishes. While in an ideal situation, the form will be an outcome of the assessment, too often the form drives the process itself' (Stainton, 1998, p 143). Standardised forms fix the categories through which an individual and their story will be told. 'Service users are managed through networks of question schedules that subordinate them to the assessment's pre-determined agenda of categories' (Webb, 2003, p 76).

Similar concerns were expressed in recent research undertaken following the introduction of the 'integrated children's system', the national IT system in children's services designed to produce more standardised and accessible records. Social workers complained of the system being too complicated, time-consuming and prescriptive, and that it was difficult to grasp the key features of a case because the information was split into various different sections. The system was seen to rely on a form-driven, tick box approach which failed to address important questions while asking others that were irrelevant, resulting in 'bland analyses' (Gillen, 2008).

Computers are reducing potentially complex situations to binary coded categories, although Grint and Woolgar (1997) argue that these codes are often already embedded in everyday practice. The linguistic practices governed by the codes can be seen to provide a simplified construction of the complexity of lived experience. They can also, however, no longer be seen as representations of the real world at all, but rather as attempts to construct an imaginary world through the arbitrary juxtaposing of signifiers and meanings (Simpson, 1995). Baudrillard (1981 [1988]) refers to such a world as 'hyper-real', where the real and the imaginary become confused, and the symbol or sign comes to be more 'real' than its meaning. The signifier of an event has replaced direct experience and knowledge of such an event.

Regan (2003, p 89) argues that the community care reforms were sold on the basis that they would bring about 'quality services', 'value for money' and 'consumer choice'. These 'essentially arbitrary, abstract and decontextualised set of signifiers formed a powerful system of signs, or communicative frame, which structured the value (meaning) of community care and in doing so successfully emptied out alternative forms of interpretation of the new legislation. "Quality", "value" and "choice" continue to be used interchangeably and repeatedly in all reforms and strategy documents'. Regan goes on to argue that making the benefits of the reforms 'real' involved the imposition of 'simulcra' or fantasy models.

The record can now be viewed as part of an attempt to create an image of a world that does not exist in the lived world of either the practitioner or the service user, but is nevertheless necessary in order to maintain the illusion of more efficient and effective service delivery. There is a gulf between the rhetoric and the reality of current social care provision, and the record, as the accountable evidence for how that provision is organised and delivered, is crucial in either maintaining the illusion or acting as witness to its essential fantasy.

In the extract below, Postle (2002) quotes a care manager describing the situation he faced when a woman with whom he worked reached 65, and was therefore no longer entitled to the care scheme for younger disabled people at a subsidised rate:

> This is the situation. I've got £130 and I'm told it's a strict limit. I've got to be upfront with you because I can't go through the sham of an assessment and then say "What I'm really here about is getting the cost down". That's totally unfair. So I had to give her the choice. If you want these carers to come in the morning, the ones who've been coming in for 12 years, we're gonna have to cut the care package elsewhere to justify spending that amount of money on the morning carers. She views the carers as friends and so she exercised her choice to keep them. I had to completely slash the rest of her package and now three hours on a Friday is the only time she gets out all week. I came back and I tried to argue for more but I couldn't get away with it…. So this myth of a needs led assessment is complete garbage when you come up to a limit on a care package. (Postle, 2002, p 340)

Postle described such dilemmas as commonplace. This is the lived reality for many practitioners and service users but the rhetoric tries to convince us otherwise. The record is the place where all the dilemmas in the social work role, trying to reconcile the rhetoric and the reality, are focused.

Recording dilemmas and professional discretion

Howe (1991) argued that professional discretion in social work has been increasingly constrained as a consequence of greater managerial control. However, the issue of the extent to which professional discretion features in modern-day social work raises more complex questions than a simple equation, which assumes more managerial control equals less discretion. In one sense social work is clearly more circumscribed and accountable, but in order to understand the full implications of this issue we need to examine the work undertaken by Lipsky (1980) on the use of discretion among workers in the public sector. His original contention was that workers are often left to deal with policy contradictions, with resources that are inadequate to implement those policies. It is in trying to work with the resulting confusion and contradictions that practitioners then exercise discretion. It could be argued that discretion in this sense is simply the exercise of individual judgement in the face of confusing and conflicting expectations, which is informal and not legitimated. Professional discretion, on the other hand, is the legitimate application of a particular body of professional knowledge and skills. It may be useful to consider recording dilemmas in relation to the former rather than the latter.

Evans and Harris (2004) accept that social work practice is organised within a legal, policy and managerial framework, but 'it is an unwarranted assumption to present this framework as coherent, complete and unambiguous and as being understood in exactly the same way by all those involved with it' (p 887). They also argue that attempts to further elaborate rules and guidelines do not necessarily clarify, and can indeed add to the confusion and uncertainty by introducing more conflict and contradiction between the proliferating procedures.

Guidance material might try to square the circle of an agenda of financial restraint and ever-increasing user choice, but practitioners may still be left vulnerable. The confusion created by the House of Lords decision in *R v Gloucestershire ex parte Barry* (1997) is an interesting example. Gloucestershire was challenged on not meeting a need that had been assessed. The authority's defence was resource constraints, and so the issue of 'unmet need' became the subject of legal deliberation. The majority decision was summarised:

> ... the authority need provide only what it can reasonably afford, and can assess or reassess the individual client in the light of financial constraints. But ... if the need is found to exist, the authority must meet that need, even if it lacks resources.... Following the Barry case, the Department of Health issued a Guidance note (LASSL 97/13) telling local authorities not to use the judgement as an excuse to take decisions on resource factors only. Decisions must always be based on needs assessment. (Brayne et al, 2001, pp 317-18)

The issue was then further complicated by the Laming letter CI (92) 34, in which the Chief Inspector advised on the recording of 'unmet need':

> This highly charged and explosive political issue – service users with access to their records pointing to the difference between their identified needs and the services provided – needed careful handling by professionals. While practitioners were enjoined to take a rigorous approach to assessing need, they were warned to be careful in their recording practice not to raise unrealistic expectations on the part of users. (Evans and Harris, 2004, p 886)

Recording is clearly identified as a potentially sensitive and problematic feature in this controversy. Workers may be left exercising discretion in response to conflicting and contradictory directives, but the record leaves them peculiarly exposed in having to account for the way in which they have exercised that discretion.

Harrison (1999) argues that relying on individual discretion to try and make sense of vague and contradictory policies can be a useful political strategy. When things go wrong, and it is established that procedures have not been duly followed, then blame can be more easily laid at individual practitioner level. It is also in the interests of politicians and senior management to distance themselves from the difficult and awkward day-to-day decisions around resource allocation, which they create by imposing strategic plans without the budgets to pay for them.

Discretion, understood in this way, can be seen as an enduring feature of public sector services, where the gulf between the rhetoric of policy and the reality of resource-constrained provision makes for inevitable dilemmas in the day-to-day work of practitioners. It has been argued that recording is in an unusual position in terms of professional practice. It is the space where workers have to give a coherent account of their work. If their work is only possible through the exercise of discretion which, by definition cannot be made explicit without acknowledging the extent to which the individual is individually liable, then the question arises as to how to record a process of work that cannot be fully acknowledged. Contemporary social work raises many dilemmas for practitioners and it would seem that the competing and conflicting agendas which impact on the production of the record may add yet more dilemmas.

Recording: a problematic issue

The recent case of 'Baby P', while it did not highlight the issue of recording in the same way as the inquiry into the death of Victoria Climbié, might be seen to raise more profound questions. There was widespread revulsion at the fate of this small child and disbelief at how such a catalogue of failures was possible. Although the issue of information sharing was raised once more, what emerged in the popular and professional debate was a sense of frustration that social workers were spending too much time recording and too little time in face-to-face work with children and their families.

This reveals a fundamental contradiction in the attitudes taken to recording. On the one hand, it is seen as an administrative chore that takes up too much time and prevents professionals from getting on with their 'real' work. On the other hand, it has been acknowledged in numerous previous inquiries that professionals cannot work effectively without being able to refer to accurate and reliable recording.

However, as we have seen in the research that has been done on the subject of records, there is cause for some considerable doubt as to the quality and reliability of the information recorded. As the records are produced for organisational purposes this imposes constraints on what can and cannot be said. Information is increasingly ordered according to categories that may have more to do with the requirements of audit than professional decision making. Yet public services are required to be accountable and to be able to demonstrate their efficiency and effectiveness – their funding depends on successful achievement of set performance indicators. Practitioners are finding themselves ever more involved in these processes, with the record assuming greater significance.

At the same time the power of the record is recognised and also a concern to work more openly with service users in sharing the information that is held about them. This raises its own dilemmas for practitioners as to how they reconcile their ongoing work with service users, and the explicit acknowledgement, which the record represents, of the process of surveillance to which those same service users have been subjected.

While many of these issues have been identified and discussed, there has been little attention paid to how this impacts on individual practitioners and their approach to the recording task. Too often the focus of research into recording has concentrated on the practice of recording and evaluating that practice. It is time that we heard social workers' accounts of their experience of recording. Through my research I wanted to provide them with an opportunity to explore the different, and it would seem, potentially contradictory and conflicting influences which impact on that task. The recording task is seen in the context of the role of the social worker in modern-day adult social services. We saw in Chapter Two that the social work role is fraught with ambiguity and tension, and practitioners are working with those ambiguities and tensions on a daily basis. At the same time they may also feel a dissonance between the rhetoric of community care and the reality of their lived experience. Much has been written of those role conflicts, but little attention has been given to how those might impact on the writing of the social work record.

The record in social work is seen as a neglected area with generations of commentators lamenting this neglect, but nothing seems to change. I am concerned with trying to understand why recording continues as an issue that is acknowledged as significant, but is still ignored. As the record becomes increasingly important as the evidence on which individuals and departments will be held accountable in a society preoccupied with managing risk, the record becomes more powerful in bearing witness to how those contradictions are managed. The record can be seen as the product of an attempt to reconcile a number of competing agendas into one coherent account. The extent to which that is seen as problematic or otherwise is the focus of investigation.

FOUR

Setting the scene

This chapter sets the scene for the following chapters in which the research findings are discussed in detail. It provides a brief account of the organisation of the research in order to enable the reader to appreciate the scope of the investigation. We then move on to some of the more general issues identified by participants in respect of their feelings about the subject of recording; so many different issues are raised that it is sometimes difficult to maintain a coherent discussion. This preliminary presentation is an attempt to provide a summary impression of social workers' attitudes to and experience of recording. The chapter demonstrates the extent to which recording remains a submerged subject for many practitioners, as well as highlighting their essential ambivalence towards it. Recording is seen as a chore, but one that has crucial consequences, and so, even before we start to explore the complexities of the recording task, we begin to recognise its contradictory aspects through these initial views expressed by the participants.

Research organisation

The investigation was in two stages and involved 50 semi-structured interviews with mostly qualified social workers in 14 departments, followed by 460 completed postal questionnaires from qualified social workers in a further 79 departments in England and Wales. The research focused on practitioners working in adult services. It was recognised that the issues identified by 50 social workers, while they might be very interesting and throw fresh light on some of the complexities around the recording task, risked being seen as limited to a small number of perhaps unrepresentative individuals, who had a particular interest in the subject. Finch (1986) acknowledges that social policy research in the UK has favoured quantitative over qualitative methods. It was important to be able to compare the findings from the interviews with a much larger and, it is hoped, more representative, sample of social workers. The postal questionnaire was formulated from the interview findings and Association of Directors of Social Services (ADSS) approval was given for the research. The 50 interviewees were drawn from a mixture of shire and metropolitan authorities within a 50-mile range of Oxford. A further 141 departments were approached in respect of the questionnaires, with over half agreeing to participate. Each department then distributed 10 questionnaires. A return of 460 on an original distribution of 790, and a potential distribution of 1,410, represents a very respectable response rate. All regions within England and Wales were included. Interviewees and respondents were self-selecting.

Although the interviewees opted into the research, and as a consequence there was little opportunity to ensure a representative sample, the sample did reflect a broad range of characteristics. It was originally intended that only qualified social workers were interviewed; seven, however, of the final 50, did not hold a social work qualification. All the interviewees worked as care managers and held a caseload. Experience ranged from 12 who had been qualified for five years or less, 19 who had been qualified for between six and 14 years and 12 who had been qualified for more than 15 years. Twenty-nine of the interviewees worked in older people and physical disability teams, 11 in hospital teams and 10 with other adult services, that is, learning disability and mental health. Four of the interviewees had a supervisory/management role, but still held a caseload. Thirty-nine worked full time and 11 part time. Nineteen had worked with more than one authority. Forty-one were female and nine were male. Forty-two of the participants were white and eight were non-white. Comparisons with national figures and individual authorities suggest the sample was representative in terms of the above characteristics.

The questionnaire respondents also demonstrated a broad mix of experience. Over half (55.8%) worked in older people and physical disability settings. Learning disability (16.9%) and mental health (16.4%) made up another third, while hospital social workers (8.4%) and sensory impairment (2.5%) made up the remainder.

Length of time qualified in respect of the questionnaire respondents may be more easily indicated in table form (see Table 4.1).

The main focus of the research was the semi-structured interviews, each lasting on average one-and-a-half hours. These were exploratory and intended to give practitioners the chance to reflect on the recording task. (For details of the interview schedule see Appendix 1.) The postal questionnaires were used to establish the extent to which the interview findings might be representative of the views of a larger group of social workers. (For details of the postal questionnaire see Appendix 2.)

Table 4.1: Length of time qualified

Length of qualification	%
Less than a year	8.2
1-5 years	33.6
6-10 years	21.5
11-15 years	16.6
16-20 years	8.4
More than 20 years	11.7
Total	100

In my training on recording practice I emphasise the importance of including direct quotes from service users and others in the record, in order to provide the reader of the record with direct evidence of what the various parties involved have said. This enables the reader to hear the range of views expressed, including the practitioner's. Only in this way is the reader able to form an understanding of the situation described. In the same spirit I quote extensively from the interviews, allowing the voices of the practitioners to be heard. I acknowledge that I am in a powerful position to select the quotes that will be heard, but at least the reader will be afforded the opportunity of distinguishing between what the participants have actually said and my understanding of what they meant, and the analysis I drew from that interpretation.

A difficulty that is sometimes identified in qualitative research is that it does not always indicate how typical certain responses were, and the tendency to rely on illustrative examples compounds this problem. As Silverman (1985, p 140) put it, 'The critical reader is forced to ponder whether the researcher has selected only those fragments of data which support his argument' (Silverman, 1985, p 140), and encourages qualitative researchers to 'count the countable'. As Bryman (1988, p 143) concedes, this is surprising advice from a writer like Silverman, who has been such a critic of the quantitative approach in sociology, but simple counting techniques enable the qualitative researcher to survey the data and to 'provide the reader with an overall impression of those data'. I will try to provide the reader with such an impression. In addition I will include the questionnaire data where it is relevant to the discussion as a further indication of how far an issue is characteristic among the wider body of social workers. The questionnaire data are presented in simple frequencies (the data are presented in full in Appendix 3, available online).

Recording: a submerged subject

Recording remains something of a submerged subject for many social workers. It is something they are expected to get on with. They do not expect to be engaged with the subject, other than to complain they do not have enough time for it. That has been the general attitude of people who attend my training, until they are given the opportunity to start reflecting on the more problematic aspects of the recording task. It is only then that they become animated and begin to discuss the dilemmas they experience.

Social workers rarely have the opportunity to reflect on the recording process. Prince (1996) noted that a pattern emerged in her research in which social workers started off describing recording as boring and a routine chore, but:

> ... once relaxed and allowing themselves to take a unique opportunity to consider what social records meant to them, both clients and social workers talked in a flood, with emotions of anger, fear, cynicism, confusion and anxiety expressed freely. Thus dismissing record keeping as boring seemed to have become the usual way of pushing all its inherent difficulties, complexities and conflicts well away from painful scrutiny and examination. (p ix)

The research challenge was to provide such an opportunity, to help participants make explicit thoughts and attitudes that previously may have remained implicit, without influencing their responses to the agenda that was being set.

Incorporated within both the interview schedule and the postal questionnaire was an exercise that I use in my training. The intention was to provide social workers with material that would prompt them to think about recording in terms of professional practice issues, rather just as an administrative routine. The exercise uses a vignette and involves a comparison of two different ways of recording information about a particular service user.

Version A

Miss Vera Miles, aged 81, is a quiet lady who has recently moved from sheltered accommodation into residential care. Although very reluctant to leave her flat, her increasing confusion was putting her at considerable risk. She was diagnosed with Alzheimer's disease eight years ago. Miss Miles has no family, although she does frequently ask for her mother, who died when she was 12. She worked as a librarian for many years and was an active member of the Ramblers' Association. If prompted, she enjoys talking about the past.

Miss Miles has suffered from arthritis for over 15 years, which has particularly affected her fingers and hands. She is still otherwise very mobile and spends a lot of time walking around the building. Despite her confusion, she seems to be settling in to her new home, smiling at staff and other residents, and relating well to her keyworker, who she now appears to recognise. Miss Miles responds positively to one-to-one social contact, but can become anxious in larger groups or in more noisy environments.

Miss Miles needs help with personal care, but likes to choose her clothes if given the opportunity. She needs some assistance when using the toilet, but occasionally does not always give sufficient warning to get there in time.

Version B

Miss Miles is aged 81, single with no family. She suffers from Alzheimer's disease, arthritis and a degree of incontinence. She recently moved from sheltered accommodation where she posed too serious a risk to herself and others. She spends long periods aimlessly wandering around the building, frequently calls for her dead mother, has poor short-term memory and lacks orientation to time and place. She requires personal care and toileting. She has been assigned a keyworker. Miss Miles becomes very agitated with large groups of people, sometimes shouting and shrieking during social activities.

The exercise invariably provokes considerable reflection. On the one hand, there is a sense that the more concise version is desirable because time is limited for both writing and reading the record. On the other hand, there is an acknowledgement that Version B restricts itself to a purely negative description of the woman, concentrating on what she cannot do and the problems she presents. Version A is usually seen as a 'nicer' version which includes details of her past and what she can still do, describing her as a person rather a case, but there are questions as to how relevant that information might be for the purposes of social services. In my training I am concerned to promote the value of person–centred recording and to explore the consequences for the service user of a negatively focused record and how that might influence practitioners' expectations of the individual.

The exercise is fundamental in encouraging practitioners to look at recording as not purely an administrative issue but one that profoundly affects service users and our perception of them, the decisions that are made about them and what happens to them as they go through the care system. I considered this exercise as vital in prompting that process of reflection in both the interviewees and the questionnaire respondents.

In my research role I was nevertheless conscious that my position as a trainer in recording practice might interfere and constrain the responses of interviewees. I was concerned not to prompt an interviewee into a particular response, but to leave them to come to their own conclusions after having read the vignette along with other stimulus material used during the interview.

A chance to talk

When an activity is both familiar and routine as well as being something people prefer to avoid, it is difficult to excite much interest. The reaction of the social workers to the interviews was invariably one of surprise. Many said that they had not imagined how it could take one-and-a-half hours to discuss recording. It is "such a part of daily work, don't think about it" (interviewee 29). "Never really thought about recording" (interviewee 30). "Recording becomes part and parcel of your everyday" (interviewee 48).

The experience of being interviewed and being asked to discuss the issues around recording provoked a series of reactions. Some said how much they had enjoyed it, "That was really good fun" (interviewee 43). One described himself at the end of the interview as "exhausted" (interviewee 34). Thinking about all the possible different reasons for recording, one joked, "I'm getting more concerned!" (interviewee 50). Having the opportunity to articulate a number of frustrations, one interviewee exclaimed, "This is so therapeutic!" (interviewee 26).

In addition to these emotional reactions there were also the reflective comments on the extent to which the interview had stimulated their thinking in relation to the subject: "Speaking to you makes me revisit where I'm at with recording" (interviewee 48).

One interviewee articulated this sense of a topic suddenly assuming a significance that had remained obscured. Towards the end of the interview the weary but excited comment was made,

> "God this is difficult!… it's good 'cause it makes you think…. It's not boring!… It does make you think, …, until I've started today recording … is a chore that I have to do … and I'm very aware of why I'm doing it and, very aware of what I put into it … but until you actually sit down and think of all these things … it's just part of the job." (interviewee 20)

There were specific reactions to the different stimulus material, which again illustrate the extent to which interviewees were finding themselves confronted with issues that resonated, despite not having previously considered them. The influence of the different readerships on how people might record was a specific issue of interest in the research; I had anticipated it might be one that they did not think about, but would recognise when asked to reflect on it. The following comment again demonstrates the way in which social workers carry out recording with sometimes only a partial awareness of the influences that may impinge on that process:

> "It's insidious, isn't it, you don't realise how much you're sucked into readers' points of view – we don't spend enough time thinking about it." (interviewee 50)

Sometimes interviewees were sufficiently engaged with the subject that they asked to keep copies of the different stimulus material, in order to take it to their teams to promote discussion of the issues raised in the interview:

> "It would be really interesting … if I was able to share this with the team.… I can just see this bringing up lots of useful, meaty discussion in a team meeting." (interviewee 7)

The vignette Versions A and B made a particularly powerful impression. One interviewee kept returning to the sheet; its impact had been especially disquieting:

> "It shocked me – I would like to keep it … just to remind myself what I shouldn't be doing, … I've fallen into that trap.… It really hits you … I mean that has really shocked me to see it written like that. It has really made me think." (interviewee 32)

This example again raises the issue of how far the interviewees felt their practice was being scrutinised and possibly found wanting. It should be emphasised that this particular interviewee offered these reflections without any prompting. Simply reading the two versions had made her more aware of issues she recognised, but had, over time, become less focused on.

For many the interview was a stimulating experience, if a sometimes unsettling one. They were asked to think about a routine, taken-for-granted activity in a way that was making many aspects of that activity more explicit, and potentially more problematic. There was nevertheless a sense that these were issues that they recognised. There was also a sense of relief that this largely neglected activity, which they were expected to just get on with, was actually receiving some attention.

Essential but pointless: attitudes to recording

Recording conjures up strong feelings among social workers. Despite it being a topic they say they do without thinking, once they are given the opportunity to express their feelings, they present a seemingly never-ending set of contradictory and ambivalent attitudes. At the heart of their ambivalence is their relationship with the service user, or perhaps what they might more accurately describe as their lack of relationship with the service user. They expressed a constant tension between time spent in the office with recording and administration, and time spent with service users – 70.7% of questionnaire respondents said they felt more like administrators. This was often seen as inevitable, although there was a sense that it was something they regretted:

> "And the other day I had a day out when I saw three clients, ... and I came back the next day and I said, 'What a fantastic day I had. I actually saw my clients!' ... more often than not most of us are in the office, and I just think it's just a strange way of working.... I haven't had time to think of a way that it could be better, but you've got people who are qualified in their area of expertise, yet ... spend huge amounts of time recording." (interviewee 48)

Regret was sometimes mixed with resentment given the pressure social workers experienced, aware that waiting lists constantly represented yet more work urgently requiring attention, and yet still they had to spend so much time on the recording:

> "Generally a lot of social workers, they know how important it [recording] is ... but they resent the time it takes to do it.... As waiting lists get longer ... and you wonder how fair is it to be sitting in the office for three quarters of the day ... recording." (interviewee 35)

It is interesting to note that only 42.2% of the questionnaire respondents said that they resented the time they spent recording, although many comments suggested the percentage would have been considerably higher if the question had referred to the *amount* of time spent recording.

Even though recording was seen as a time-consuming chore that took time away from seeing service users and slowed down the work of processing cases, there was an awareness that without it service users would not receive a service. It was a necessary activity that ultimately served the interests of the service users:

> "I don't want to be in front of the computer until 3 o'clock in the afternoon and I've seen the person at 11 o'clock in the morning. I don't want to do that, but I know that in order for something to happen – this is the way it has to be." (interviewee 6)

It nevertheless remained a chore, albeit a necessary one, agreed by 79% of questionnaire respondents, which many social workers found "irksome and tedious" (interviewee 37).

> "It's like ironing, it has to be done, but no one likes doing it … you want to put it off … but you know it has to be done and you want to do it properly." (interviewee 9)

> "You never catch up. This is one of the sad things. Like housework, you just keep doing it." (interviewee 10)

These negative feelings were often exacerbated by the belief that the recording systems used involved unnecessary repetition and duplication. This, together with the sense that the process of assessment was a formula-driven activity, could make the exercise seem even more meaningless:

> "I just find them a bit depressing because they're so incredibly repetitive … you write on the assessment, then you write something very similar on the care plan … you seem to repeat yourself a lot.… And because you're sort of limited in what you can offer – particularly with care plans – you do find that you just have set phrases … it could be anybody's care plan really." (interview 43)

Despite the frustrations there was also a recognition that the record could relieve the pressure on workers. They were often involved with taking information from many different sources in any one working day, and the record was a means to ensure that all the information was captured:

> "All this stuff is in my head, once it's on the computer … then I can move on." (interviewee 7)

> "The more cases, the more stuff I have in my head, the more I need to write it down." (interviewee 14)

Many social workers remained uncertain as to how much information they should be recording, and in what detail. They were all too aware that the record would be the only evidence of the work they had done:

> "If you haven't recorded it you haven't done it." (interviewee 31)

Where there was a constant stream of information, sometimes the record was an important reassurance, even to the worker, of a task accomplished:

"Recording is important as evidence of having done something ... convincing myself I did it." (interviewee 40)

The record as evidence was also a potential source of anxiety. Often dealing with complex situations, communicating with many different people, it could be confusing trying to recall all the different items of information that could be recorded. Social workers depended on the record to demonstrate that they had thought of all the possible factors relevant to a case, and that they had communicated with everyone accordingly. This, in itself, becomes a pressure. It is not only carrying out the tasks, but documenting that you have done so:

"I find the case note recording a burden ... and each year.... I find I'm recording more and more because of the usual thing, making sure that I've covered everything." (interviewee 28)

Social workers do not work in isolation. It is more commonplace now for social workers to hold a case for a relatively short time and so, as the case is passed on, the record becomes highly significant in communicating to other colleagues what has happened and what has been done.

Recording was seen "As a necessary evil, which I don't think is probably uncommon, it's something you've got to do, because the file is going to be passed on to somebody else ... and they've got to know what you've done" (interviewee 29).

Despite the recognition that the record was the means to provide the service user with a service and the evidence to demonstrate how that had been achieved, there was still a belief that the preoccupation with the record was motivated more by concerns over liability – 94.7% of questionnaire respondents believed recording was important to cover their backs:

"I'm a bit ambivalent ... necessary to record ... what you're recording is hopefully going to contribute to a good service for the individual ... people have a right to know what's written and held about them ... they can challenge.... Sometimes we're asked to record things not for the sake of the service user but, I think, to protect the department, protect the service, and to protect the councillors." (interviewee 27)

It would be easy to conclude from the extracts so far that recording was seen in a wholly negative light, and so it may be surprising to discover the extent to which many workers actually took pride in the task – 87.2% of the questionnaire respondents said that they took pride in their recording, although it is interesting to note that this percentage declined with length of experience:

"Recording is quite satisfying ... you are demonstrating what you have done ... it's good to have it all there ... it's important we are telling the story in a way that makes things happen." (interviewee 37)

"I'm quite proud of my file ... I like the paperwork to be up together ... actually makes me feel good to know that any of my colleagues can open any of my ... cases." (interviewee 38)

"I like to do it well ... there is always the sense that it's public." (interviewee 40)

There was an acknowledgement that the record was something that demonstrated professional competence – 95.8% of questionnaire respondents saw recording as a professional task. Colleagues could see it , and it had status as a 'public' record. The record was something that they wanted to do well, not just as a means to an end, but there was an intrinsic sense of pride being expressed in these comments. Sometimes this sense of pride could become another source of pressure. When time was limited, it was not always possible to record to as high a standard as would have been liked:

"I wish I could spend more time thinking ... about what I'm going to write in the record ... thinking about words I am going to choose." (interviewee 32)

Some people struggled with the pressure to measure up to their own self-imposed, exacting standards to produce the perfect record:

"I try very hard, [I'm] quite an obsessional person, so I actually try quite hard to produce something that I think is a quality assessment." (interviewee 34)

"I like my work to be perfect in terms of anyone reading it." (interviewee 20)

Some people did actually enjoy writing for its own sake:

"I'm a wordsmith, I love words.... I can paint things with words." (interviewee 26)

It is worth saying that the above comment was made by someone who had, nevertheless, earlier in the interview still described recording as "irksome" (interviewee 26).

Attitudes toward recording were complex. Recording highlighted the uncertainty in the social worker's role. Social workers were instrumental in decisions that would have potentially profound consequences for people's lives, and the record was crucial to this process of decision making. The value of the record was closely tied to the value of the outcome for the service user. If the intervention had been effective, then the record would be evidence of a job well done; if the intervention had not been so effective, then the record could provide ready ammunition for retaliation on the part of the service user or their families:

> "My view and experience of recording is: get it right and it's brilliant, get it wrong and it causes no end of pain for you, the department, the service user and their families." (interviewee 38)

Most social workers were all too aware of the central importance of the recording task, and yet they were often confronted with the seeming futility of the effort:

> "In situations where colleagues and even managers don't read the file to get the information that's on there, I wonder why I bother." (interviewee 47)

This sense of futility combined with the awareness of how crucial the record might be in certain situations produced a powerful cocktail of feelings:

> "I do wonder, all this recording we do, you know you've got to do it because it's going to, one day there will be that complaint and you'll get a phone call from the inspector, as I did ages ago ... and you know like 'ugh!' ... in those instances, yes it is very valuable.... There is so much of it. It's probably about 80% of the stuff that we share now, that never gets looked at again ... it is on the one hand pointless, on the other absolutely essential." (interviewee 36)

This was a view that echoes some of the earlier literature on recording: 'a great deal of the materials that accumulate in organizational files is never referred to, never read, and never acted upon' (Wheeler, 1969, p 13). This is one of the fundamental contradictions in recording, as we will see in the following chapters.

FIVE

The demands of recording

Focusing on the ambivalence expressed by social workers highlights their complex attitudes in relation to recording. It begins to point to the tensions experienced in relation to the recording task. In order to understand the way in which those tensions arise from fundamental contradictions in that task, we need to move on from a descriptive account to one that analyses social workers' experience of recording in terms of the different factors they have identified, organising those factors within a framework that explains the complex relationship between them.

Analysing social workers' accounts of their experience of recording suggests there are a number of pressures, or *demands* (see Figure 5.1), inherent in the task. These pressures or demands arise from the different requirements placed on the record. The most obvious requirement is actually gathering and recording the information about a service user in order to supply a service. This involves communicating with the service user and colleagues and establishing that an individual is eligible to receive a service. These requirements are essentially concerned with the *functional* aspects of recording. Recording is the means necessary to provide users with a service.

In carrying out the functional aspects of their work social workers, along with many other groups of workers, are accountable for what they do. The records may be subject to legal scrutiny. They are accessible to the service users themselves, and they are also the basis on which an individual worker's and a department's performance is evaluated in terms of efficiency and effectiveness. These requirements are concerned with the demand for *accountability*.

The final area of demand arises from the social workers' perceptions of what constitutes principles of good practice in respect of recording. These ideas arise from the basic *values* that underpin professional social work practice, which are concerned with respecting the service user, recording from a person-centred perspective and reflecting the service user's story. Social workers are trying to meet these three areas of demand in their various recordings.

Value demands

This section encompasses both the professional values which underpin social work and the influence which client access has on the way in which social workers record. Client access straddles the demands of values and accountability, but will be discussed under values as the principles of openness and sharing of information with service users are incorporated within social work principles of good practice (Topss, 2004, Unit 16). Social workers are aware that most of what they record could be read by service users. Some documents are routinely shared,

Figure 5.1: Demands of recording

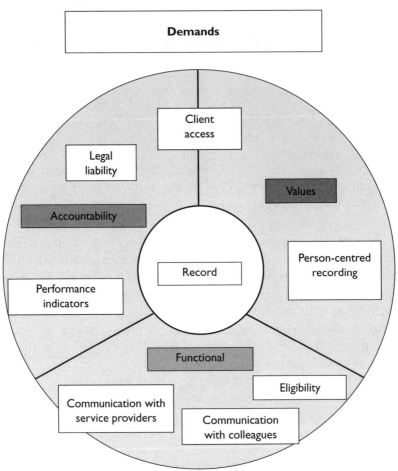

while other records can be seen following a formal access request. Social work values emphasise respecting the service user and these are demonstrated in person-centred recording, where the record describes the person and not just the case.

Person-centred recording

In both the interviews and the questionnaires the vast majority of the participants expressed a preference for a person-centred description of the service user. Comparing the two descriptions of the same service user included in the vignette (on p 44), where Version A gave the person-centred description and Version B concentrated on the problems the individual posed, 40 of the interviewees said they preferred Version A, while 10 thought both versions had strengths and weaknesses, and that either recording might be appropriate in different contexts. Among the postal questionnaire respondents, 70% preferred Version A, 10% preferred Version B and 19.6% believed it depended on the purpose of the record.

Version A was described as "more balanced" (interviewee 16), "holistic" (interviewee 4), "positive, social care model" (interviewee 7), "provides more context" (interviewee 8), "what she could do" (interviewee 9), "more objective" (interviewee 10), "thorough and detailed" (interviewee 13), provides "insight, … gives … background, tells you why she is where she is" (interviewee 27), "information about her previous life, her interests … how her arthritis affects her, what she is able to do … that she likes to have choice in choosing her own clothes" (interviewee 3) and "opens up thoughts about what support she might need to cope" (interviewee 37).

Version B was described as "pejorative, detached, cold" (interviewee 50), "appalling" (interviewee 2), "rushed" (interviewee 3), "value judgements" (interviewee 8), "blunt" (interviewee 9), "what you get from a GP" (interviewee 14), "makes assumptions" (interviewee 19), "sterile" (interviewee 21), "institutionalised statement" (interviewee 26), "a bit terse" (interviewee 27), "harsh, impersonal" (interviewee 29), "quite damning" (interviewee 33), "makes it look a rather hopeless situation" (interviewee 37), "clinical" (interviewee 38) and "bleak, she's a problem" (interviewee 47).

There was an overriding concern that Version B, through an exclusive focus on the negative aspects of the woman and her situation, distorted the account, which might have damaging consequences for the care she subsequently received. Version A was seen as maintaining a respect for the individual person, acknowledging that her history might be useful in understanding her and her needs, and that it was important to recognise what she could still do in order to help her keep her independence.

Many of the interviewees not only described Version A as more detailed, but they believed it also revealed important information about the individual that was not included in Version B. Version A included information about her past life, which they argued might be useful in understanding her in her present circumstances, particularly as she had been diagnosed with dementia. Such information would also be helpful in establishing a relationship with the woman. It included information about what she could still do, which was important in order to ensure that those capacities were encouraged and retained, rather than diminished still further by a care package that fostered dependency. As a consequence of such a description, it was felt that professional carers would be more positive in their view of the woman, and so have higher expectations of the quality of life she might be able to enjoy. Such humanistic principles of care have been argued by Kitwood (1998) and Kitwood and Bredin (1991).

Of the 10 participants who said that both versions had their merits, there was a concern with the record being "factual" (interviewees 5, 6, 44). There seemed to be an equation with "facts" and "succinctness" (interviewee 41). Version B was seen as being "short and concise … it's factual" (interviewee 20). The concentration on the "facts" was seen as making the record more accessible. "Version B would be more suitable because it's very straight and to the point … you can immediately pick out all the key bits" (interviewee 45). However, the same worker acknowledged that "if you're sending it [the record] to the people ... providing the care, Version A would be much better" (interviewee 45).

However, this very distinction between fact and opinion was one that was highlighted by those clearly preferring Version A; "aimlessly wandering" was seen as a "judgemental" statement (interviewee 23). There was a concern that too little detail could lead to assumptions being made; "arthritis is mentioned but it doesn't link ... to how it affects the person. Again, a degree of incontinence could mean anything from very, very frequent to once a week ... so again that's a subjective judgement" (interviewee 8).

In comparing these two different accounts, describing the same individual, workers were identifying what they considered to be the principles of good practice in recording. While most of the discussion endorsed the person–centred approach, as well as the importance of distinguishing the status of different information, there was nevertheless a concern with ensuring the information remained accessible to colleagues by concentrating on what was judged to be relevant. But those judgements about relevance might vary, depending on who would be reading the record. There is already an indication of the impact of the different readerships on the record.

Despite the majority of interviewees indicating that they preferred Version A of the vignette, when asked which version they saw most often when reading service users' records, 26 said Version B predominated, 13 said it depended on the purpose of the record, and nine said Version A was more dominant. A similar picture was found among the postal questionnaire respondents, with 42% saying that Version B predominated, 35.2% saying that it was dependent on the purpose of the record and only 22% saying they were more likely to see Version A. These issues will be explored further in Chapter Seven, when we focus on dilemmas in the recording task arising from an interaction between the competing demands and the various constraints on recording.

Client access

Analysis of the interview data in respect of social work values highlighted the extent to which the record was shared with service users. Only four interviewees said that they did not consciously think about the service user when writing the record, while the remaining 46 saw the service user as a principal focus in how they approached the record.

Social work departments are now legally obliged to share copies of the assessment of need and the care plan drawn up from an assessment with the service user. It should be noted that the implementation of the single assessment process, which occurred during the period of the research, meant that some departments were only just beginning to routinely share their assessments with service users, while others had been doing so for a number of years.

While service users can expect to receive copies of assessments and care plans, the rest of the file can only be accessed with a formal request. That file would then have to be prepared by a social worker, with advice from the legal department and the information governance officer. Any information from a third party (someone not employed by social services) who did not want that information shared with the service user would have to be removed. Any information that, by sharing it with the service user, might make the prevention or detection of a crime more difficult, would also have to be removed, as would any information thought to be too distressing or damaging for the service user to read. These categories of information may be actually recorded under 'restricted access', or identified as 'restricted' in the preparation of the file for access. Despite the facility for restricting certain information, the ethos of good practice over the years has been to move to a position of more 'open' recording, and many workers did describe this sense of recording as if the service user was on their shoulder, reading as they wrote, for example:

> "I always record as if the service user is sitting next to me … so that I could say: what do you think of this?… I'm very careful not to stick labels on people, and everything I write I feel that I'm open to be challenged on, that's clear.… I can substantiate what I'm saying, and if it's something someone else has said … I put it in inverted commas." (interviewee 40)

> "I'm always thinking, if I'm going to put something down on an assessment, would I be happy with someone reading it … I have this view of someone sitting on my shoulder, and I suppose that's probably sharpened up and you could call it a backside-covering job, but since much more openness to data, I probably am much more careful about what I actually physically write down. I might've been a bit freer with my views before." (interviewee 34)

It is interesting that the concern to represent the service user accurately was also equated with 'backside covering' in the context of client access, which straddles both the demands of 'values' and 'accountability'. There was a sense of responsibility to ensure the information was accurate, that the details were correctly recorded:

> "… it's also a way of presenting somebody's life to them as well.… I mean, people will pick you up on things like 'Actually I'm not this person's niece; I'm her cousin'. Or 'I'm not her son; I'm her stepson'; representing something that's really important to them, … the fact that they're a step-family and not a blood relative family.…" (interviewee 46)

> "You can interpret events in your own mind, but I think the important thing when you go out to assess somebody, because basically the service user or client has their own copy of the assessment now, whereas in

the past that didn't used to be the case, so it's improved practice, and everyone's mindset within the department, whatever we were writing down, the service user is going to get at the end of the day. It's their own assessment." (interviewee 5)

"You should never write anything anyway that you wouldn't want that service user to read. It does make you think about how you word things." (interviewee 20)

This concern with transparency extended to ensuring that the record contained no surprises for the service user, that the record only included information that had been discussed with the service user. Speculation was viewed with disapproval:

"I try to write with bearing in mind that that person has access to their file. So I try to make sure that there's nothing in there that I haven't actually discussed, or had an open discussion with them about. I try very much to make sure there isn't 'I think this might happen', because I wouldn't want it written about myself." (interviewee 21)

Even when social workers were taking care to attribute information accurately they may still encounter problems. The following example illustrates the difficulty in recording what the service user has said in terms that, while it might clarify the status of the information, it may communicate to the service user that the information they have given is subject to question or doubt:

"… if I tell you that I had polio, why should you dispute it with me?… Why would you need my doctor to prove that I had polio?… And the way you word it, could also be quite disturbing because.… 'What does she mean: I claim I have this? I've reported I've got this. What does she mean: I've reported it?'. You know, 'I have got it!'. So there is that, when you're recording information: if it is there the user is … going to read it. How do you record what they've told you in such a way that it isn't demeaning to them?" (interviewee 18)

It was recognised that sometimes information may be problematic. It may be upsetting for the service user to read, but it may be judged necessary in order to accurately describe the person and their situation and so indicate their level of need, which anticipates the functional demand of recording. In such situations good practice was seen as using factual evidence to support whatever was being recorded, so even though the service user might not always like or agree with what is written, the reliance on the evidence makes the record and the worker less vulnerable to challenge. Nevertheless the tension between providing an accurate record and one that did not jeopardise the relationship between the worker and service user could make for significant dilemmas in recording, which underlined the record as part of a process of surveillance (see Chapter Seven). The following example illustrates how the awareness of clients' right to access again connects with the values and principles of professional practice:

> "Access to records, although it's been around for a number of years ... it's becoming more and more sort of relevant as the years go on, because people are talking about data protection, ... people are wanting to see records more ... I'm always aware that somebody could read the record, so I have to be careful about what I write, and I do try to be objective, and if I make a comment I try to justify it with an explanation, because often when I look at records, you know just say 'unable to manage personal care needs', but it doesn't explain what ... so it's very vague references... or it'll say 'clothes appear neglected', well, explain why....You know that would differ from one person to the next, so someone if they saw a few stains on clothes might record, ... 'clothes being neglected', whereas with another person it would have to be that they really were dirty.... So I try to quantify what I say, backing up evidence." (interviewee 32)

The discussion so far has illuminated what social workers consider to be the fundamental values governing their approach to recording. While that discussion has hinted at some of the tensions workers may encounter in trying to observe these principles, a fuller examination of those difficulties will follow in Chapter Seven.

Functional demands

The functional demands cover three main areas. The record must establish the needs of the service user and then whether those assessed needs meet the *eligibility* criteria bands operating within a particular department. Central government established the overall eligibility framework, but each department may set its threshold at a different point within the bands of 'critical', 'substantial', 'moderate' or 'low'.

The record is also the means by which a whole range of professionals, who may be involved in assessing a particular service user, communicate. So *communication with colleagues* and other agencies is also part of the functional demand.

The record is also the means by which social workers *communicate to service providers* (those who will actually be providing the care to the service user) what care should be provided and how it should be delivered.

Eligibility

The interviewees, when given the stimulus material 'Purpose of recording' (Appendix 1b) and asked to rate the different items on the list, all identified

'Up-to-date information on service user's needs and eligibility for services', and 'Statement of purpose and plan of work' as highly important. No other items on the list of purposes were so consistently rated. This demonstrates the central importance of the process of assessment and establishing eligibility in recording and the social work task:

> "The purpose of the social work assessment is to identify what a person's needs are." (interviewee 3)

The recorded assessment and statement of eligibility is the basis on which crucial decisions will be made as to whether an individual will receive services or not. The mechanism for making such decisions in most departments is for a resource or budget allocation panel to consider requests for funding submitted by social workers, in respect of the individuals they have assessed. As budgets are rarely sufficient to meet the demands made on them, as we shall see in the next chapter, this is invariably a competitive process. The specific dilemmas that this process may generate are explored in Chapter Seven. The present discussion concentrates on the formal process and how it operates in order to demonstrate the procedural demands on recording.

The overriding concern in establishing eligibility is to demonstrate levels of risk. While the government guidelines in relation to eligibility emphasise 'risk to independence', this is often interpreted as actual physical risk:

> "You're asking for funding because you are trying to manage a risk so you would be focusing on ... in terms of like health and safety ... you know that that's what budget holders make decisions based on.... Risks, that's what they're looking at." (interviewee 40)

As well as a clear identification of the risks, the request to the panel needs to address all the possible questions the panel might ask in respect of a particular case. Social workers do not usually attend panel meetings, and so the panel decision crucially depends on the written information in the form of the panel report. There was a concern to have covered all the angles, to include all the relevant information, to have considered all possible options in how the needs might be met, otherwise the request was sent back and further delays ensued.

The previous interviewee continues:

> "... and also you know your budget holder ... you've got to be clear, because if they make the wrong decision and you haven't given them a clear sense of what the risks are, ... then it's very difficult then to actually say, well it's their fault, because it's why didn't you make it clear to them, ... but also the other side of that is that if you don't fill all the gaps and make sure that they're aware of everything, then they may question something or not prioritise something, you'll get a reply

back with perhaps a question, and you'll think, well I knew the answer to that, ...why didn't you kind of second-guess that they would have looked at that, ... I always treat it as writing an assignment, you need to cover everything and make it clear, because otherwise you're going to get it right back ... then it doubles your work." (interviewee 40)

"You know that you have to have considered ... certain things; otherwise it gets thrown back at you. So you make sure that those things are in there." (interviewee 12)

Some workers had attended panel meetings, and that experience emphasised the need to ensure reports not only covered everything, but were also to the point. There may be a large number of requests for consideration at any one meeting, and workers realised that they had to ensure that their report made as effective a case as possible:

"I've sat on the panel so ... I really ... know how their thinking is going to be, so ... I've got to knock down things in this assessment to get through to the key to whatever I'm after...." (interviewee 34)

"I tend to summarise and be more concise, because I realise that they're probably getting through 50 requests for funding, and I want to make a strong argument. I don't want to take pages and pages in doing it because I know after the first couple of paragraphs it ... I have to give the information that I think they want, and I try to second-guess the questions they will be asking, because quite often the funding ... it will come back with those questions on if I haven't answered them." (interviewee 38)

From these extracts it can be seen that workers have a keen sense of writing for the panel, addressing their concerns and priorities, and adopting a style that is appropriate to busy readers who have limited time to absorb the information. For many workers, writing panel reports raised very real dilemmas that highlighted the tensions between the functional and value demands. With the former, the emphasis was on concise recording that focused on risks, while the latter underlined the importance of a person-centred approach that might emphasise individual detail. These dilemmas are discussed further in Chapter Seven.

Communication with colleagues

Of the 50 interviewees, only three said that they were not thinking about colleagues when they recorded. For the rest, the awareness that colleagues would require the file to understand what had been happening with a particular case was a significant concern. This connected with their own experience of reading other people's files and the reliance on easily accessible relevant information, particularly in situations where that information was urgently needed:

> "... inevitably social workers come and go, they change, and so it's quite important that when you pick a case up ... what's gone on before." (interviewee 27)

> "... if something goes pear-shaped over a weekend or in the evening, then the out-of-hours duty team need to have as much up-to-date information as possible about that person's situation." (interviewee 46)

The file communicates to colleagues what actions have been taken, and unless that has been documented, they would not know what had been done:

> "There's no point in it being in your head." (interviewee 7)

The issue of duty was repeatedly raised in this context. When workers take 'duty' calls they are often dealing with urgent situations, where there is no allocated worker, or the allocated worker is not available. In such circumstances the worker is totally reliant on the file to provide the information on what has happened previously with the case:

> "... a third of the time is spent on duty ... [what is] really important on duty is good recording because you spend half your time unpicking it, and you're on duty for a morning, then you could spend a lot of time reading what somebody else has already done, if it's not really clearly laid out." (interviewee 28)

> "You know if you're on duty and following someone else's work, and they haven't even used an A4 sheet of paper and there are post-it notes all over, and scraps of names, and you know and you can't follow it." (interviewee 31)

There was a recognition that they were dealing with situations which, if not urgent, might often be fast moving in terms of events, and if the recording was not up to date, it would be difficult for anyone else to know what work had been done, or what might need to be done:

> "Because people in the community – especially older people – their health changes almost on a daily basis – their frailties, their needs, the risks ... when you're away, you need someone to pick it up.... You have to be clear with the information you're leaving; so they need to know who the home care provider is, how many calls.... So certain

information you want your colleagues to instantly be able to see...." (interviewee 17)

This concern to ensure colleagues knew what was going on with a case was particularly important with workers who were part-time, or who worked in a specialist capacity:

"For us that's really important, because if I'm on holiday, or taken sick, or just in the normal way, ... my colleague X does Mondays, Tuesdays, I do Wednesdays, she quite often does Thursdays and I do Fridays here.... We have to write down what's happened, what's the next thing you need to do." (interviewee 28)

"... there's only myself and one other worker in the team, ... doing physical disabilities. I am quite conscious that if I don't write things clearly, they [colleagues] might not understand it, because I know when I first started working with people with physical disabilities, and you hear all these abbreviations for medical conditions, and you think, 'What on earth does that mean?'. I try not to do that, because I think, ... if I'm on holiday this lot [other team members] are going to have to pick it up, and they need to be able to understand it.... I try to make everything as clear as possible, because I don't want an older person's social worker coming along and not seeing where I'm going with it.... Treating it like one of their cases.... They won't necessarily think of doing that themselves, because it's not something they do on a regular basis." (interviewee 9)

Here the worker was explicitly using the file to ensure that colleagues continued to work with the case in a particular way. It was argued that working with younger physically disabled people encouraged a focus on rehabilitation, whereas working with older people made that less likely, and the worker was using her recording to distinguish her particular approach to any other colleagues working with that case.

There was also a sense that the file recording demonstrated a basic courtesy between colleagues. This was about professional self-respect, wanting colleagues to feel that you were competent, and that you appreciated and understood that everyone relied on good quality information in order to do their job:

"... I'm conscious that, when I'm writing, I want people to be able to go into my files and say, 'Right. X has done this, this, and this; and this, this, and this needs to be done'. I try and keep it clear." (interviewee 45)

"I record every telephone call, every conversation, every letter, every piece of information that comes in to me, because if you don't and you hand the case on to someone else, they don't know where you're going, and if it's a long case, because sometimes we can hold cases for up to a year-and-a-half, I often do a summary as well every so often ... because if you're on leave ... and something crops up, then you need to be specific, you need to let people know where you are with that." (interviewee 44)

This highlights the issue of the problem of holding the case for a longer period. Despite the overall emphasis on a fast turnover of cases, there is still a limited amount of long-term work, even in older people's teams. It was recognised that the longer a worker held a case the more likely they were to see the file as their own and not consider other colleagues.

The file was expected to demonstrate a certain professional standard, but it also raised the issue of colleagues' responsibility to one another to pass on information that was not only important in being able to work with the case but, at a fundamental level, was instrumental in protecting colleagues from potential risks:

"I've been handed some really cruddy files, where the information is rubbish, and I think 'You ought to be ashamed of yourself, producing that tripe. It gives me no information whatsoever'. I'd rather give too much information than not enough, and I want to make sure that I gave that vital bit of information; ... that vital thing that ...'this person lashes out at any social worker who walks through the door' ... these are the vital things that people need to know.... So as long as those things are down and clearly written, I feel I've done my duty by my colleagues. I wish they would feel the same as me." (interviewee 46)

In contrast, there was also a degree of scepticism about the value of the information in the file, not because it was inadequate, but because it might reflect more of the worker's own judgements about an individual service user which might not be reliable. This underlines yet another contradiction. The record was an important means of communicating important information, and yet that record was constructed by an individual and would therefore be compromised by their subjective perception. So the question arises as to how far the record could be seen as a reliable account:

"There has always been a constant tension about that one, part of my head says, no, no, I'd rather go out without prejudiced notions and so I won't read it. And another part of me says, what an incredibly stupid thing to do because ... it may turn out, ... it's going to be some guy who is incredibly antagonistic and there is a background of violence." (interviewee 39)

Many interviewees recognised the difficulty of recording objective information. As a consequence there was a tendency to distrust the information in the file. This might arise from experiences where the information in the file did not match the individual service user as perceived by the worker, or it might simply be a reluctance to be influenced by anything other than own individual professional judgement:

> "You can read something, because there's two sides to whether or not you read a case file before you go out and meet somebody, or you go out with this blank canvas and then you assess them from what you know." (interviewee 48)

The concern may extend to not wanting the record to blunt or distort your perception of what was happening with a service user and their situation:

> "I prefer not to see people with preconceived ideas. Apart from anything I like to think that I'm fairly observant, and I think if you go in with preconceived ideas you stop looking for the unusual things." (interviewee 35)

So at a fundamental level there was again ambivalence about the value of the record. On the one hand, much effort goes into providing information in order to enable colleagues to provide continuity in working with a service user; on the other hand, because the record is the product of someone else's perception, this renders it potentially unreliable, which may be to the detriment of the service user. Despite such misgivings workers still rely on the record. There is a tension between the subjectively produced record, and the record as an objective assessment.

While recording is essentially a means for workers to communicate with one another without the need for direct contact, the point was made that, even if you spoke to a colleague about a case, they might not remember, and so the record becomes the only source of information anyone can depend on, including the individual who originally wrote the record, but now cannot recall what happened:

> "I've had experiences of being on the other end of it, when things aren't recorded, and it's such a nightmare to try and work with, because you don't know what was going on; unless you speak to the person, and half the time if it is in the past they can't remember. If it's not there, it's very difficult to work with." (interviewee 47)

In a situation where social work is increasingly organised around short-term interventions with service users, sufficient to undertake the assessment and set up the care package, the record assumes greater significance in being the source of information on which successive practitioners rely, to know what has happened and what is currently happening with a case. Interviewees were concerned with the effectiveness of the record in communicating to colleagues about the work that had been undertaken. This was to ensure continuity, as well as demonstrate the practitioner's competence.

Nevertheless, there was also a distrust of the record. Some interviewees acknowledged that the record depended on the subjective perceptions of previous workers, and as a consequence, the record might be seen as less reliable. Some referred to the dilemma of whether to read the record before they went out to assess a service user, with the concern that the record might prejudice their view of the individual, where, on the other hand, the record might include important information, which might be crucial for ensuring their own safety. So even within the functional demands of recording, there were tensions as to how useful the record was as a source of reliable information.

Communication with service providers

Service providers are discussed separately from colleagues because they raise different issues. While communicating with colleagues is about letting them know what is going on and what has been done in a case, communicating with service providers is about ensuring that they have the necessary information to understand a service user's needs and how to meet them. Social workers rely on the care plan to communicate this information:

> "It's important to know what the client's needs are, what their level of function is, what their abilities are, and what they're struggling with. And information on their health that is relevant: if someone's a diabetic, or something like that. What's important to the service user, and what the risks they're involved with." (interviewee 5)

> "I think they need to know the level of support that the person needs, and I think from that angle, health and functional ability and current support are the three main issues. We do risk assessments to outline any issues with regard to health and safety with regard to accommodation, the situation and location to the property. Service user's health and behaviour patterns etc to ensure the carers who go to them are safe, and aware of their needs." (interviewee 24)

In addition to the basic information in relation to the service user's areas of needs, there was an awareness of the importance of sharing some information about the service user:

> "I tend to be very detailed about what the client needs, … because … if the care plan and the care package doesn't work, it comes back to me to sort out, so I try to include a lot of detail there. And I think it's important for providers that you do give some history of the background, because…. I think, well they're the ones that are going

to be talking to the client, they're the ones that are going to need to establish and build that relationship, so they need to know background information to start conversations." (interviewee 45)

However, judging how much information might be appropriate to share with service providers could be difficult when it might infringe the service user's privacy:

> "Well yes, you do have to give them chapter and verse. They want to see the ins and outs of everything, in order to make a decision as to whether they can meet that person's needs, which is fair enough.... It's the same document that goes ... that encapsulates the person's situation, so again when you said: 'Who are you thinking of when you write the assessment?', I'm thinking: the person themselves is going to read it, and the provider is going to read it. What right does the provider have to know all the intimate details of somebody's life; what use is it to them to know that they don't get on with Auntie Nelly?" (interviewee 46)

These dilemmas around the different readerships sit at the core of recording practice: who is the social worker writing for? Information that is appropriate to share with one party, the service user, might feel inappropriate to share with the other, the care service provider, and yet they may be given the same documents. Here we can clearly see that competing audiences have implications for what may be left in and what may be left out of the record, which then may render it less relevant for one audience as opposed to another.

One of the main concerns in respect of recording for service providers was the contractual side of the record. Issues around specifying liability arose in their relationship with service providers. The care plan is the basis of the agreement between the provider and the social services department as to what the provider will actually do in respect of working with a particular service user. Clearly meeting individual need sits against a backdrop of structural (service) conditions that implicitly and explicitly shape what and how needs can be met:

> "On the care plans you ... make it absolutely clear what it is that you're asking them to do. And I think that's something that I definitely learned over time, is that ... something that seems blindingly obvious to me, that I would expect them to do, if you don't write it down, they won't do it.... You've got a service user who is blind, who has no mobility, and you've got on the care plan to make them a cup of tea when they get there in the morning. But if you don't write on it 'and then to take the cup away and wash it up', you can guarantee that they will leave the cup next to.... So you have to be kind of very direct ... but again it depends on the service provider." (interviewee 43)

This concern was not just prompted by ensuring that providers would fulfil the requirements of the care plan, but that they would work in an appropriate way with service users:

> "I know if I don't put it on the care plan, they don't know what to do.... I prefer to be an enabler than to send the care package in to take over. I suppose, if somebody is able to do something, I will make sure that that goes in the care plan, because the last thing I want is the care assistant going in and saying, 'Oh, I'll do that – it's quicker' ... taking every last bit of independence away. So ... my care plans are quite full and specific." (interviewee 35)

While they were concerned to share more person-centred information with service providers, they were also expected to use the record, in the form of the care plan, to clearly delineate the contractual expectations in respect of the provider's responsibility in fulfilling the requirements of a particular service package. Many felt that this legalistic aspect to their role was alien to their professional social care values, and was sometimes contrary to commonsense ideas of what should be involved in care provision.

The issue of the contractual relationship between social services and service providers negotiated by social workers anticipates some of the themes in the next section, which looks at accountability demands in the recording task.

Accountability demands

Legal liability

When asked about how much they were thinking about lawyers when they were recording, less than half the interviewees said this was a significant consideration, although many answers betrayed an ambivalence. Some would initially respond by saying they never or rarely thought about lawyers, and then go on to recount a story where a colleague's record had been involved in an investigation of a complaint, and how that had impressed on them the importance of recording. For many the legal accountability of their record was an issue that was not an immediate consideration but it was something they were vaguely conscious of:

> "Not much at all, it's only in that kind of back of your mind sense of how things went wrong, if it was a complaint." (interviewee 3)

For some there was a contrast between present and previous roles, where certain areas of work were seen to be much more likely to involve legal scrutiny:

> "I think it's somewhere in the back of my head, ... less so now, but certainly when I was doing forensic psychiatry, my God, I might find

myself on the front of *The Sun*, so it's much less these days, although I am aware of legal obligation...." (interviewee 39)

"I think when I was working in childcare you would have been much more conscious." (interviewee 37)

Even when workers were not in the front line of mental health or childcare work, there was still an awareness that all their records were legal documents and should conform to the rules of evidence:

"... when I first came into the post, and this is sort of 10 years ago, and I was working on the older persons team, and somebody said to me, 'Don't record anything that can't be read in court'." (interviewee 48)

The stories that the interviewees shared often involved investigations after service users had died, or there had been an access request that then prompted a complaint. These stories represented in many workers' minds the nightmare scenario, where their work was going to be judged solely on the basis of the file evidence. Workers dreaded the possibility that the record would reveal or suggest that they were in some way at fault. They might be confident that their actual practice was acceptable, but there was the doubt as to whether they remembered to document everything that they did. It may be the seemingly insignificant detail that did not seem important to record, or they simply forgot about, which becomes the crucial detail on which their professional reputation may depend:

"I think once you've been through situations where there has been threat of legal action, or media interest, and you've had managers looking at it from that perspective.... I can think of a case ... somebody unfortunately died in a fire, but they had refused assistance from the social worker three days before to move them out of their flat. And that was well recorded: the visit was recorded, the conversation was recorded ... a complaint was made by a neighbour, that we didn't do anything for this person, and that was the cause of their death.... I was actually involved with managing that social worker at the time, and thankfully he had recorded his visit." (interviewee 8)

"I did have an incident with a client that I used to have, she was transferred to a different department ... I had her for about four years and after four months she committed suicide ... there had to be a coroner's inquest etc and it meant, because I was with her the longest, I had to write the report, because I had done all the work in those four years, and I had to trawl back in her case file, read everything and write an extensive report.... So I learnt in a sense how doubly important it is that the case files are up to scratch." (interviewee 33)

"I have been in a situation where a colleague had a complaint. You know, there'd been various complaints at various times, but a close colleague had a complaint, and because I was actually the care manager I was involved in the complaint. And because of my colleagues and my case records, we were able to prove that the complaint was unfounded. And the whole thing was so unfortunate and traumatic; and in fact the colleague left." (interviewee 35)

Social workers recognise that there are certain situations where they can anticipate that service users may be unhappy and likely to lodge a complaint. In such situations the record may be approached with more caution. Many suggested that they recorded in more detail in cases that were expected to be contentious. Withdrawal of service is an issue that causes difficulties. Service users may have been receiving services for some time, but because the department changes its banding threshold for its eligibility criteria, service users may find they are no longer eligible for those services. Workers have to manage such changes and recognise that this is a situation where their recording may be crucial in documenting how the decision has been made in order to justify that decision if there is a subsequent challenge:

"I had one particular service user, who we were withdrawing services from, who was incredibly vocal, and knew her rights and her position … she decided to challenge the decision to withdraw services and took it to X Law. My assessment was then picked over by our legal team to within an inch of its life." (interviewee 43)

Some cases will be seen as contentious simply because of the people involved, either the service user themselves or their families. They will be seen as more challenging or likely to be dissatisfied with the service. This may not only lead to more detailed recording, but also more prompt recording:

"When I have belligerent relatives saying: 'I want this, this and this and why haven't they been doing this', and really pissed off with so and so, then I will tend to get it down fairly quickly." (interviewee 39)

"Only in a difficult case. Only if, … from day one if … we've got this case … every office has got cases which just … float around, and everybody knows the client and their family, so I would say, not on every case do I actually record everything … every single detail … mainly the ones that I know could go to complaint. But then any case could go to complaint really, couldn't it?" (interviewee 45)

In this sense recording almost requires a capacity for clairvoyance. Sometimes it is not possible to predict if a case is going to become contentious. The worker may then find that there is a complaint in respect of a case that they thought was straightforward and had not considered such detailed recording would be necessary. Sometimes it is the nature of the work itself that is seen to more particularly raise the issue of accountability. Adult protection is an area where it is crucial to document the evidence in preparation for legal proceedings:

> "... we do quite a lot of adult protection investigations and, and if you have that, and if you know that it's something that potentially could end up in court, or that there might be some sort of arbitration, or it could go further, you would want to be very clear and specific about things." (interviewee 1)

The issue of liability and litigation, linked to an increased perception of risk, is seen as something that both individuals and departments have to be more aware of these days. There was a sense that the public were more likely to consider legal action, and this heightened the feeling of anxiety in relation to the record:

> "I'd be thinking about how's the department done, ... their duty in respect of the person that the lawyers looking at the records in terms of possibly being sued or whatever, ... nowadays you think about that side of things more than you, ... it's something that's developing, and records could actually land someone in very deep trouble.... I suppose we'd always have to think about intervention and the fact that ... what's written down is written down and it's there for all to see, ... if you haven't done something right, it's there." (interviewee 32)

This concern over accountability becomes more complex where social services are working with other agencies. The position of the hospital social worker can be especially problematic. On the one hand, they may find themselves under pressure to process a patient's discharge, with the threat of the delayed discharge financial penalty for their department if they do not comply within the designated period. On the other hand, they may have real concerns as to the safety of the discharge for the service user. They may feel that the record is the only means to ensure that there is documented evidence that they have acted professionally and in the best interests of the service user:

> "... because we're not the lead agency in a hospital setting, ... with the policy on delayed discharge and people being placed into interim placements and me being asked to sign up to it, ... when I was recording if things hadn't gone well for that service user or there was issues of conflict between the medical staff or myself and the family, I recorded taking that into account...." (interviewee 30)

"I mean in some cases that give you the heebie jeebies, a gentleman who insisted to go home and wouldn't have the service, so the record demonstrates that we've done everything we should possibly do ... offered him services, pressed him to have services, twisted his arm behind his back to have services." (interviewee 29)

The record may also be used to exert pressure on professionals from other agencies to ensure a particular response:

"And I've got pushier in my recording, and I used recording as a tool and rather than saying: 'Well, are you going to visit the person and can you give me an opinion on their injuries?', when we've had a report of new injuries on somebody. I am much more assertive now and I say: 'What do you want me to record in the direct records?' ... because we have a county at risk policy which is health and social services, ... 'What do you want me to record in that record?' and ... I use it as a very strong tool." (interviewee 31)

There appeared to be a curious attitude to legal accountability. While social workers might feel anxious over their own accountability in relation to the record, they also recognised the power of the record to influence the behaviour of professionals from other agencies. They were able to use the record in situations where they felt they had less authority as a means to exercise influence over others and achieve a particular outcome. The concern with documenting risk and the extent to which it was being effectively managed acted as a powerful sanction in negotiations with other agencies, where there might be considerable arguments over questions of responsibility and liability.

While some workers said that lawyers were not at the forefront in their mind, there was a widespread awareness of the record in terms of accountability. The 'back- covering' element of recording was significant, as social workers experienced the pressure of knowing their records could be subject to legal scrutiny at any time.

While some workers acknowledged that calculations would be made about which cases to record in greater detail, on the basis of anticipated contentiousness or complexity, they were also aware that even the most straightforward cases could take unpredictable turns. This made it very difficult to identify what level of detail was required in every case. Some interviewees suggested that it was the experience of having their files subjected to legal scrutiny, following a complaint or investigation, that had made them more wary, and inclined to record in greater detail. It was conceded, however, that this contradicted the functional demands to process cases as quickly and efficiently as possible, with the minimum of recording necessary to either decline or provide a service. This resulted in an uneasy tension, where workers accepted that they were unable to record in the detail required for legal scrutiny in every case. Instead they relied on their judgement to successfully discriminate between those cases that might be subject to legal dispute, and the rest. There was a sense that this depended as much on luck as judgement, given the level of risk involved in many of the cases they dealt with. Despite the considerable damage that can be done to individual and departmental reputations in such situations, the continuance of high profile tragedies and subsequent inquiries are testimony to an uneasy acceptance of doing the best you can and hoping you stay lucky. So defensive recording was practised in certain cases where challenge was anticipated, but the sheer pressure created by the volume of work meant that the level of recording, in many cases, left the worker potentially vulnerable.

Performance indicators

Many of the interviewees expressed much frustration together with a sense of reluctant resignation at the priority given to collecting statistical information to provide evidence of meeting performance indicators. Here the demand on the record was to provide information to satisfy the processes of audit and inspection.

The interviewees accepted that part of the purpose of recording was to provide evidence that they, and the department, were working efficiently and effectively, although there was some doubt as to whether the measures employed were particularly meaningful. There was resentment at the amount of time that could be taken up with recording additional information, solely for the purpose of proving that centrally driven government targets were being met. Nevertheless, many were aware that, without that evidence, their department's funding might be reduced and so there was a cynical acceptance that this was necessary to achieve a desired end:

> "I can see the point of that but frankly I find it really time consuming and annoying…. It doesn't feel like the best use of your professional expertise." (interviewee 22)

> "We're encouraged with that one, … that one is pushed. I wouldn't say I don't think it's important, because I understand why we have to do it. Our primary concern is still the people that were working with. So although … we know that we have to, and we do try and be aware of those things, it … feels like that pales into insignificance when you're talking about an 89-year-old woman who is being abused by her son, … whether or not we tick the box for the government…. I think social work and computer systems and government recording statistics and all those sort of things, it can be quite difficult to marry them … together really…. When you go home with eye strain because you've been working at a computer all day and you're qualified as a social worker." (interviewee 4)

In addition to the feeling that this was largely an administrative activity which was not the best use of professional time, there was a concern that the software packages being used to record information on service user files were often designed more to suit the requirements for statistical information than to work more effectively with the service user – among the questionnaire respondents 62.6% felt that recording systems were designed more to produce management information. A similar figure was found among those respondents who held managerial responsibility:

> "I'm not enamoured of the way that certain of the software is being developed in order to provide statistical information in terms of government targets. I think that the software ... is now being developed less as a tool for professionals to do their job, and more as a tool to provide the statistical returns for the government. I think it's the wrong way round and ... I think that when you're looking for the software that's available, it should actually be there to facilitate our job, and then if people need statistical analysis from it, they should find a way of interrogating it without it having to impinge on what we have to do." (interviewee 3)

> "Our forms are now designed around, ... to include tick boxes for that we're meeting certain targets." (interviewee 13)

> "... with these performance indicators ... at the moment the government has decided that certain indicators are important, so that's given ... to the county councils and so forms tend to reflect that, and again they're not necessarily about the quality of the service." (interviewee 27)

Many workers were sceptical about the validity of the statistical information. There was a feeling that this preoccupation with statistics did not, in the end, say anything very meaningful about what was actually happening to service users:

> "... you can manipulate statistics to whatever you want to prove really, can't you?" (interviewee 19)

Many workers expressed a resigned attitude, accepting that, if they did not provide the required information, they would be reminded by managers, and ultimately would not be able to close cases until all the information had been properly logged:

> "... there are certain parts of the IT system that pulls through on central data, and they come back and say 'You haven't recorded this and we need it'.... So we do get stuff back that needs to go on the appropriate data sections." (interviewee 24)

"I do what I'm asked to do because I won't get a case finished and closed off if I don't, so I do it." (interviewee 25)

Many felt frustrated at what they felt was valuable time being diverted in retrieving information, when it was assumed that, having previously completed the required paperwork, that information should already be available:

"We have computers.... I find it a real PAIN, that I get emails asking me to collect things out of file ... for the life of me I can't understand why, having completed all these forms ... they then ask me to get it out of the file again. But ... they do." (interviewee 18)

There were some lone voices:

"I don't know whether it's my management background or not, but I think that targets are important, because the more stars we get, then the more money we get, ... the more creative we can be." (interviewee 38)

Far more typical were comments that suggested a reluctant acceptance in respect of providing statistical information, recognising that, if funding was dependent on such information, then it was ultimately service users who lost out if the information was not forthcoming. Nevertheless it was still seen as an extra chore, when there were so many other priorities, and the job was made even more difficult by inefficient information systems:

"... it's a big priority [for the department], because we've got to meet our performance targets, and therefore we're overloaded with horrible forms which require us to tick boxes to show we've done things, if we can understand what they actually mean, half the time you can't in relation to a particular process you're doing ... we know we have to justify what we do and account for it, but our whole IT systems are lacking, instead of doing these things as it were automatically as part of.... What seems to be essential recording you've got a whole extra burden.... And people feel very frustrated and very angry about that I think it doesn't seem like a priority when you're trying to get things done for people. When there's a huge amount of material to produce anyway ... then you've got this other lot, but a lot of it is down to bad systems." (interviewee 37)

Performance indicators were seen as yet another pressure which seemed removed from the day-to-day concerns of the social worker, and yet they realised that they could not ignore the issue They worked with systems that demanded this information, and without it there was a risk that there would be even less funding available for already overstretched services.

The previous interviewee later returns to the theme, emphasising the extent to which recording such information was in tension with what she saw as her professional priorities but, nevertheless, recording such information was part of how her individual performance would be monitored and evaluated:

> "Oh god ... I've failed again this week, because here's a list of activities that I haven't moved on, activities meaning ticked a box, not activities meaning doing anything that matters ... management pressure, they've got performance targets to meet ... and that gets passed down to us and it's just stress." (interviewee 37)

Conclusion

This chapter has identified the complex and contradictory demands in the recording task. Social work values emphasise the importance of person-centred recording and greater sharing of the record with the service user. Sometimes, however sensitive or potentially embarrassing, information has to be recorded in order to meet the functional needs around establishing eligibility, accurately stating the level of need and risk identified, and this may be difficult to then share with the service user. The record is the evidence of the surveillance process to which the service user has been subjected, and confronting service users with that evidence can be potentially uncomfortable for them and the practitioner.

Person-centred recording requires an account of the individual, including their strengths and their weaknesses, but this may be in tension with the functional demands of service provision, which are concentrated on minimal information to ensure service delivery. Here the emphasis is on information that is quickly accessible and that focuses on the reasons for the agency's involvement with a case. Invariably this is concerned with emphasising the risks to a service user. This is the basis on which eligibility will be assessed and is assumed not to require the more descriptive information about an individual. A tension remains, however, even within the functional demands, with the information required by service providers being more detailed and person-centred in order for the care workers to be able to work appropriately with the service user.

The functional demands of recording are then seen to be in tension with the concerns around legal accountability, which require far more detailed recording in order to comply with the rules of evidence and demonstrate that work has been undertaken according to established procedures. Here the concern is with producing a record that adequately documents for legal and audit purposes, that individual practitioners and the organisation have properly discharged their duties and responsibilities, and that the record will be sufficiently robust in situations of challenge. The functional demands mean it is not possible to record in this level of detail with every case, and so judgements are made as to which cases might be subject to challenge, acknowledging that this relies somewhat precariously on the worker's ability to make such predictions.

The case record is also increasingly being organised in terms of the statistical information required to demonstrate that targets have been met, in order to ensure continued funding. So the record is designed to collect information according to an overall organisational agenda, and yet still produce a meaningful account of an individual and their situation. The audit society is transforming the service user file, creating tensions with both the values and the functional demands on recording. A more specific focus on these dilemmas is left until Chapter Seven. Before that the discussion moves on to consider the resources/constraints that interact with the demands, facilitating the recording task or making it still more difficult.

SIX

Resources/constraints impacting on recording

This chapter explores the resources/constraints that impinge on the recording task. These conditions can be seen positively or negatively, depending on whether they are seen to be facilitating the process of recording or not. More often they are experienced as constraints and exacerbate the tensions already identified. A more detailed discussion of the interplay between the demands and the constraints, which produces particular dilemmas for practitioners in writing the record, forms the focus of the next chapter.

The resources/constraints provide the context in which the demands operate. They bear no particular relationship to each of the demands, but simply encircle the demands and provide the context within which the demands compete and the record is produced.

Developing recording practice covers everything that may have an impact on the worker's sense of competence in recording (see Figure 6.1). This includes the process of *learning to record*, the availability of clear and consistent guidelines in relation to recording procedures and the ongoing *management feedback* on practice.

Time available for recording extends not only to the issue of how much time, but the quality of that time. Interrupted time may be seen as less valuable than undisturbed time in relation to recording. It includes the overall issue of pressure of work flow and the organisation of work.

Change is almost a continual state of affairs in many modern work settings. In respect of social workers and recording there are two principal areas of change that are relevant. First, the way information is collected and shared within social services and other agencies, and the increasingly widespread introduction of *IT* in recording. Second, the changes in the *social work role* in relation to care management, an issue that still reverberates for many workers, despite care management being introduced nearly two decades ago. These changes may be seen as welcome improvements or regrettable developments, in trying to maintain professional standards in recording.

Budget and service provision impinges fundamentally on the social worker's capacity to deliver the services they believe the service user needs. Because the availability of resources is something beyond their control, and is unpredictable, the size of the budget and the range of services available are crucial in determining how they negotiate within these limits. The record assumes strategic importance in succeeding in what many perceive to be a competitive process.

Figure 6.1: Resources/constraints

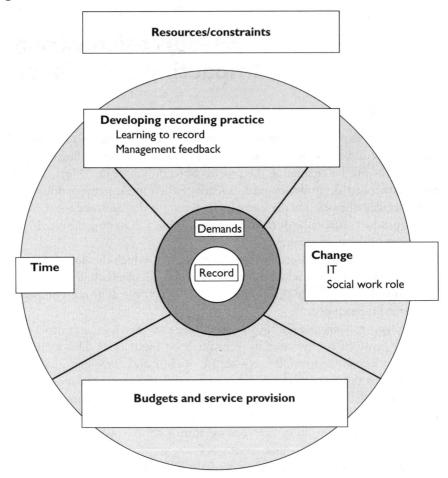

Developing recording practice

In this section I first discuss the experience of learning to record described by social workers, and then move on to their perception of management direction and feedback on recording practice, as well as the value of policies and procedures on recording. In looking at these areas I want to not only explore the process by which workers develop their skills in recording, but also look at how they come to identify what constitutes 'good practice' in recording. It is only through the process of learning and feedback on practice that the expectations around what constitutes good recording emerge.

Learning to record

The majority of interviewees had not received any formal training in how to record, either as part of their qualifying training or in the form of in-house training since they started work. Only nine identified any relevant training on the subject. Of the questionnaire respondents only 30.3% said that formal teaching had been a significant influence on their learning to record:

"Negligible, I would say. Not enough." (interviewee 48)

"Nothing." (interviewee 28)

"I've recorded for many years, I've never had any training on it." (interviewee 32)

"It wasn't a high priority [in qualifying training]." (interviewee 39)

"Very little that I can recall in my qualifying training … that's probably what most people would say, … but by the time I trained I was already very used to recording because I worked as an unqualified social worker.… As an unqualified social worker, nobody told me that I had to record anything … [I] just was started and was given my first case in the first week, … and nobody said a word about what I had to do and I was just left to get on with it, and after a day or two I thought I'd better write some of this down.… Really, I taught myself to record." (interviewee 40)

Although this last comment suggests a rather extreme situation, it does indicate the way in which recording is a task that is so taken for granted that a newly appointed unqualified worker was not given any explicit instructions about recording, not even that she was expected to actually record information in the file. Many interviewees described a process of informal learning where skills were acquired rather than taught. This view was also apparent among the questionnaire respondents, with 95.9% saying that 'doing the job' had been a significant influence on learning to record:

"… as you sort of gain experience you begin to know what's more pertinent." (interviewee 17)

"…you kind of learn the trade as you go along." (interviewee 33)

The interviewees made a distinction between the knowledge-based qualifying training and the practical skills that were learned on the job. Competence in assessment and recording developed from experience. The next extract describes a complex process, where lack of experience leads to uncertainty over what and how to record certain information. Information may then not be recorded but, with greater experience, confidence develops in what it is appropriate to record, and how to write that information. The record may not only reflect, but also actually determine what is discussed with the service user:

> "You get more confident, so you record things which you didn't feel you could record before.... Like medical conditions. When I first started.... 'Should I be recording that? Oh no, I don't think so' ... maybe they don't understand what that is. But now I will say to the client, 'Oh, you've got a heart condition. Do you understand what ...?'. So now I would record that they have a heart condition ... and, 'the client's understanding is this'.... I think it's lack of knowledge when you first qualify, because your knowledge is very basic when you qualify....And what you learn in university is nothing in reality to what you learn when you're on the wards, or working with a client.... All the case studies that you do at university, they're very superficial really, you may have worked through how you could have resolved that situation, but nobody told you how to record things, or what you should have recorded, or what the client might have wanted you to record.... I mean I've only been qualified just over three years." (interviewee 19)

The link between greater competence and experience is based on increasing familiarity with dealing with a range of social work situations. Workers described a process of learning to record through the examples set by the files they read. Among the questionnaire respondents 61.5% said that reading other people's files had been a significant influence on how they learned to record. The reading of other people's files helped to identify the expectations in respect of recording:

> "I think we all learn from each other, and we learn by example." (interviewee 48)

> "... the way you learned ... was you just looked at other people's files." (interviewee 10)

Workers identified models of good practice in their terms and tried to emulate the example they set:

> "So 80% of my working life is about recording, yet there's no formal training done, well, certainly when I did my training there wasn't any sort of formal training; you tended to ... pick up from other, more senior practitioners." (interviewee 8)

The experience of working with information recorded by other colleagues also demonstrated effective and less effective ways to record. Could the information be easily accessed and understood? Was the information relevant and useful in working with the service user? As with the discussion on communicating with colleagues, certain areas of work, namely 'duty' and 'out of hours', provided very valuable learning opportunities in identifying examples of good recording:

> "… we're so used to doing duty….And we're so used to making sure that we note everything down. We do it a lot. So I think we're quite good at it….Because we know that … cases get passed around a lot…. I think, that makes us … good at case recording." (interviewee 9)

> "… I work for the out-of-hours service [the emergency service], and … it isn't until you look at other people's recording that you realise…. I mean it does pull you up by your bootstraps, because you suddenly think, 'Fantastic. This person has just recorded just the information I need'…. You can look at other practitioners' recording and you just think, 'Oh, my goodness …why haven't you been pulled up by your manager?'." (interviewee 48)

Although the workers could identify what they considered good and bad practice in the records they read, they were nevertheless questioning why inconsistent standards in recording appeared to be tolerated by management. This theme will be developed further in the next section. So the sense of confusion as to what is acceptable is further reinforced. Does the inconsistency arise from different managers having different ideas, or is the inconsistency simply an indication that management is not very concerned with the standard of recording in the case file? Workers were left feeling frustrated and confused.

While many workers relied on their own judgement, based on what they thought was important, left to devise their own recording strategies, there was still a sense of uncertainty, of not really knowing whether they were getting it right:

> "I've never really given too much thought about recording, but I do think that I have developed my own format by maybe looking at others' recordings, … if I contact Dr Bloggs I will put Dr Bloggs' telephone contact number down. I will take the name of the person I spoke to … it's basic patterns I have established and habits that you get into but, who knows, maybe somebody else finds my recording rubbish, I don't know, I've never had any feedback on mine." (interviewee 30)

Such uncertainty can lead to feelings of confusion. Seeing different ways of recording in the files may lead to anxiety over what was the right way to record. This was shared by questionnaire respondents, 68.4% of whom reported confusion because of inconsistent standards in recording. This illustrates the ambivalent and contradictory aspects of recording, where social workers were left unclear about what constituted a good record, where what may be appropriate for one readership might not be appropriate for another.

Although recording skills were assumed to develop on the job, longer experience did not necessarily result in a greater sense of confidence about what to record and how to record. Indeed the sense of confusion over the problematic nature of recording seemed to increase with experience, with twice as many of the questionnaire respondents with over 20 years' experience (49%) saying that recording was complicated by different readerships, as compared with 24% of those with less than one year's experience. Of those qualified less than a year 51% thought that recording was confusing because of inconsistent standards. The percentage again rose rather than declined with experience, with at least 69% of all those with six or more years' experience agreeing that inconsistency led to confusion:

> "I felt like I've lost my way. As I say, I write quite descriptive things in my notes, ... and lots of other people don't, and you do start to query whether you're doing it right or not.... Some people instead of writing ... proper sentences, just like little bullet points, and you think, well, maybe that's more helpful for the people.... So I think sometimes confusion can set in afterwards, and probably doing it all right to begin with." (interviewee 41)

For some the effectiveness of their recording was a straightforward matter of: did it serve the purpose? Was it adequate? In terms of assessments and requests for funding, the effectiveness would be measured in terms of whether the information was adequate to make a decision:

> "If your recording isn't OK, somebody is going to come to you and say, well, you can't make a decision based on this, and then this is what's lacking, that is what's lacking.... And so you do learn [what are the] expectations by doing the job." (interviewee 3)

For a small number of interviewees managers had played a significant part in their learning to record, although this was the case with half (50.5%) of the questionnaire respondents. These managers had often not just given instruction and guidance on recording practice, but had also motivated staff to value recording as an important skill:

> "I had a very thorough, very clear manager who led by example and I've learnt with skills from her in what to do and what not to do." (interviewee 31)

> "My first team manager, when I joined my present post, was very good at going through what you'd written: she'd get the red pen out and [laughter] sort of quite happily say, 'What's all this waffle?', and she very much helped me improve my recording style, which hadn't

been addressed in the previous job, which I don't think was bad; it was just more long-winded...." (interviewee 13)

"I haven't actually done a recording course, but my team manager in my longest post, which was 18 months, actually taught recording.... So she was an absolute stickler for things being done strictly by the book, and seemed to be happy with the way that I did things ... as a fairly newly qualified person when I first went to her team, and with her having been my practice teacher in my first placement.... She carried on in that role of ... saying, 'Well, I think you ought to do this', ... but once you started doing it her way, then she was OK." (interviewee 46)

This is not an uncommon reflection of the way a manager's direction will be perceived. There was a sense that if you were doing it the way the manager would do it, in the style they would write, then you were doing it correctly. While the requirement to follow the style of the manager could be felt to be constraining, there was nevertheless a feeling that a manager's interest was something to be appreciated.

When training on recording was mentioned, it was seen as of limited value. Some of the interviewees had qualified around the time of the introduction of the Access to Records legislation in 1989, and described a concern with the issue that they have not experienced since:

"Oh, it was a long time ago. I can't remember, but it was looking at significant points and the way that we needed to record. And with the access to records – you know, we've done Access to Records training." (interviewee 35)

"Great swathes of us did that training, but yes, I haven't done anything since." (interviewee 38)

Value was placed on clear, constructive guidance in respect of recording expectations, but this was a rare occurrence:

"I used to work for a local authority which was very clear about what you should be recording when, ... eventually it becomes inculcated in your practice....These are the things you have to comment on, this is what is expected of you and it was very much a tool for practice." (interviewee 25)

Formal training courses were often concerned with issues of format or confidentiality, or they were considered to be too general:

"... there was quite a bit of input about the physical layout." (interviewee 34)

"It wasn't a course that was specifically tailored to care managers or social workers. It was a generic course for all workers in X ... it was more about confidentiality of the client, rather than how to word things." (interviewee 45)

Occasionally examples were cited of training courses that had been especially valued:

"One of the things that always sticks in my mind from years ago, when my training course was actually done by a coroner, and that was quite an interesting course, and he went through recording practice ... especially at times when professionals have come into court and their recording has been looked at." (interviewee 2)

As the previous discussion on accountability suggests, giving evidence in a coroner's court was likely to be seen as a particular ordeal by many social workers. It is not surprising, therefore, that such a practically focused course, which directly addresses highly relevant concerns, should be so positively recalled.

For the majority of practitioners recording training was non-existent or inadequate. Some were grateful for the interest and guidance of an especially enthusiastic manager. Otherwise they relied on their own experience of what appeared to work, and followed on from examples of what they saw others record in the file. Underlining this rather haphazard experience of learning to record in social work was the contrasting experience of people who had previously recorded in other professional capacities. Those individuals placed greater reliance on the training they had received in these other careers. Of the questionnaire respondents 34% said that the training and experience from other work roles had been a significant influence on learning to record:

"Now I think that goes back to my nursery nurse training, where you wrote and observed everything." (interviewee 21)

"Actually, as a social worker, I have never received any training on recording.... I'm also a qualified psychiatric nurse, and for that I have, I mean in training ... get quite a bit of input on recording." (interviewee 22)

"And I do record things in detail, but I think, in my view, because of my past experience of recording things ... when I was working as a nurse...." (interviewee 19)

This lack of a systematic or standardised approach to learning to record left workers unsure as to what was expected, and confused by the variations in recording practice that they encountered in the file. Learning from experience was accepted as the way practitioners developed their skills in recording, but it was recognised that sometimes experience delivered a very hard lesson:

"… it's from bitter experience really, because it's often the bits, … that somehow you think, 'Why didn't I write it down, I could have sworn I wrote that down…. Why didn't I write that down?'. So it does happen and it's, especially in the early days, it was always the bit that you wanted…." (interviewee 40)

Management feedback

Only a small minority of the interviewees reported receiving any useful feedback from their managers on their recording practice. The overwhelming majority felt they received confusing and inconsistent messages, both in terms of management expectations and policy guidelines. Many felt their managers were less concerned with the content and quality of their recording, and were much more preoccupied with checking that the necessary boxes were ticked in order to provide statistical information for performance indicators:

"70%-80% of [supervision – regular one-to-one meetings between worker and supervisor] is about … you haven't filled in those, … you need to fill in this bit." (interviewee 39)

"I'd say, really from my line manager, not a great deal, I mean it gets audited, but I think it's … more or less about completing modules. [laughing] Have you actually done it…. I think it seems quite functional." (interviewee 23)

Some interviewees found this concentration on 'functional' information frustrating. Many interviewees felt that feedback on the quality of their recording would be useful, and would help them to improve, but too often the feedback remained at the level of spelling and grammatical mistakes, which often seemed petty:

"I remember one thing she picked me up on when I was a student, and I wrote 'loo' instead of 'toilet' or 'lavatory'." (interviewee 46)

"He usually just points out the spelling mistakes. [laughter] Honestly I'm not joking. I send my manager an email to say, … I've assessed Mrs Such and Such and he'll come back and he'll say to me, 'There's four spelling mistakes in the summary assessment', because I'm not very good at typing. But he never says, 'That's a really good assessment', or

'That's a bad assessment', or whatever … just the spelling mistakes …
my manager changed six months ago, and the manager I had before
… used to say to me, although he did tell me the sentences were too
long, he did say to me 'That's a really good assessment', or 'That was
really thorough', or … 'You've obviously spent a lot of time with
that person', or whatever…. But, my new one just tells me about the
spelling mistakes." (interviewee 9)

Sometimes the lack of feedback was seen as an indication of the manager's
confidence in the worker's practice. The assumption was that if there was no
feedback then there were no problems:

"I think we work on the assumption that if there was a problem they
would get back to us." (interviewee 24)

Many interviewees felt that managers were either too busy to read the files or
not sufficiently interested. The following comment was made by a manager who
saw recording as an important issue, but who did not believe that view was shared
by all managers:

"… if you have a line manager or a supervisor who's looking at your
recording, and who is picking it up in supervision, … and who is
saying, 'This is important. This is how you should be recording. You've
got to do it right', then the standards will raise…. But if you've got a
manager, or a line manager, or a supervisor, who's just not doing any
of those things, and who sees it as just an administrative task, and it
doesn't matter what you put … then you're in trouble. And I've had
managers who just didn't care, … and it's scary." (interviewee 49)

The variation in supervisory or management experience may not only be in terms
of the manager's commitment to recording, but also their standard of what is
acceptable in terms of recording practice. This adds to the sense of inconsistency
described by many interviewees:

"… she [manager] was very clear and very motivational about and it
wasn't a negative experience at all, it was a very positive experience
of having a positive leader who could see you working, and admire
and try and follow…. That's been a challenge since, because there
have been some managers who haven't had the same standard…."
(interviewee 31)

The daily experience of reading files where standards of recording vary so
considerably was an ongoing demonstration of that inconsistency:

"And you see … that people's records are so different because … we do get files passed on from other people … whereas I spend a lot of time recording, another person won't record anything at all, … I think it's the manager's responsibility to make sure that we are recording things…. And that they're done properly, and I think … sometimes people haven't been told when their records, … either that they are writing things down inappropriately, or that they're not writing at all, or that … their writing is completely illegible…. Often people aren't picked up on that." (interviewee 32)

One of the frustrations that workers experienced in relation to feedback on recording was that, while they were told what they hadn't done, they did not always get specific guidance on what they should be doing:

"And I said to her this morning, 'If you think I'm doing too much recording, … let's make this evidence based. You look at my file and tell me what you think was unnecessary … or has been over recorded, and we'll have a discussion about that'. I think there is an inevitable tension between a lot and a little." (interviewee 37)

The reluctance to give clear guidance may also arise from the manager's own lack of skill and confidence in recording, not to mention the judgement about how much was enough, given the tensions already identified in the preceding chapter on demands:

"I've had managers who've been more focused and interested in it, and the quality of what you're putting out; other managers … in their view they're giving you more autonomy, but they're leaving you to get on with it. And … I do see work where I think, 'Well, who's monitoring the quality of what we're all doing?' … it's not necessarily bad, or unprofessional recording, but not as good as it could be, or … consistent…. But, I mean, it depends on the particular manager's own abilities in recording and interest in it. I mean, they might read something and not think it's an issue…. They're not necessarily experts in recording themselves." (interviewee 13)

Ultimately if workers feel that managers are not checking the quality of their recording except in terms of the information for the performance indicators, there is little incentive to make it a priority:

"In health you almost felt you had a legal duty to record in this way, and you were given continual reminders … and you don't get that in social services, there is no one on your back saying 'this is what you've got to do'." (interviewee 22)

A source of significant frustration and confusion was the experience of moving from one authority to another and encountering very different recording systems or policies. This intensified the sense of there not actually being a correct way of recording, just many different ways, each developed within a local context:

> "When I came here to X, I wondered what I was coming to, because every area had developed its own way of doing things, and certain things were standardised, but there was a lot that wasn't." (interviewee 25)

> "When I first came to the team, I thought, 'Gosh, you've got a wonderful assessment report; nobody uses it'. [laughter from both] ... because having come from X, where their assessment ... is all on the computers, and they have ... three lines where you're supposed to write the client's home situation – three lines on the computer. Having a joke, having a laugh!... And the client's needs, you had five lines.... And the medical condition – three lines.... So I came from that system to here and thought, 'Brilliant assessment report!'. And then you look on the files, and people would write maybe two sentences in a box.... So they had the scope to write so much, but they'd write so little. Now I understand why they do that, because it's so paper-driven, [laughter] and they haven't got time." (interviewee 36)

Time was identified as a significant issue in how workers negotiated the recording systems they encountered, which is discussed further in the next section. Workers may be more or less critical of the recording systems they were required to use, but a major influence in how they worked with that system would be the time they had to record. Even within one authority, the introduction of a new system of recording, especially electronic systems, may add to the sense of confusion and even anarchy:

> "I think we're all doing it wrong, but to be quite honest, I don't care. As long as the service user has got the assessment which I've written and the care plan that I've written, and they're getting the services.... I do them because I have to do them, but whether I'm doing it right or not half the time I think, 'Well, I'm just guessing'. Everybody seems to be doing it a different way." (interviewee 43)

Management guidance and feedback, was, for the most part, considered unhelpful, with a few notable exceptions. Many interviewees complained of managers preoccupied with stylistic considerations, which usually translated into directives to follow the style of the manager. The overriding management priority was with the completion of information that would contribute to achievement of the performance indicators. Perhaps the most eloquent comment actually came from a manager, frustrated by the lack of clear guidance on recording:

> "So recording isn't a straightforward task; you really have to think and, you know, when you're here at sort of 5 o'clock on a Friday afternoon, and you've got three hours' worth of visits to record, and they're all high-risk situations, and you're tired, it's pants. So there would be a plea from me (which I'm sure – I hope – my colleagues would agree with) … give us some concrete training." (interviewee 49)

This comment is a poignant plea for clearer guidance on what was expected, and for the training to equip workers with the necessary skills to meet those expectations but, as the following sections demonstrate, there are further constraints that add to workers' difficulties in meeting the recording challenge.

Time

It is no surprise to find the overwhelming majority of interviewees complained of lack of time given the pressures of the work. Forty interviewees said they spent more than half of their time recording, and 12 of those said it was at least 75% or more. Lack of time was a very definite constraint as far as most workers were concerned.

When asked about how much time they spent recording, many interviewees responded with a variety of exclamations:

> "Oh! Days! [laughter] … it's probably a common moan among social workers that we feel that we spend more time at our desks writing than we ever do seeing people…. At least 50 per cent…. Probably more like 75 per cent, I would say." (interviewee 13)

> "Masses. Masses and masses and masses…. When I first went to the review team I was working on something like 10 to 15 [assessments] a week, and now I'm going to five…. And that's down to recording." (interviewee 26)

Of the questionnaire respondents, 78.8% said that they spent more than half their time recording and of those, 22.5% believed they spent 75% or more of their time recording.

Other research echoes these figures, where 75% of 1,000 social workers said that they spent more than 40% of their time on paperwork, and it was the most significant factor in causing one in four of them to seriously question their future in the profession (Revans, 2007). This anticipates some of the issues raised in the next section, which explores changes in the role of social work.

For some interviewees the pressure on time resulted in working beyond their contracted hours in order to make sure the information was on record and in the file:

> "… I make sure every single point is in, and that does mean that I do an awful lot of hours outside of my hours…. Because I'm frightened that one day … someone will pick up my case, I will not be around, and they wouldn't be able to sift through it and find out exactly what I've done, what day I've done it on, because it wouldn't be in my recording." (interviewee 10)

There was a widespread perception that the paperwork had increased over time. This was said by workers with long experience, and even by those who were comparatively recently qualified. It was acknowledged that asking people how much time they spent on an activity may not be the most reliable indicator of the actual amount of time spent, especially when that activity was one they would rather not be doing:

> "I spend most of my time, … because you do quite a quick visit…. And … you're phoning so many people afterwards because of that visit…. And it all has to be recorded, and then you've got the assessment. I mean the paperwork has increased … we do too much … I don't know, there's a balance, that's the trouble…. I mean … it's a less pleasurable side of the work, so it's always going to seem like it [takes longer]." (interviewee 15)

> "I think it's probably more likely two thirds. This is a vast change from when I started in social work, where you probably could give a proportion of 30% time recording, 70% face-to-face with clients." (interviewee 3)

> "It's hard to know. I mean, just to give you an example: if you went out to an initial assessment visit, perhaps that visit might take an hour-and-a-half or two hours – your first visit to a client…. And then that could generate three or four hours of paperwork, depending on what you're arranging for them … because the actual assessment form that we use, if you fill it out thoroughly, that takes quite a time to fill out; then you've got the support plan, and then perhaps a memo to the resource panel to go with your support plan…. And then the record sheet, and then perhaps you're putting in a day care application, so that's another application to write out." (interviewee 16)

The tension between time spent in face-to-face contact with service users and time spent recording was a crucial factor in the attitudes workers held in relation to recording, and so it is no surprise that this theme is once again a preoccupation. There was almost a palpable sense of the relentless pressure in the way interviewees described their work:

> "I think, because it's a busier job now, there was more time to think about what you were writing years ago when I was a social worker. Very, very busy, you're assessing people, and you have an awful lot of forms to fill in, and processes that you have to go through, to get them a service so … and you're doing it as quickly as you can, because there's so much to do, you really haven't got the time to spend running over something, … there's more scope for mistakes, there's more scope for things being missed out because you're writing it quickly." (interviewee 32)

Many described a sense of recording as a constant process of describing and accounting for every activity:

> "Well, I'd say 70%–80%, because I'm recording when I'm assessing, and I'm recording when I get back to the office, and writing letters. So I'm constantly recording something, because really every activity – it's the same in X – every activity there has to be a record of; a letter going out, a letter coming in, telephone call made, telephone call received, it all goes onto the record, … what the content of that conversation was, what the follow-up action might be." (interviewee 8)

> "So anything that moves, you log it." (interviewee 34)

Time management was very difficult, because the nature of the work is that emergencies are part of the working day and can constantly disrupt planned schedules of work – responding to crises is part of the job. These may be in the form of new referrals from unknown service users, or it may be that a situation develops with a known service user; in either case, delay is often not an option:

> "You could have your day all planned out and it's completely different when you come in, because you can get an urgent call from a family." (interviewee 44)

It was not only the actual amount of time that was the problem, it was also the quality of the time. Many interviewees described the difficulties of trying to complete recording when they were continually being interrupted. Recording was done in between dealing with the numerous enquiries that would constantly be coming into a busy social services office, all of which have to be recorded. This required them to shift from one case file to another, moving from one screen to another in the case of electronic records, which then disrupted attempts at trying to construct a coherent record. Before the previous call had been recorded the phone might ring again, and all of this might be happening in the middle of trying to complete an extended assessment report:

> "I could do with a secretary.... That's what it feels like some days, and I think the frustration that we all feel is that ... you can be in the middle of something and you get interrupted; and I think that's when recording just ... and you put the phone down and then the phone goes again." (interviewee 12)

Even when they had arranged uninterrupted time to get on with a piece of work, they may then be seen by their manager as the most available person to deal with the unexpected emergency. This underlines the dilemma for many workers. While they tried to value recording as an activity and give it priority, they did not experience it as a priority as far as management was concerned. There was a sense of workers trying to protect precious recording time from all too frequent management incursions:

> "... you can diary your week, or diary your day, ... have every best intention to do recording, and then, ... you get a phone call to say your client is sort of standing naked in the middle of a roundabout. And then you have to go. And I think ... because of the time pressures, there have been times when both myself and other colleagues have penned into our diaries 'keep free for admin', and then managers assume that's the day that can be accessed for other things.... But in fact it's not. It's as necessary as going out and meeting the client.... And it should be valued a bit more.... And again, ... it's a difficult situation for managers, because if they've got one person in who's sitting there and blanked out their diary to do their recording, nobody else in the office, they're going to ... there's times when I've thought, I think I'll go and work from another office and hide, so I'm not available, because I've got to do this recording." (interviewee 48)

Recording was always the time that could be re-allocated should something else arise. Given the unpredictable nature of social work, this was a frequent occurrence. As a consequence, recording, despite management's emphasis on the importance of maintaining up-to-date records, seemed to be the lowest priority. Workers experienced a seemingly impossible tension where they were expected to give priority to recording on the basis that if they hadn't recorded it, they hadn't done it, but at the same time be endlessly available to be interrupted, often by management, to deal with whatever crises arose, whenever they arose.

Interviewees described a process of constantly trying to juggle competing priorities. The concern was to set up the care package, particularly in hospital, to enable the patient to be discharged. So as long as the assessment and care plan had been written, any other recording, including 'observations' as part of the running record, could wait until later. However, if they were not done reasonably promptly there was a sense of them getting out of control:

> "You're always trying to ensure that the person who is going to be discharged next, their files are up to date, but you may be holding information about another person in your head, but you just haven't had a chance to record." (interviewee 2)

> "Observations, I try [which is a running record] ... I try to do that as I'm going along, because it just gets overwhelming. And I live with notes all over my desk.... Very cryptic, and I think, 'God, who the hell is that about!' [laughter from both] I can't remember. And as for the assessments and care plans, I try ... we do it quickly, because they have to be sent out to the providers before the care can start." (interviewee 43)

> "... someone may have a very good understanding of recording, and what's necessary, ... and that a case record needs to make sense, but they don't have the time." (interviewee 49)

> "... you've got another client waiting to be seen that will take priority, and unfortunately that's across the board I think for everybody." (interviewee 11)

This sense of frustration is echoed among the questionnaire respondents, 83.6% of whom said they did not have enough time to record in as much detail as required. With all the other priorities, recording becomes ever more difficult to keep up with:

> "You miss some of the recording ... or you're getting overwhelmed by it. Oh God, I've got to write three days of ... almost cynical to the point of saying 'do not ring me up because if you knew how much paperwork you're going to cause me'!!" (interviewee 39)

This sense of frustration may lead to an acceptance that only so much is possible in a working day. Despite the awareness of the number of cases still waiting to be allocated, there may be a straightforward equation between number of cases, available time and the level of recording. The same interviewee continues:

> "[There is] ... this ongoing dilemma of all these cases unallocated, and you've got to keep up to date with all this lot ... [it] is fine if you're given that number of cases, yes I can do that amount of work, or you can give me as many cases as you want, but I'm not going to do all the recording on it." (interviewee 39)

For some this results in a lowering of their own standards, which they regard as regrettable, but inevitable. The next interviewee had made a conscious accommodation to the pressures she experienced. She felt her recording was adequate, but not at the level she had previously maintained, or at the level she would ideally like:

> "My recording isn't at the level I would want it to be at now. I've had to go slightly lower than when I started, because there is no time to do it." (interviewee 17)

For many the change to new systems of recording, particularly electronic systems, meant more time was spent becoming familiar with the system and learning to use it:

> "That would be difficult to say at the moment, because we are still getting used to the computer system, so we are slower than we used to be: I mean you could rattle off a really good comprehensive assessment document in, say, three quarters of an hour to an hour; but when we first started with the new system, it was taking us all morning. [laughter] … it had us all in despair." (interviewee 46)

For many interviewees and questionnaire respondents (65.1%) it wasn't just the amount of paperwork that they complained of, it was, in their terms, the unnecessary duplication, the sense that they were filling in forms for an arbitrary and bureaucratic process that was not even rational:

> "… I'd love a system analyser to come into the team and just sort it all out: sort out the procedures, because the duplication is incredible … it would free up so much time for us to do the jobs that we're paid to do really." (interviewee 36)

The interviewee was keen to provide an example of the amount of paperwork that could be generated from a fairly simple referral for meals on wheels. There was almost a sense of delighted satisfaction being expressed in illustrating the ludicrous absurdity of the process:

> "… there's [the] panel front sheet, which is your summary and where you're noting down your risk factors, and how this is the only service that prevents those risks, or minimises those risks.… And then you've got your assessment, which could be a three- … or four-page document. Then you've got your care plan.… That goes to panel. Then for the Home Care Department, they also get those three … documents. You have the home care referral, which is another two-page document, which is something that writes down the client's details –

even though the details are already on the first two.... You get your safe manual handling assessment, which you have to do. I had to do a safe manual handling assessment for somebody who's taking a client shopping – on carrying shopping bags! And then, ooh, you could add on to that if the person needs help with their medication, that's another form that the person has to sign for.... If the person needs a key safe they have to sign the key authorisation form, which is another form that goes along with that.... There's also a risk assessment form, if you've really got time to do that ... that's highlighting any other risks that haven't come under the manual handling risk assessment form." (interviewee 36)

While there was a sense of the paperwork becoming an end in itself, there was also a feeling that the proliferation of the forms was a response to an increasingly targeted system in which resources were ever more rationed:

"Because we have more forms to fill in ... more ... more reasons to justify why we're asking for that service." (interviewee 20)

Although so much time was spent writing the record, interviewees reported spending much less time reading the record. In part this was because of lack of time although, as was seen in the section on communicating with colleagues earlier, lack of time was not the only reason. It was often felt that there was too much information in the files to be able to access the useful or relevant information very easily:

"I don't know that we necessarily have time to or do look at old files when we go back and revisit people. So the information might be there, but sometimes if there's too much of it you wouldn't go back and look at it again....You can't actually find the important bits within a huge file that would give you the information you need to update it really." (interviewee 41)

"... you don't sit and read them at length unless you were taking ... over a case. But there is a lot of searching for the right bit of paper." (interviewee 37)

Sometimes a judgement might be made that much of the information in a file going back several years may be less and less relevant as time goes by:

"... I never know how much of a file – especially if it's a thick file – how much to read, because, ... what happened 20 years ago might be totally irrelevant now." (interviewee 12)

It was recognised that making assumptions about what might be relevant in a file might be difficult, and so there was a tension between dismissing older, historical information and possibly overlooking something highly pertinent to understanding a service user, or spending precious time wading through the entire file in case there might be something significant:

> "... some of these old files have got some very, very interesting information in them, ... but it could be the first one that could have very relevant information that this person might have had a mental health problem ... years ago, and some of that information might have been lost." (interviewee 32)

There was a distinction between the information that formed the service user's story in the file and the information that enabled the worker to see what actions had been taken in the management of the case:

> "That's extra ... reading case files, I do in unpaid time, it's the only time to do it. If you read a case file ... it has to be something I do after everybody's gone, ... as long as I don't get locked in the building, because reading case files is a real, real luxury during the working day, so you tend to get in early and read a case file, ... it's very rare to have the time to sit and read a case file especially in the sort of work I've come from, ... you might read them as a story and ... that's wonderful to do that if you've got time, but you might be reading, thinking: 'I want to know how we arrived at this, how that ended up like that', so you'd actually be looking for certain letters, certain headed note paper, certain organisations, professionals so you'd be reading it ... in a different way. That usually is during working time, because you'd be doing it with a purpose." (interviewee 40)

The focus here is on the information necessary to understand the case and not the person's story. This returns us to the issues raised by the comparison of Versions A and B. While most interviewees preferred Version A as the person-centred account that was more consistent with social work values, they tended to see Version B in the actual records, as this was the account that focused on the problems. When time is precious there is little opportunity to do anything other than what is absolutely necessary to process the case and focus on the work that needs to be done in order to get the client the services he/she needs:

> "I want to read, because I want to see what work was done, so I'm not repeating myself.... And that could be hugely frustrating for the client." (interviewee 36)

"Well, I wouldn't say I spend much time reading files.... And I think that's ..., annoying ... because I think we have in X, this culture of collecting this massive amount of information.... But you actually wonder if it is ever read.... I mean a number of times when cases are allocated, and no one even tells you that there's a file that thick that you can have look through...." (interviewee 3)

Time represented a considerable constraint that undermined workers' ability to either record or read all the information they might want to. Despite attempts to work more efficiently, there was a sense of unrelenting pressure and many competing priorities, which contributed to recording becoming, for many, an activity that sank further down their 'to do' list, but which remained a constant source of anxiety because of the potential consequences that any investigation or inquiry, scrutinising the record, might have for their professional reputation.

Change

Changes in social work have had a profound impact on what social workers do and how they do it. This is especially so in relation to recording. Changes in the expectations around what has to be recorded, and in the systems used to record that information, have transformed the working routine for most workers. This section looks first at the impact of computers on recording in social work. It then moves on to explore the changes in the role of social work in adult services itself, namely the move to care management, which has had a profound impact on what social workers now do in adult social care and has increased the significance of the record. The dominance of care management in adult services since the introduction of community care has led to more short-term work with a faster throughput of cases, as well as a more explicit process of decision making in terms of allocating resources, all of which has made recording a higher priority and a more complex task. I want to explore how workers have responded to their changing role, and how that might influence their approach to recording.

Information technology (IT)

IT, and specifically computers, has not only impacted on how social workers record, but also on what they record and their sense of the file as a more accessible document. The introduction of IT has proceeded at different rates in different local authorities. With the introduction of the electronic social care record there is now an expectation that all recording is on electronic systems. However, many departments are still working with combinations of electronic and manual recording. Only five of the interviewees were working with solely manual records and only six with completely computerised systems; the rest worked with a combination of both. A similar picture was found with the questionnaire respondents, 22.7% of whom worked with purely computerised systems, 7.8% with purely manual and 69.5% with a combination of both.

Some of the issues that arose in relation to the introduction and use of computers have implications for the concerns around time and how it is used. This will echo some of the themes identified in the preceding section. Attitudes towards recording on computerised systems were more ambivalent than divided. Many interviewees expressed both positive and negative attitudes and many, while identifying considerable advantages in using computers, felt the process of implementation had been very difficult. This was again found among the questionnaire respondents, with the highest levels of satisfaction with the recording system used (51.9%) being expressed by those using purely computerised systems, while only 30.6% of those using purely manual systems were very satisfied. However, there were again many comments from the respondents about the difficult and often distressing process of implementation.

One of the overriding advantages of computerised records was seen as simply being able to read them. One of the main complaints of manual recording was the problem of illegible handwriting and this was an issue identified in the Laming Report (House of Commons, 2003), investigating the death of Victoria Climbié.

> "… you can read it, whereas a lot of the paper files, you couldn't always read people's writing." (interviewee 24)

The more negative attitudes revolved around a sense of frustration at either the individual's limited ability to work with computers, often compounded by a lack of training and support, or frustrations with the limitations of the system itself. There was an acknowledgement that often it was more experienced workers who found it most difficult to adjust to the new technology:

> "… some workers aren't comfortable working on computers…. In the last four years, … due to changes in the department and due to increasing IT, we've lost some really good old-fashioned social workers who weren't comfortable with the new system." (interviewee 31)

For some it was a simple matter that they found it quicker to write than to type. Few had received any training or support on basic keyboard skills:

> "… our forms are now on computer, which is fine if you're good at typing, but I'm very slow." (interviewee 25)

The pressure on time and the degree of difficulty experienced in using computers may lead to an accommodation where less was recorded:

> "… if you're not happy typing you're probably going to type the minimum, aren't you, because you really want to finish the damn

thing and get it out of there. You know, it could make a difference." (interviewee 47)

For some their level of skill was not sufficient given the demands of the software system they were required to use, and this was compounded by the complex way in which workers often recorded, working on several files at the same time:

"… because invariably the phone will ring and I will get distracted, and I would have to keep switching programs on the computer to find the right folder for the person I'm talking about, and it would get lost." (interviewee 30)

For others, recording on a screen was more difficult because they could only focus on one section of a piece of work at a time. This complaint also applied to reading the file on screen:

"And it's just a physical thing in our system, you cannot view a page at a time, … you only get … the question that you're actually answering. So if you're trying to think … 'What have I put down already?' it's actually quite difficult to get the whole of that up here in your head as to the structure of the report." (interviewee 34)

A consistent complaint even from those who were relatively enthusiastic about computers was the lack of training available:

"One big, big criticism I have of social services (and you've probably had this across the board) is the huge lack of training for an IT system.… I said to my service manager, 'You wouldn't go into NatWest and then go and draw some money out, and they say, "Well, I actually haven't been trained in that. If you can just pop up and see Maureen, she had half an hour last week, and she might be able to help you with your account…"'. And as a team it is farcical. It's absolutely unbelievable. We've had no floorwalkers. I'm surprised we have responded and reacted as well as we have done." (interviewee 48)

Even where interviewees were positive about the introduction of computer technology, there was a sense that the implementation had been mishandled and this had resulted in staff frustration:

"I think it's the way it's been rolled out, because I've spoken to other organisations, and X in particular, … they're using the same IT system, and they rolled it out complete. What they did was to get in specialists to come and sit in offices and sit alongside practitioners.… So I think the organisation has done itself no favours because … this is the biggest cultural change – you've set me off now ... in social work, ... since community care. The fact that we've got IT there, we're expected to use it. We're going to be losing the paper files.... The system is there; it's going to cut down on the amount of paperwork, and be so much more useful to us. Now I know there were a lot of colleagues who were stuck in the 'Well, we'll be sitting at a desk all day, and we won't have time to spend with the people that we're supposed to be meeting with', but actually there is a balance, and I personally find it a much better use of my time to sit and type my community care assessment, print it off, send it out, than to handwrite it, give it to admin, have it back in two or three days' time, and have to make some amendments.... So I'm really excited about it." (interviewee 38)

Such enthusiasm was unusual. Many complained of the inefficiency of particular systems. Sometimes these replaced previous systems that workers had become familiar with, and the adjustment to the new system was almost as difficult as the introduction of computers in the first place:

"... the computer system that we've got now is awful, and it ... doesn't work to the point where people ... think 'Oh sod it'." (interviewee 15)

"I also find that the IT system ... there are so many boxes and windows that you have to do, so it's not a matter of just sitting down, doing your assessment, and recording whatever it is ... and it just takes an awful lot of time." (interviewee 2)

"... unfortunately what we're finding is some of the documentation like booking respite care, which they've put onto a template and we should send electronically now. It actually takes you longer to do than the old handwritten one and then having done it, you find you can't actually send it now, because there's some hitch in the system, so we've retreated to the old style.... It's terribly cumbersome, dreadful, I mean having to illustrate every need, and how that need was met, and when it was met, there are pages and pages, and the next week it could all be different." (interviewee 37)

There was a weary sense that even if you struggled to learn how to use the new system, the effort might be of limited value, as there was every expectation, given the rate of change, that you would have to get used to yet another system or a modified version of the same system before very long.

A process of accommodation to working electronically could also be observed. The process of moving from a manual to a computerised system might prove challenging but ultimately rewarding, allowing for some limitations:

"It was a bit of a culture shock, because when I was in X, it was a paper office. And you had a reference computer to look people up on and get basic information, but we did all our recording, ... we handwrote our care plans – everything was on paper. And I came to W, and W was IT mad: everything ... just centres around YY [computer software system]. If YY can't do it, social workers don't do it.... That's exactly what it's like. The first thing you get told is 'Right, this is where the YY training is'.... Because you can't do anything in this office unless you can do YY.... And it was a really big culture shock, and I kept thinking, 'If I don't get the hang of this computer system, I can't do my job' ... because your assessment ... all your case recording, ... the care plan ..., the service package, all the financial details – everything is on that computer. And once you get used to it, you realise how useful it is.... You don't have to keep getting up from your desk and running to the filing cabinet. Or, every time somebody rings, you go and get the file out and write down that they've rung. You just push a button and it comes up.... Until the computer crashes.... Then all hell lets loose. But it is quite efficient, but because it's a computer system there's no means by which you can be flexible.... So if the computer won't let you do it, you can't do it. Like if you're handwriting a care plan.... And you want to put something on that care plan, you just write it on. We've got pick lists on our computer, and if it isn't on the pick list, you can't put it on the care plan. So if it's a bit unusual, or it's slightly away from the norm, you can't put it on." (interviewee 9)

Computers are so dominant in the previous interviewee's new local authority that it is not possible to work until you have some competence in operating them. Many advantages were recognised, but there was still an unease that the system might impose constraints on how you recorded and, on occasions, may leave you with no record to refer to at all, at least temporarily. In an emergency situation that could have serious consequences.

Interviewees drew a distinction in terms of how far computerised systems facilitated the accessing and the inputting of recorded information:

"To be honest I hated it when it first came online, but ... having had a few cases, people who have gone home, gone to an area where they're using YY, so the worker has been able to document the case straight on to the computer and then that person [comes] back into hospital, and me having access to the assessment ... has been brilliant. 'Cause it's saved an awful lot of time in terms of trying to find files." (interviewee 20)

When asked about putting information on to the system the response was less enthusiastic, although this was mainly because of having to operate a computerised and manual system at the same time:

> "At the moment it's [laughter] another, extra pain in the backside thing to do, ... because not everybody is online. We're having to do both, we're having to make sure it's on the computer, but then printing it off so we've got a paper file." (interviewee 20)

The problem of dual systems can be compounded by workers having the option to record electronically or not, so it is not clear where the information might be:

> "I use a computer quite a lot to record things.... But, there are other groups within the department who still don't use their computers, who you still have to give the information manually. So you're using both systems. And I find it quite time consuming." (interviewee 18)

Computers were also seen as making the actual process of writing easier by providing a quick and easy means of correction:

> "One of the advantages, ... with recording on the computer is deletion.... You write a sentence for instance, and you read it back, and you think, 'That's not really how I want it phrased', and it's quick enough to delete, whereas when you're filing a recording you really don't want to be, ... crossing out and it just looks so messy. You'd tend to leave that sentence there, but you might reword it another way further on." (interviewee 2)

Alternatively there was the sense that the computer record was more visible and workers might feel more anxious about their recording being instantly accessible to colleagues. So if there were remaining errors not already identified, they would be there for all to see.

Electronic recording emphasises to social workers the status of the record as a more visible and accessible document, which can be instantly seen by colleagues and other staff working in an organisation:

> "But I know that even more than ever, what I have written is going to be read.... And then, so at the drop of a hat, someone's going to press a button and read what I said.... So it has to be right. And that does put pressure, ... the legality of what I'm saying and.... Well, it's maybe my spelling that's worrying me more than the litigation side of it [laughter].... It's very embarrassing to have it quite so up in your face.... If I read some of the stuff I've written – oh dear, oh dear. Yesterday I said so – was it 'somebody gave birth to'? And she

gave birth, and I don't know what it was I was meaning to write, but I wrote 'stork'! 'She gave birth to a stork'!… [laughter] Oh lord. I thought I'm going to have to go back in and alter that, and every time you go back in, and it's version number two, and you think, 'Oh flip'. So you read it and you read it, and you read it, and you…. So it takes time." (interviewee 26)

And sometimes the problem was as basic as there not being enough machines:

"And we are very lucky in our [section] 'cause we're a small [section] and we've all got access to a computer. In our area teams, they're not so fortunate, they've got three or four people sharing one computer. Again recording is even harder." (interviewee 20)

There were complex reactions to the introduction of computer technology. There was considerable frustration over the process of implementation, with practitioners complaining of lack of training and systems being overly cumbersome and unreliable. Nevertheless the advantages of computerised records were also recognised. Electronic recording made the retrieval of information more straightforward, although there were some misgivings about the way in which recording was being overly prescribed by checklists and standardised formats, determining what was included and excluded from the record. This issue is explored further in the next chapter. Electronic recording also emphasises to social workers the status of the record as a more visible and accessible document, which can be instantly seen by colleagues and other staff working in an organisation.

In many respects technology was seen as a means to try and resolve the problem of ever-increasing pressure and insufficient time to record properly. Of the questionnaire respondents, 70% said that they felt 'more like administrators' and this again was a theme repeated in their additional comments. So while computers may enable more efficient working, there was also a sense that they more clearly underlined the greater administrative function of the social worker.

Social work role

Since the introduction of care management in 1992, there has been a division between the assessment of a service user's needs and the provision of services to meet those needs. Social workers in adult services primarily work as care managers, assessing individual needs and matching services to meet those needs. Before 1992 social workers would hold cases for long periods, providing social work support. At that time there was a much less clear distinction between assessment and service provision. With the advent of care management the emphasis is now on short-term work and fast turnover of cases, together with the requirement for explicit and transparent decision making in relation to the allocation of services, which has made recording an essential part of the process of delivering a service to users. It is only by understanding the different attitudes between social workers regarding the nature of their work, and the perceived impact of these changes on service users, that it is possible to put their attitudes toward recording into context.

For many interviewees care management represented something different from social work, even though only 24% of the sample interviewed qualified before the introduction of community care. Most said that care management meant that they no longer did 'social work'. The majority of interviewees saw this as a regrettable development, including those who had qualified since the introduction of care management in 1992. Others saw care management in a more positive light. Whether seen positively or negatively, care management is crucial in defining what most social workers now do and in understanding the implications that has for recording.

Care management means a short-term involvement with service users. The objective is to assess the needs and put together a care package to meet those needs, and then review that package. If the care package is working satisfactorily the case can then be closed. There is little opportunity for longer-term work with service users. Often this means responding to crisis situations:

> "… we crisis work; we don't have the opportunity to plan…. But I think that there's a huge level of frustrations from care managers around the lack of opportunity to plan, and you're just dealing with things on a daily basis, and not even looking at your diary for the next day … a good analogy is … the plates in the circus when you've … got them on the pole, and then, … you think you've got them all going and then … one of them starts wobbling and you have to rush up, and that's really all you do." (interviewee 4)

Short-term work means there is little opportunity to develop a relationship with the service user in order to fully understand their needs. This makes the recorded information even more crucial, as each time a service user is referred to social services their case may be allocated to a different worker:

> "I think … there's less opportunity to get to know service users really well." (interviewee 27)

> "They [care managers] can't really get a handle on what's going on with anybody because it's all about going in and going out … which is why I will say recording is so important, because if the last person didn't write it up properly, what do you base your next decision on?… It is all about money and recording … the recording has come up as an important thing because the worker's not there, evaluating throughout." (interviewee 26)

There was a sense of disappointment and frustration with the limitations care management placed on what the worker was expected to do, with many practitioners seeing themselves enmeshed in a largely bureaucratic process:

> "Care management isn't the job that I thought it was going to be.... It's a lot more office based, and we're more negotiators and navigators of the system.... We don't really get time to do what I think is social work, if you like: to actually sit down with the client ... to really develop a good solid plan of care. It's quite often you go out, you do your assessment and get the funding, you set the care up, you go back six weeks later – job done." (interviewee 45)

> "I don't do the nice bits of talking to people, ... my job is to get people out of hospital ... I hate it." (interviewee 20)

Many interviewees felt that care management emphasised the functional needs of service users and overlooked the more complex emotional needs that social work skills were specifically designed to address. There was a sense of regret that social workers were no longer involved in providing a service to users. Counselling was repeatedly identified as a skill that was part of the social work repertoire and yet, as care managers, social workers were seldom able to offer that as a service themselves – they would usually refer a service user on to a professional counselling service. The record therefore becomes the crucial means of communication, both in order to justify an intervention and to ensure that those who carry out the intervention understand what the service user needs. Information sharing is vital when the process of social care is so functionally separated:

> "... I think the expectation is that you refer on to bereavement and counselling services to other services, and maybe there is less time now for workers to be so involved in more of what I consider social work casework. We're very much more ... looking at ... appropriate resources to meet the needs ... and it's only those more complex cases that ... I have the opportunity to practise my social work skills which I do hold one or two of those sort of cases. But what concerns me is, are we giving people enough time to think about loss, you know, somebody goes into a residential home, that's one person left behind, what does that mean to that person?" (interviewee 2)

> "... with my most cynical hat on I might say that we would be deemed to have done a satisfactory job if someone is propped up, warm and fed.... It's very much get in, quick fit, get out...." (interviewee 34)

Time is precious, and workers are conscious of how they were spending their time. With the pressure to process cases as quickly as possible in order to get on to the next one waiting on the unallocated list, it could be difficult to judge how much time was appropriate to spend with one service user. There was also a sense that care management was more consistent with the emphasis on measurable outcomes in order to evaluate the effectiveness and efficiency of a particular service:

> "... care management gives you much more of a focus, and an action plan with an identified outcome, which the government likes for their ... returns, it negates the value of that other side of social work which can't be quantified in the same respect, which is counselling people.... And I think that side of social work is being dissolved, and undervalued, and missing, to the point where we are just purchaser providers. We are there to assess, and somebody else goes in and does that. And that's not always appropriate.... If there's an 85-year-old, who's just lost his wife, and he's losing his memory, he doesn't necessarily want to go to a counselling service in X." (interviewee 36)

This raises the question as to whether a service user is being best served by having to talk about their needs and concerns with one individual (a care manager) in order to be assessed, and then rely on that person to accurately record and pass on that information to someone else (a care provider), and then for the service user to resume the process with the care provider. This is made particularly problematic where the issues are highly personal and emotionally complex.

Because social workers only hold a case for as long as it takes to set the care package up, and then conduct the review after six weeks to ensure everything is satisfactory, should something change, or the service user experiences problems after that point, the case would have to be referred and re-allocated. This would usually mean the service user would be assessed again by another worker. The record again is the means by which this becomes possible. The allocation of the case is independent of who might have previously worked with the service user, because the record is assumed to convey the necessary information for any new worker to understand the history:

> "... you close a case, somebody rings you up three months later, well theoretically they go through the whole process again, and it won't necessarily come to you, whereas part of my head says, they ring me up I can deal with this, and they [service user] have some sort of relationship with you, sort of trust ... and we start again, because you're now a customer, whatever that means, again the whole notion, the whole language has changed, and all the tools of social work have been devalued, the use of casework, the use of relationships.... [We are] provider, gate-keeper, resource allocator." (interviewee 39)

Many interviewees saw themselves as gate-keepers of ever scarcer resources, involved in a process of assessing someone's eligibility in order to decide what services they might receive, if any. So the functional demand of record in terms of establishing eligibility was one of the most significant aspects of the care management role and the recording task. The frustration stems not only from the less rewarding nature of care management, but from the perception that it is less effective in actually addressing the needs of service users. Its critics saw it as essentially superficial in its approach:

> "It's always been care management ever since I qualified, ... it's assessment, care plan, apply for services, monitor, review, and as soon as it's stable – out and on to the next person.... Sometimes it does feel almost like going in, put the sticking plaster on, and get out again and hope it holds for a while." (interviewee 16)

> "... there's a greater emphasis on being the broker for services, ... sometimes it becomes a clerical task, because you're just filling in application forms and even when you're trying to find the right residential home, you can't find the right residential home, because there is no choice, because you're stuck with one home." (interviewee 50)

So while much time and effort may be spent in trying to apply for and arrange services, it is not possible to provide the actual service you might wish, or feel is most appropriate. While certain valued aspects of the social work role have been lost, it was felt that these aspects had been replaced by other, perhaps less attractive aspects. There was a widespread feeling that the administrative aspects of the work had become more dominant, with 70.7% of the questionnaire respondents saying they felt more like administrators. This echoes the perception, already discussed in the section on 'Time' earlier, that most workers felt they spent the majority of their time with administration:

> "I feel like social worker, care manager, secretary, administrator, clerk, there are so many roles all mixed up into one. Because when I sit here trying to alter templates on the computer and I think, well, I didn't actually train to be a secretary.... I feel frustrated about it, I've been qualified for five years and I really, I really, really, really enjoyed my training and I think I had a really charmed time. I've spoken to other people, I don't know, it feels like we've been a bit cheated." (interviewee 30)

This inevitably led to a sense of frustration that precious professional time was not being best utilised by being diverted into so much administrative work. Qualified social workers were not only spending the majority of their time recording, but also with many aspects of routine administration, which might have previously been undertaken by clerical staff:

"… having been in care management for 10 years, I have seen that the admin support has got less and less, … I think there's a huge amount of kind of admin work that could be taken off care managers so they can go out and do what they're able … they're qualified to do. Because we would arrange meetings, we would minute those meetings, we would chair those meetings, and we would type those minutes up, which doesn't seem to probably be the best way to manage our [time] … as professionals." (interviewee 48)

Some interviewees went further and questioned whether the care management model, which employs the technical-rational approach of assessment, was actually appropriate for understanding people's needs:

"I think care management is very much a linear process. You go in and do the assessment, you do the review, you make any changes, you close the case. Whereas I think a good social worker, if you had the time to do it, would be.... I mean care management makes the assumption that everything goes straight down the line; whereas with social work, we go in and do the assessment, we might set some goals, go around the houses a few times, then try to move onto the next stage." (interviewee 14)

Care management was then seen to impose a simplified, rational process, which could be recorded, on an activity that was inherently messy, often unpredictable and sometimes confusing. Some felt that the only way they could retain a social work dimension to their job was by resorting to specific strategies:

"I do sometimes try and resist that and do the extra things that I feel we should be doing.... I probably keep cases open a little bit longer." (interviewee 16)

"… to an extent social workers in hospital … still do some social work.... I would define that in that sometimes maybe we just talk to people and we don't offer them any services, all they want is to talk through the situation, look at their options and what are their possibilities.... But, see, an area worker wouldn't do that because nobody would get through the system to just have a discussion with somebody.... They would have to have enough risk factors to make them a high referral to get that conversation.... But I would say that conversation is social work. And maybe at the end of that conversation you do nothing, maybe you give them a couple of telephone numbers, maybe you say: 'Right, ok, you're alright for the minute, we've talked it through, and if things get a bit worse this is the number to call'." (interviewee 29)

This points to the distinction between working in hospital and working in the community. In the latter, someone would not even get to talk to a care manager unless their situation was considered a sufficient priority. Members of the public can talk to someone not specifically experienced in working in social care, and from that discussion, they may be advised to contact other agencies, 'signposting on' as it is known. Only if their situation was considered of sufficient concern by a contact centre worker would their details be recorded and referred on to a care manager. It would not be until that point that they would have the opportunity to talk to a care manager. In hospital, patients, by the very nature of their situation, can talk to a care manager.

Some described the struggle to maintain professional social work values:

> "… you've got to hold on to social work values, it's really important, and it takes a lot of energy [laughs], and I expect lots of other social workers have said exactly the same thing." (interviewee 40)

> "We don't have time any more really for doing the real listening, the real empowering and enabling people to actually meet their own needs; or to do things for themselves. The counselling bit has definitely gone.… You're there as a signposting person. And sometimes I sit here at my desk and think, 'Yes that's what I'm doing, I'm processing people', which I actually find quite distressing really; … it's not what I came into the job to do. And you have to fight hard, and become a little bit devious to put some of those other things back in, in a way." (interviewee 21)

Doing social work was regarded as a privilege which might be 'allowed' by managers or arise as a result of a more specialist role, which was then envied by colleagues who were working in a more routine role:

> "I do get a chance to do quite a lot of social work.… I mean the other girls in the office are always saying to me, 'It's not fair!', because they've got the older people; their caseloads are twice the size of mine.… Because management decide, well, the older people cases are more simple – they can have twice as many; whereas the young ones tend to be more complex – they can have half the amount, and they can do a bit of social work." (interviewee 9)

Of the 50 interviewees, less than 10 discussed care management in more positive terms. Some believed care management was a more effective and efficient means to deliver a service to users. They preferred a more focused way of working, where the primary purpose of the care manager was to assess and broker a service for the user. They accepted the centrality of the record in this process:

"Care management is essential in keeping you focused; in measuring both the quality of the service provided by yourself, and by the team, ... it actually fits what we're supposed to be doing.... So there's a logical flow to it, ... I'm person-centred, but actually I also work in a task-centred way, and I think the two can work together." (interviewee 38)

While the frustrations within the system were acknowledged, there was a belief that the care management model provided a more effective framework for dealing with those pressures, and again there was a sense of relish in the challenge:

"... we do have to think more about budgets; we do have to think about service provision; ... when you've done all your assessments ... and you're thinking of the perfect way of helping them to solve their problems, or realise their ambitions, or whatever, and then you hit the brick wall that is resources and money and what's available out there. Or how are you going to provide that service for them. So I think we do have to think much more outside the box; ... to look at different ways of providing the things that people will need, or helping them to find things that they need, which I quite enjoy." (interviewee 35)

Sometimes the issues of service user dependency and the pressure on professional time were cited as reasons for care management not only being inevitable, but a better way of working, while also acknowledging that social work skills were necessary in being able to work effectively as a care manager:

"I like care management, and certainly since I've been managing the team I've encouraged them into a more purist care management approach ... less use of social work skills ... but not total lack of social work skills, because I do believe that you need to have social work skills, because those are the skills that value people ... a purist care management is the bang, bang, bang. You're a step back, you're more of a broker, your business is done more on the telephone, you have your basic contacts, assessment reviews, stuff like that, but essentially.... For me the difference is, ... a few years ago, a social worker would have taken Mrs Trent to the library to change her books and get a coffee and spend some time chatting with her. A care manager won't do that. A care manager will get someone else to do that.... I don't have a problem with the care manager role, because the job is still done ... we couldn't cope with our level of business if we were social working. We don't social work any more; we can't social work any more; but you can still, particularly in this field, you have to have good social work skills, and you have to use them to build those relationships with people." (interviewee 49)

This extended discussion on the continuing debate within social work as to the value of the care management model is crucial in understanding workers' attitudes to recording. For some, the development of care management has provided an opportunity to work with a more focused and purposeful approach, and so it may be seen as a resource. For others, care management is something that prevents them from practising as social workers, and so it is seen as a constraint. Either way the record has become a critical task which dominates their work and on which the effectiveness of their intervention with the service user depends.

Budgets and service provision

This final section on resources/constraints again may not seem to be directly connected with the subject of recording, but it is crucial to understanding the world in which social workers operate. Ultimately they see their role as one of trying to meet the needs of service users by providing services. Among the interviewees, perceptions of the adequacy of the budgets and services available were found to have a profound impact on their attitude towards their job and how they approached it. For many there was a feeling of having to struggle to maintain their professional values in a system increasingly driven by hard economic 'realities'. The frustration over care management was closely linked to the experience of insufficient resources to meet the needs of service users.

As has already been identified, it is for the social worker to make an effective case through their recording for the allocation of resources in what is seen as a highly competitive situation. Social workers do not make decisions about resource allocation. They present the recorded evidence to management, and it is on the basis of that documentation that a decision will be made. Social workers often view themselves as having to defend the interests of service users against a management preoccupation with budgets and targets, where the pressure is to maintain a rapid throughput of cases:

> "I think the authority's agenda, or goals ... are very different now to how social workers are trained as professionals.... And a lot of senior management aren't trained social workers necessarily, and they have different pressures on them, in terms of budgets and government targets, ... and it's ... doing your best to advocate for the person – for their needs – but fitting it into the services that are available." (interviewee 13)

> "The department is interested in, well they have to be interested in throughput, ... and that's why I'm not a manager, because I wouldn't like to have to have that pressure, and I do feel for them, because there is that huge pressure." (interviewee 40)

There was an ongoing tension between the perceived priorities of senior management, which were concerned with the efficient management of resources, and the social workers' concern for the individual service user. Professional social work values focused on the person and on representing their needs. These values were felt to be under threat when the political and economic priorities of management dominated:

> "I know obviously our managers have all been where we are and do care about people, but ... they're managing the budget, and they've got the budget in mind when making decisions, whereas us social workers, we're that much closer to the service users ... you've been out, you've met them, you've heard their problems, you've heard their stories, and it's really hard to make that distance, like the managers can, so that can be quite difficult." (interviewee 9)

> "... it feels to me that the department – it's focus is on keeping in budget, ... that seems to be reflected even when managers who I've known as social workers have moved up.... And they've gone up because they want to fight, and they think, 'Right, we can do this. If we move up we can do this'. And you watch them getting sucked into that sort of bureaucratic bit, and they lose that – or a lot of it. And I just feel that's really very sad. I think it's survival." (interviewee 21)

Often there was an understanding of the pressures on management and, to some extent, those pressures were acknowledged by workers themselves. They also wanted to demonstrate an efficient delivery of service, but often felt frustrated at the lack of resources that undermined their efforts:

> "... the department's priorities are ensuring that waiting lists are low, ... the requirements are met, ... making sure that X gets their three star authority rating. Whereas my priority is making sure that Mrs Smith down the road has got her morning care, so she can live in her own home if she wants to ... we have a really fast pace of work up here, and there is a lot of pressure to get it done, ... to get it right, because we work for X and we want X be the best authority, ... but at the same time we can't make it one of the best authorities without support and resources. We've got ... two qualified social workers in this team, and there's 13 of us altogether, ... and the rest of us are unqualified, so how much do they expect us to...?" (interviewee 45)

One of the small number of non-social work qualified care managers continues:

> "There's a lot of pressure to do the same job, because we have the same caseload, we take on the same type of clients as the qualified

workers ... and we are expected to do that without being qualified, and still help X to get its three star rating and meet the National Service Framework older people standards." (interviewee 45)

Some acknowledged the tension, but felt there was a bottom line position that they felt they needed to hold:

> "I mean ultimately if ... we get a deadline, then I'll work to the deadline for what my line manager and my service manager want. And I've got very good relationships with them, and I totally respect that they have different criteria, different pressures to work under, but if push comes to shove my allegiance would be with my clients.... And I've said [to my manager] my priority will be with those people. It won't be doing your spreadsheet." (interviewee 48)

There was a sense of inevitability about the direction in which social services were heading, which individuals might try to resist, but it was recognised by many that, ultimately, this was the system they had to work within:

> "... you feel as if you're on a conveyor belt...." (interviewee 11)

> "... it's going more that way, especially with the new government targets, where they don't expect us to have waiting lists. But it is a dilemma for the managers because obviously they want us to be practising well, ... but they've got to make sure that we haven't got long waiting lists, and I suppose that they're under pressure to get us to change our way of working, to get that quicker throughput, so that the targets are met." (interviewee 16)

The tension between good professional practice and the pressure on waiting lists was acknowledged. The solution was to work more quickly but the fear was that compromised the quality of work done.

The tension between social work and care management surfaced again unsurprisingly, as in many workers' minds care management was about rationing scarce resources. Most interviewees felt that their role was primarily concerned with establishing an individual's eligibility for services, in other words, they acted as gate-keepers, with the recorded assessment being the basis on which eligibility was decided. Many interviewees described experiences of having to fight on behalf of certain service users, but acknowledged that this demanded a level of energy and determination that was not possible to sustain on a routine basis:

> "I have done an assessment on someone and identified a resource that they wanted, and I thought would be really good for them, and I had to fight for months and months to get the funding for it. And it

worked in the end, but they made me jump through so many hoops to prove why it [alternative options have to be identified and ruled out] wasn't suitable, that it becomes a battle to get something, and you can't battle like that on all of your cases because ... you couldn't keep up that level of intensity." (interviewee 14)

It was accepted that there needed to be a process to allocate scarce resources in an equitable and rational way, but the processes that had to be followed in order to ensure the appearance of an equitable and rational distribution were themselves seen as consuming valuable time. The conundrum was that, if the time-consuming processes were not followed, the limited funding would be further cut:

"... there are limited resources, and there needs to be some process and some means by [which] you're going to allocate resources as fairly as possible, but on the other hand you've got all these people's needs. The difficulty is, the dominant bit is this allocation of resources and the needs of the agency overwhelm. You're spending 80% of your time sitting in front of a computer filling in all this stuff and there's all these large number of unallocated cases, and the reason they're unallocated is because you're doing all this rubbish, most of it is admin. And you think, I shouldn't be doing this ... this is mostly government-driven, and this is about funding, so the cynical part of me says this is absolute rubbish, but if I don't do it I understand [at] the end of this process there'll be less funding, and that's important to have." (interviewee 39)

There was a clear link between the increased level of recording and the need for documented evidence to ensure funding. As more attention was focused on maintaining an explicit and accountable process for establishing eligibility in order to distribute and target scarce resources according to agreed criteria, so the record assumed greater significance, both at the individual case and at departmental level, as a means to document and justify the process of decision making and resource allocation.

For many interviewees there was a strong sense that older people's services received less in funding proportionately than other client groups. This reinforced a feeling of inherent unfairness in the way the limited resources were made available and intensified the anger at the way the system operated:

"Well, there's a certain amount of money ... and they divide the cake up, ... maybe not the way that I would choose sometimes. So I think elderly tend to get discriminated against, and it's a Cinderella service really." (interviewee 50)

"I would say that older people's care is appalling. I mean I think it's actually criminal. They are being sent out of hospital when they are ill, because of the pressure on beds, and they [health service] will deny that.... And yet you have younger people ... who are in here for ages and ages ... and they are walking about, and you say, 'What about these younger people? Why aren't they delayed discharges then? Why is it the older people, the very sick and frail that you are targeting to move out, move on, and put into temporary beds?'... And that's the other issue: moving people around. People are being moved around constantly, and that is very, very damaging. And actually I think people die through this." (interviewee 1)

Hospital discharges was one of the most potent and emotive issues for many interviewees. In order to address the problem of bed-blocking (patients taking up hospital beds who are medically fit to go home), the government introduced a system of reimbursement charges which health can make against social services if a patient is not discharged because of delays caused by social services. This has placed social workers under considerable pressure to progress hospital discharges as speedily as possible. However, many interviewees complained that, alongside even tighter controls on budgets, they were also having to deal with ever increased expectations on the part of service users. These expectations were being fuelled by central government:

> "So they spend a lot of time now giving people information, telling them their rights, encouraging them to use them, go to the carers' service, go to the users' network, go to the advocacy services, go to CAB, go wherever it is, that results in people making more demands for services, so on one hand we're trying to squeeze them and the eligibility criteria, because we haven't got the resources; on the other hand we're saying to people, 'come to us, come to us, these are your rights, don't ask for more ... and also, if you don't like it, you can challenge us, and this is the way'." (interviewee 37)

Workers felt angry and frustrated by the mixed messages they observed being given to the public. Practitioners found themselves in an increasingly difficult situation, where they were expected to work within the constraints of a resource-limited service. The public, on the other hand, were being led to believe that their right to choose was fundamental to how they might expect services to be delivered:

> "... as of last week, we've been asked to give out letters just basically saying, you need to go to a home. You can go to a home of your choice later, but basically you've got to vacate this bed and go. And I'm talking to a son about this, and he's been on the website, ... the website is saying there is choice, you can go to the home of your choice and I am thinking for Christ's sake ... mixed messages or what? You know here is the government charging us god knows what for not providing

a service, and yet on the other hand they're saying well of course you can go where...." (interviewee 25)

The same individual returned to this theme at a later point in the interview:

> "My aim in life is to get them the best deal out of this rotten system....
> I understand the constraints the department is under and I understand
> what I have to do, it doesn't always sit comfortably with me, I think
> the whole issue about delayed discharge is impossible because ... I'm
> being set up to encourage people to go to places they don't want to go
> to, or to take services ... they're not necessarily happy with ... by the
> system but as a social worker I should be saying: 'You don't have to do
> this. There is no legal power, they can't make you'." (interviewee 25)

So workers felt caught between an awareness of why they were working within the constraints they were, and a sense of anger at what they perceived to be a fundamental dishonesty in a system that encouraged service users to believe that they could expect what was not available. The dilemma for practitioners was how far did they then make those contradictions and tensions in the process explicit in the record.

Some felt that by referring to their professional code of practice they could help resolve the contradictions in their position. The code of practice could be used to support what at times might seem a beleaguered position:

> "But I think what's interesting about this social worker registration
> is that ... [it] has actually got duties that are put upon you as a social
> worker that may well actually help in those sort of dilemmas.... A
> responsibility for the patient and if the hospital seems to override that,
> then you can say: 'Well, I'm sorry I can't go along with this because
> I'm a professional, I'm a practitioner and my code of ... practice would
> not allow me to do that'." (interviewee 27)

As we saw in the discussion on accountability in Chapter Five, some workers will use the record to put pressure on colleagues from other agencies in order to ensure a certain course of action is agreed. Documenting the distance between your assessment and that of others can be a powerful lever in negotiations with other agencies, where questions of responsibility and liability might arise. But for most, the day-to-day reality is negotiating within a difficult situation, in which all they can reasonably do is try and get the best they can for their service user:

> "And very many pressures come from above, and the expectation
> [that] you need to be performing and reducing delayed discharges....
> We are the frontline people who are dealing with the service users
> and their relatives, and we're hearing what they're saying.... You have

service users or their relatives saying: 'I don't think my mum should be discharged from hospital because' … I mean in most cases we do understand what they're saying.… People have to be given time, or listened to, and as much as we try to listen, at the end of the day – accountability and delayed discharges." (interviewee 2)

While hospital social workers found themselves in the front line over delayed discharges, there was also a recognition that they were often in a more privileged position than those working in the community when it came to budget requests. Because of the cost of reimbursement charges to departments, there was a perception that hospital discharges would get a level of service provision that would not be possible in the community. The subsequent withdrawal of the services may be because the individual no longer needs them, but there was a sense that budgetary considerations were a more significant influence. The record then becomes a significant means to provide the evidence on which those difficult and potentially contentious decisions around service withdrawal are made. Inevitably, where service users are faced with the loss of services to which they feel entitled, they are more likely to contemplate challenging those decisions:

"Well, that's always a very tricky one, isn't it?… I'm in a position where maybe services are being put in when they're [service users] in hospital, but at home being taken away because they are not eligible. So it's always a hot potato, I think." (interviewee 30)

"… when you're asking for money to get people out of hospital … it's more likely to be forthcoming than [working] in the community … you're more likely to be fighting and arguing, and nagging people for funding for services in the community than you would be in a hospital setting." (interviewee 46)

Time and again interviewees described their frustration at not being able to deliver a level of service that they felt the service user needed and that, ultimately, decisions which would have profound consequences for someone's future were being made on the basis of cost:

"I think it's very difficult … we distinguish very much on the money side of things, whether someone is offered support at home and whether it is suggested that they go into long-term care, which is very sad." (interviewee 24)

"I think it's a very natural thing, social workers want to make things better and we've got a limited number of prescriptions that we can offer to make things better, and we don't very often have the resources to look at other bits, which we should do." (interviewee 29)

While the eligibility criteria did focus on the social and emotional needs of service users, many interviewees felt the reality was that 'risk' was not interpreted as 'risk to independence', as it should be according to 'fair access to care services' eligibility criteria, but 'risk to life and limb'. As a consequence physical and functional needs were seen to be given priority over social and emotional needs:

> "… it doesn't necessarily mean that we have the time or ability to look at individuals' social needs, … our focus nowadays is, probably because of the number of service users have gone up and our limitations is shrinking…. It's the pressure of demands basically…." (interviewee 42)

The budgetary restrictions might not only mean that there was not the money to pay for the services, but sometimes the services themselves were not available, or a postcode lottery operated:

> "… it's really difficult sometimes, because you might know what would best meet your service user's needs, but the department doesn't provide it. Then how do you advocate on that person's behalf to get what your employer doesn't provide…. The department has these strategies, and they have these goals, and mission statements and everything else. But at the end of the day the department is completely terrified of budget…. So at the end of the day that's the bottom line, isn't it: we've got a budget, and we have to stick to it…." (interviewee 9)

The tension between the rhetoric of the mission statements and the strategic initiatives with the day-to-day reality of budgets subject to greater constraints is difficult to reconcile, which makes the job of recording that process even more problematic. How far do you make the contradictions explicit in the record? Interviewees described themselves as working in an environment which was subject to ever-increasing pressure, where the demands became ever more complex and where it was difficult to feel that doing a worthwhile piece of work was possible:

> "… again it's more complex, … what we can do now or are expected to do is greater. A few years ago we didn't have direct payments [money paid directly to service users, who then organise their own care], and now we've got direct payments for everyone. So that is in itself a highly elaborate system that we have to try and negotiate. We didn't do nearly so much work with health, and health has moved in a way to push vast amounts of responsibility towards us, as they've ditched … long-term clients and people with high dependency, and we've had to try and cope with that…. Clearly there is a strong emphasis on collaboration and partnership which is good, on the other hand there is so much more to do, and so many more choices to make, and

so many more things to have to negotiate, and in the contexts of big pressures about cost and throughput, a massive cry for health to get people out of hospitals, appalling discharges that no one could look at and say, well, satisfactory, but yet someone lands here and we've got a crisis, ... it should never happen but it does. It wouldn't have happened in that way 10, 20 years ago, and all the problems over long-term care for people, whether they're in institutions or community 20 years ago, health had these long-term facilities available ... and it was there, and it was safe, and you didn't have to argue about being paid for the bloody things and tied up in knots." (interviewee 37)

Here there is a direct reference to the extent to which greater interagency working means that practitioner time is increasingly taken up with negotiation, including questions over which agency or area of service is going to pay in a particular situation. This again highlights the significance of the record in documenting this process, in order to evidence the way in which responsibility and hence liability has been decided.

For many there was a sense of applying all too superficial solutions to situations that demanded more in terms of time and resources than it was possible to provide:

"We're nearly always chasing empty coffers. It's really a big part of the work.... And you're ... writing letters and doing this and doing that, and it's not getting anywhere, and it's very depressing. So you ... try to ... put sticking plasters on these wounds. You know, you're ... not getting anywhere." (interviewee 15)

Not only did this lead to a sense of treading water, but in some cases a feeling that, because the emphasis was on the most needy situations, individuals were left until their situation deteriorated before anything could be done. For many workers this is contrary to their professional principles, not to mention their humanity, but the restriction on preventative work means that the eventual intervention will inevitably cost more than it might have done if addressed at an earlier point:

"Certainly in some cases ... you know what's going to happen. Two years down the line, and you can almost see it, and it's that disheartening.... Because you know that the request for what you want is not going to be met, and you know it's going to drag on, and you know eventually it will end up in – I don't know – an abuse case or something. You know, you can see it happening. You can't say that, you can't record that, but you know." (interviewee 15)

This underlines the way many workers felt that it was not possible to use the record to document the complexity of the situation. Speculating on how a situation may develop and deteriorate over time is not part of the purpose of the record as it is understood by most workers. Service users' situations are often complicated by many factors that interact in ways that assessment criteria with their emphasis on simple cumulative calculations of risk factors may not be sufficiently sophisticated to recognise or properly evaluate.

The final comment illustrates the beleaguered feeling shared by many workers. The interviewee described a small incident which might seem trivial in the broad scheme of things, but which demonstrates how the tension between the rhetoric and reality are inescapable:

> "... they took all our computers one weekend ... and ... put all this new system on so that we could all have the same server, ... and when we came back every one of our screen savers was now this subliminal message about us serving the community. And the dogs, and the family, and the grandchildren, and the houses, and the seaside views had gone; and we can't have them back. And I'm thinking.... Why do we have to have this? Don't we know that we serve the community to make it healthier, happier and some other stupid statement? And it's that: they've lost touch with people and reality.... And if you don't look after the people who look after the people, then you've lost the plot; and I think they're losing it. And thank you government – especially this government ... they have served themselves by trying to make it look as though they have made things better, but the people they have served have been themselves, and they have not served the public well." (interviewee 26)

There was a sense of resilience, distress and anger that captured the mood that characterised many of the comments on the theme of resources and budgets.

There was an overwhelming feeling that the restriction on budgets and resources placed social workers in invidious positions in relation to their work with service users. This feeling of frustration was compounded by a perceived lack of honesty in the system, where there was more concern to maintain an appearance of improvement. The rhetoric, however, did not match the reality, and the record was not expected to reflect that tension.

Conclusion

In the preceding chapter we saw how the recording task was made problematic by competing demands and tensions. In this chapter we have seen how those tensions are then compounded by various constraints. Social workers are rarely taught or given any clear or consistent guidance in how to record, or indeed what constitutes a good record. This leaves them uncertain as to what is expected, never sure whether they are recording correctly or not, and potentially vulnerable in a situation where there is a complaint and the record is challenged. Neither do they feel they have the time to record adequately, wrestling with many competing pressures. There is a contradiction between the importance placed on the record by management as evidence to meet the demand of accountability, and the low priority given to recording time by management.

In addition, while IT has benefits in terms of the greater accessibility of information, it has also imposed its own burdens by requiring practitioners to accommodate to software systems that are often overly cumbersome and likely to change on a regular basis. Social workers also described a sense of frustration with the care management role, where they felt they were able to make little impact on the lives of service users, and their role was reduced to an administrative process of assessment and form filling. The frustration was further increased by the pressure on budgets and resources which often left them competing for all too scarce resources. While all of these frustrations were seen to make the production of a coherent record more difficult, it was what practitioners saw as a basic dishonesty between the rhetoric and reality of social care that made the recording task even more problematic. The competing demands, exacerbated by the constraints, led to specific recording dilemmas. These recording dilemmas are explored in the next chapter.

SEVEN

Recording dilemmas

We have explored the varying demands in the recording task and established that the record is written for different purposes and different readerships, which results in competing tensions in its construction. In addition there are significant constraints that make the challenge of recording even more complex for social workers. Lack of clear guidance and feedback and too little time lead to confusion and uncertainty over what is an acceptable standard of recording practice. The experience of ongoing change may exacerbate that sense of unrelenting pressure still further, although it may also afford opportunities to work with greater efficiency and effectiveness. The record is expected to provide a coherent account of a professional service when, for many practitioners, the daily reality is under-funded and limited service provision. The record is also expected to be robust when subject to challenge, which is more likely in an increasingly litigious climate. I now move on to examine how tensions in the recording task directly impact on how the record is written, and at the same time explore those tensions, with particular reference to the preoccupation with risk, the record as a form of surveillance and the record as part of a process of governance.

Three main areas of tension will be discussed. First, we explore the dilemma around recording funding applications, where social workers perceive that the risk-dominated agenda in community care requires them to describe service users in the worst possible terms in order to secure funding for services. This contradicts principles of good practice and leaves social workers confused and uncertain as to how they are able to both serve the interests of the service user and adhere to professional standards. Second, we consider the issue of recording sensitive information, where social workers confront the requirement to accurately record information about service users, but still share those accounts with the service user, even though the account maybe upsetting or disturbing to the service user. Third, we examine the impact of increasingly formula-driven assessment procedures, which are seen by many practitioners as 'tick box' exercises, and which compromise the quality of information recorded for professional purposes. The final section looks at how some practitioners have used the record to try to reconcile the fundamental dilemma that many experience between their roles as advocates of the service user and representatives of the department.

The worst-case scenario

As noted earlier, the majority of the interviewees and the questionnaire respondents preferred the person-centred description of a service user (Version A) and felt that this version, more than the negative, problem-centred description

(Version B), conformed to good practice principles in recording. It is interesting, then, to find that Version B was perceived to be more widespread. The question that then arises is to what extent is the prevalence of Version B a pragmatic and expedient response by social workers to the inherently contradictory demands of the recording task, exacerbated by the various constraints experienced by workers?

Social work, by virtue of its very purpose, is concerned with the problems people experience. It is only when people are encountering difficulties in managing their lives, by virtue of ill health, infirmity or disability, that they may seek the support of social services. It is therefore inevitable that the focus will be on problems. As we saw, however, with the construction of case records in Chapter Three, this can lead to a tendency for the record to only include information that confirms the definition of the individual as a problem. The record is constructed to reinforce that categorisation and that can then lead to a distorted picture, where any information that is contrary to that construction is excluded. The service user is seen entirely in terms of the problems they present, which emphasises a perception of neediness, where any potential strengths or positive aspects about them are ignored. Expectations are lowered on the part of workers and this can have damaging consequences for the subject of the record.

Such a construction may lie at the heart of many helping interventions, be they social care or health-based. Nevertheless the practice guidance issued with the introduction of community care (HMSO, 1991) specifically encouraged holistic, balanced assessments, which emphasised strengths as well as weaknesses. It could be argued that such guidance in respect of acknowledging strengths was about prioritising needs and as such, was more concerned with targeting resources than underpinning a humanistic approach to professional practice. Subsequent developments have only reinforced this tension. As funding has been ever more squeezed, so the assessment process has become more and more concerned with establishing eligibility through an identification of risks.

It was believed by many interviewees that the purpose of an assessment as far as management was concerned was to identify the risks that an individual experienced. Eligibility for the receipt of services is determined by the level of risk established. That level of risk is identified by the calculation of certain risk factors. As Castel (1991) noted, risk is no longer located in the individual, but in the factors which contribute to someone's situation being deemed more or less needy. The purpose of an assessment is to calculate those risks rather than describe a person, and so more personal information about an individual, together with their history, while it might help to understand them and their needs, was thought to be irrelevant for those making decisions about the allocation of funding and resources:

> "They certainly wouldn't want, ... the history at all, they would just want a summary of the problems." (interviewee 25)

"… that's what budget holders make decisions based on – risks, that's what they're looking at." (interviewee 40)

This emphasis on risks was felt by many of the interviewees to be at odds with the person–centred approach that was rooted in social work values. In addition to the absence of a client history, there was also a perception that budget or resource allocation panel requests would need to concentrate on what people could not do, rather that what they could do:

> "And you'd end up with a Version B standard of information, because … the panel don't particularly care about the nice, the more positive side of people. They just want to know what are the risks; what is going to happen if we don't put these services in." (interviewee 14)

Here the concern with risk is in terms of making a judgement about what might happen to the individual should the department not intervene. The recorded assessment is evidence that this judgement has been made according to an accepted procedure. The record can then be used to rebut any challenge to that decision.

The perception that practitioners were expected to emphasise the negative aspects of a service user was reinforced by the actual design of the forms:

> "And the … new forms are negative as well. We used to have a really good assessment form where you could write a really good summary of the whole person and our forms are now about what the person can't do and ticking boxes to get funding … the panel doesn't want to know that the person is competent in some areas and that they enjoy flower arranging or walking the dog, that's not what will get you funding. And the space on the form isn't big enough to paint a whole picture." (interviewee 31)

> "I want to say it requires me to be a bit manipulative sometimes in what I say…. Like Version B…. Exactly like Version B. On all our panel sheets you don't have a lot of room to record…." (interviewee 45)

Many workers described the experience of being under pressure to compete for scarce resources for their service users, and in those circumstances it was essential to make the strongest possible case. It was believed that any positive descriptions of what a service user was still able to do would only weaken the argument for funding. Eligibility is established by confirming someone's identity as a needy service user. Any information that might contradict that designation would undermine the categorisation of the individual as eligible:

> "You certainly ... feel that you're painting a very negative picture,
> and that to put in anything positive is likely to dilute your case."
> (interviewee 21)

> "... resources are scarce ... you're almost competing with your
> colleagues to get resources." (interviewee 29)

There was an acknowledgement that, while the strategy might be necessary, it was at odds with what constituted good practice, and this underlined a sense of confusion in what was expected. Workers' daily experience of what was necessary to secure scarce resources for their service users was contradicted by what was deemed to be the principles of professional practice and espoused in policy directives:

> "I'm still confused actually, because I know that to do a good holistic
> assessment you should be looking at people's aspirations and their
> strengths as well as their limitations. I think that we obviously do
> tend to focus on people's limitations ... because we're trying to put
> together a case, to argue for the service, and I suppose you're almost
> worried that if you focus too much on the positives they won't leave
> you enough to get the service." (interviewee 16)

Workers identified what they considered a necessary strategy in order to best serve the interests of their service users, but one to which it was difficult to openly admit:

> "I still think there is room for manoeuvre, there is still room for
> interpretation, and I think probably all social workers, if their
> judgement is that somebody is eligible for, and really needs a service
> will maybe couch their recording in terms to make it more likely to
> get that, I think that happens, and I think that everybody knows that
> that happens." (interviewee 27)

> "This is a tricky one. I don't know if I should be saying this, my
> managers might not be happy with me saying this. There isn't a social
> worker out there that hasn't slightly exaggerated the situation to get
> funding pushed through." (interviewee 36)

These extracts suggest that this is something that is seen as a regrettable necessity which people do not like to acknowledge, but which everyone was aware of. There was a discernible sense of unease among many of the interviewees when talking about the strategy of describing someone on their worst day. Some would only admit to it much later on in the interview after having initially suggested that it was not an influential factor in how they recorded. While it might be difficult to openly admit to the practice, it was constantly reinforced by reading other people's assessments and identifying what worked in terms of successful bids for funding:

"... if you read assessments, they're all very much, 'he's severely autistic, ... he attacks people; he's got severe, challenging behaviour'. It doesn't say 'he's got a tremendous sense of humour; he's got a fantastic relationship with his mum', because you have to milk it as much as you possibly can to get the funds for that person. So you're not going to say, 'Yes, occasionally he has a good morning, and there aren't any issues'. You have to concentrate on what people can't do.... And it can be ... as a professional it can be hugely wearing." (interviewee 48)

Many workers felt unhappy at the necessity to engage in this strategy. It contradicted their own professional sense of the importance of valuing the person. Some interviewees became quite reflective when discussing the issue, and one was prompted to say about the practice:

"A bit wrong really." (interviewee 45)

This discomfort was intensified by the fact that in many instances these negative descriptions in the assessments would be seen by the service user themselves. This was not only recognised to be distressing to the service user, but could be damaging, in that it might add to an already overly negative self-perception on the part of the service user:

"It's difficult because I've always tried to make my assessments as positive as possible. So instead of saying: 'Mrs Smith cannot do A, B, C, D, E', I'd rather say: 'Mrs Smith can do A, B, C, but she needs help with C and D'. But if you write your assessment too much like that the managers say she doesn't need it, because look at everything that she's able to do. So you do tend to find yourself trying to be a little bit negative, and paint the worst-case scenario to get somebody the services. And that obviously goes out to the person, and they think, 'I didn't realise I was as bad as all that'. Because you've had to paint it on the worst day possible, because if you say 'Well, actually on a really good day she can do all this on a good day', she's not going to get the service that she needs on a bad day." (interviewee 9)

Many interviewees talked about describing someone on their 'worst day' or in terms of the 'worst-case scenario':

"You can be tempted to slightly paint the worst-case scenario, ... or the situation on the bad day, rather than the good day." (interviewee 13)

"... when you're doing it for panel, then it is very blunt and it tends to be on a worst-case scenario basis." (interviewee 17)

There was a concern to distinguish between emphasising the negatives and actual fabrication. The former was seen as pragmatic and defensible, while the latter was seen as dishonest. Interviewees were at pains to say that they did not engage in telling lies. It was a question of how the information was presented, what was highlighted and what was ignored:

> "I'm not going to make it up, but obviously pull out the bits of the assessment that are going to have the best chance of getting the funding for the client at the end of the day." (interviewee 47)

Exaggeration might nevertheless be justified if it was used to try and avoid a situation deteriorating. Because many workers felt that the eligibility criteria would not recognise the need for preventative work, that is, putting in services in order to avoid a situation becoming worse, it was thought to be acting pragmatically in the service user's best interests, to describe a situation as more serious than it actually was currently:

> "It can help to exaggerate something sometimes as a means to an end for a service ... because sometimes you can see what might happen in the future, but it's not necessarily happening at the moment, so a lot of our work is prevention as well.... Before you get to a crisis, and although you think, I really can't get this person what they want before it gets to a crisis sometimes, you can be a little elastic with the truth." (interviewee 44)

There was a recognition that the success of a budget request may fundamentally depend on the skill of the worker to recognise how the system worked, and to successfully negotiate according to how that system worked:

> "... the tighter the eligibility criteria gets, the better I'm becoming at writing what they want to hear.... It's awful really; you shouldn't do it really." (interviewee 43)

> "I over-emphasise certain things in order to get that service. Probably, I do. Isn't that dreadful?... I think I have to, because otherwise I won't get it.... You end up competing so hard to get those services ... but I have to nevertheless represent my client's needs as fully as I can. So occasionally maybe the person that has the best recording skills gets the resources." (interviewee 50)

At times the strategy would result in what might seem like cynicism, but actually reflects a determination on the part of the worker to keep fighting on the service user's behalf. This pragmatic cynicism can be seen as a means to survive in what can sometimes seem an absurd situation:

"I mean, if you just want to put them in care – their legs have dropped off and they're blind …and you write all of that stuff because you want them [panel] to know that they're [service user] desperately in need of being cared for." (interviewee 26)

"… last week there was like five social workers ringing round, and there were no placements; and then … one placement was found, which was far and away above what we would normally pay. And they all needed it, so they all had to justify why their service user needed it above another person's service user. So they're all writing these reports, … it sounded like these people were like days away from death … you kind of had to do that because then those decisions go higher than the team…. So it's like, well that lady can have it because she's only got one leg, and that lady's got two legs, so she can't…. It does get a little bit like that." (interviewee 43)

Fundamentally there was an unresolved tension between writing an accurate, balanced description of a service user that could be comfortably and openly shared with that individual, and writing an account that would ensure funding:

"… if you're really truly honest, sometimes, I would say, the panel will come before the client 'cause you're actually trying to get through the panel, you're actually rewriting history to fit the panel." (interviewee 18)

Even among those who engaged in negative recording there was, as we have seen, a sense of unease, particularly around the impact such recording might have on service users. This unease was a sufficient reason for some interviewees to regard negative recording as unacceptable:

"I try not to record things on my assessment that would make my client feel that they don't have anything positive to offer … it's not beneficial for them to read that." (interviewee 19)

Some went further and felt that by describing service users in the most needy terms, those service users may be seen as more dependent than they actually were. Services might then be provided which could undermine their independence:

"… if you were to present a very negative view to a panel, then people get services which then disable them." (interviewee 8)

Workers who were concerned with rehabilitation work, which by definition focuses on achievement and measuring progress, believed they needed to emphasise the potential for improvement in any funding applications (interviewee 10).

There was also a view that contradicted the prevailing idea that negative recording would be more likely to guarantee funding, and instead sought to elicit empathy from the panel in respect of the service user:

> "I do a lot of what we call extra special needs requests for increased funding from nursing and residential homes.... So I'm well aware that my use of language or style of writing might be different ... if I just recorded straight facts I don't think I would be as successful as if I put in a flavour of the person ... to draw a little bit of empathy when you're reading." (interviewee 30)

The issue of empathy was also raised in relation to cases where the needs were more complex and more concerned with social and emotional issues, which were seen as more difficult to justify in terms of the eligibility criteria for funding. In this situation a person-centred approach was seen to be a more effective strategy:

> "If you've got a lady like Miss Miles [Version A and B] you've got very definite risks.... When it comes to something more complicated ... when you've got an emotional need, then you're more likely to go into a lot more detail about who the person is and what they are like.... I've had married couples where I've had to place both of them and you've maybe got Mrs who is nursing and in here [hospital] and Mr who is residential and struggling really badly [in the] community, you go into much more emotional stuff, and then we go into much more detail about who the people ... how long they've been married and what their relationship was like and ... how long has he been caring for her and the fact that they are both struggling...." (interviewee 29)

The judgement was being made that meeting the eligibility criteria was the overriding consideration in how the service user was described and, if the risks were obvious physical risks, it was a more straightforward job in providing that evidence in your funding request. Where the areas of need were more difficult to evidence in terms of risk, the challenge for the workers was to provide an account that would still make an effective case for resources. In one sense this underlines the preoccupation with risks and negative recording in that where there are clear physical risks, there is every expectation of meeting the eligibility criteria. It is where the needs are less obvious, but still significant, that the challenge arises, which may lead workers to either resort to the strategy of the 'worst-case scenario' or perhaps to attempt a more considered and detailed account of a complex situation. However, the more detailed recording might fall foul of the time limits on those making the funding decisions to read all the information before them.

Of the interviewees, 66% admitted to couching their assessments and requests to funding panels in negative terms, while 36.3% of the questionnaire respondents stated that they would describe 'someone on their worst day' in order to secure funding. This figure rose to 44.1% among those with 6-10 years' experience, who, it could be argued, were at the optimum point in their careers as practitioners, experienced and more confident by virtue of that experience, but not yet overly jaded and perhaps more resistant to new ideas of working. Older people and physical disability social workers demonstrated the highest percentage (40.4%) when work settings were compared, which may reflect the more competitive situation experienced in such teams. Even among those respondents who carried management responsibility, 36.7% said they would do so. Given that this is an admission of what might be seen to constitute bad practice, and is certainly frowned on by management, it is significant that the majority of the interviewees admitted to the practice, as did a substantial proportion of the respondents. It is conceivable that the figures might be even higher, given the difficulty social workers might have in disclosing their participation in such a practice.

These results are echoed by recent research conducted with 300 adult services social workers, where 34% admitted to 'bending the rules' when undertaking assessments, to ensure service users met the thresholds for receiving services. As the eligibility criteria had been tightened in two thirds of the councils surveyed, social workers responded by saying that they would be prepared to exaggerate service users' needs to secure or maintain services. This was particularly the case where service users were being reassessed in an attempt to withdraw services. Two thirds of social workers were concerned that they might be disciplined for it further down the line, but would do it nevertheless (Hayes, 2007).

What emerges is a picture where many practitioners felt obliged to engage in a strategy that was based on an inherent and inevitable inflationary pressure on the identification and recording of service users' needs and risks. The system was seen to encourage the exaggeration of a service user's situation in order to ensure that individual received the support they needed.

Ultimately it is the relationship between workers submitting requests for funding and those making the funding decisions that will determine how the record is written. Where the experience of workers is that the funding is dependent on negative recording, then that will be seen as a pragmatic response in order to get the necessary resources for the service user. Where there is a greater confidence in the panel's ability to make an appropriate decision, then there is less concern to emphasise the negatives.

Most of the interviewees did not trust their panels to provide that support without their resorting to the 'worst-case scenario' strategy. In the main, the strategy was widespread even though practitioners regretted that this was a necessary response to the harsh reality of social care provision in today's society.

While the competition for scarce resources has resulted in an expedient accommodation in relation to the construction of the record, social workers are still left with an unresolved dilemma. While describing a service user on their worst day might be justified in terms of maximising the likelihood of funding, it has also resulted in many service users reading overly negative descriptions of themselves, which many social workers fear could be potentially damaging to that individual's self-esteem. This leads us to another recording dilemma. The last 20 years have seen an increasing movement towards more open and collaborative recording between practitioners and service users. During that time, social workers have struggled with how to make their records effective in obtaining much needed services, as well as being able to openly share that same record with the service user.

Sensitive information

Prince (1996) conducted her research during the late 1980s and early 1990s, at the time client right of access to records was being introduced into social services. She attempted to work in a more open way with parents, routinely sharing with them the recordings she was making in respect of them and their child. Her objective was to share as much information as possible, and yet her analysis revealed that, in the event, less than 48% of the items recorded were actually shared with the parents (Prince, 1996, p 167). This was for a number of reasons, including the legal restriction on third party information, as well as information that she judged as unduly distressing or harmful to the relationship she had with the parents. This points to the difficulty service users' right of access may pose for social workers, in their attempts to record accurate, relevant information that is, nevertheless, still possible to share with service users. The questionnaire respondents similarly indicated difficulties in sharing recorded information with service users, and many of the interviewees identified situations where they had struggled with recording sensitive or problematic information.

As noted earlier when discussing the competing demands of recording, many interviewees described the sense of the service user looking over their shoulder as they were writing the record. The record raises the curious spectre of the social worker engaged in a process of surveillance of the service user, and at the same time the social worker feeling that the service user is watching them as they construct the record. The record is the evidence of that process of surveillance, and as such it may underline for both worker and service user a potentially awkward aspect of their relationship. Copies of some documents, such as assessments and care plans, are now routinely shared with service users, while the service user can only access the rest of the file through a formal request. In this section we explore the dilemmas that can arise for workers in trying to record accurate information, necessary to describe and communicate the relevant issues in respect of a service user and their situation to colleagues and budget holders. At the same time social workers try to ensure that the record does not upset the service user, so that it is contested and so undermines the service user's confidence in the worker and the service. This involves decisions around where information is recorded and the language used:

> "Obviously the single assessment process that was introduced last year, they [service users] take that home with them – that is their assessment – so we do have to be very careful what we write on that. You have

to be careful what you write on anything, because the service user always has a right to read their records. Obviously there's a process they go through, but on the panel form you can be a little bit more detailed, because the person wouldn't go home with that record." (interviewee 20)

Practitioners face considerable dilemmas when they are privy to information about a service user as a result of being informed by another (third) party, perhaps a relative or another professional. They are legally bound not to share that information with the service user without the consent of the third party, even though that information might be highly pertinent to the assessment, and indeed, its absence might leave an inexplicable hole in the assessment:

"I'm concerned about the client reading it….Because sometimes you get information from carers [relatives]….If you do a separate interview, … you're never quite sure whether the client is aware … of how the carer is really perceiving them … and to put that in could be quite disastrous sometimes." (interviewee 18)

Professionals from other agencies may express opinions about a service user to a social worker in terms that would be inappropriate to share. They are also able to claim third party restricted status in respect of the information they share with social services, and legally withhold permission for that information to be disclosed to the service user. A district nurse was described verbally referring to a service user as:

"… taking the micky.There's nothing wrong with her. I think she just wants an easy life; she's lazy; she doesn't need services, she just can't be bothered." (interviewee 9)

When the nurse was asked to put her views in writing, she was unwilling to commit herself and sent a letter saying,

"'I'm not in a position to comment on this person's disability because'…." (interviewee 9)

So the worker was aware of the professional's opinion, but could not refer to it in any meaningful way in the assessment.

Sometimes the information is withheld because it is considered not in the service user's best interest to be made aware of it. Such information may again be given a 'restricted access' category in the file, which means it would not be shared with the service user should they make a formal request to see their file. This may involve a diagnosis that the family feels the service user would not wish to know.These are always daunting judgements to make. It is often very difficult to distinguish between information that might be simply upsetting, and information that might actually be damaging for the service user to read:

> "Some people aren't aware of the diagnosis/prognosis for a whole range of reasons…. Family become overly protective and that does create a difficulty because obviously the doctors will have documented and I will have documented their condition…. So I suppose I kind of fudge that." (interviewee 25)

> "I actually went out to do an assessment and got to the house and was quite taken aback by the situation there…. This man was terminally ill. He hadn't been told, and he's trying to get me to arrange for DFG [Disabled Facilities Grant] for an extension [to his house] … you have to be positive about most things, but he didn't know, and they didn't tell him … so how, how could I write up an assessment for him to sign…. I actually contacted the hospital, the doctors and said, look, you know, this is ridiculous….You referred this man. I've gone out to do an assessment and I CAN'T do it! … I can't write it." (interviewee 18)

In addition to information that has a legally 'restricted status', social workers often find themselves having to enquire about very personal and intimate aspects of people's lives, which could reveal potentially embarrassing information. Issues around how to record someone's difficulties in managing incontinence were routinely cited by interviewees.

Good practice would encourage workers to record such information openly, but this may lead to very real dilemmas in how to record in such situations:

> "I can't write down 'Mrs Smith has smelly knickers'." (interviewee 2)

> "People are often giving you very personal and intimate information, and I think that requires … a certain tact in how you record something, so it could be really important to put down about somebody's difficulties with their continence for instance … that's the kind of classic one with older people, and I usually say to people, … 'I am going to ask you some quite personal intimate questions and … it's quite important that if there are some difficulties you are having that we can address them, we can get them right' … and so you just might need to be quite careful about how you word things." (interviewee 27)

The physical and functional aspects of service users' lives feature greatly in older people's services, and so workers often find themselves routinely discussing these sorts of issues with people they have only just met. The contrast with other service user groups was highlighted:

"I think in the learning disability team it would hopefully be a lot different ... there'd be assessments of someone who had reached 18 and left school and you wouldn't do the assessment until you had built up a relationship with them, go out for coffee with them, meet the family.... You wouldn't be talking about, you would not go into the personal stuff and start talking about toileting and personal care, because it's just rude. Whereas here [older people's team] [laughter] ... it's very ageist." (interviewee 4)

There was also the problem of service users and their families not always being willing to acknowledge the problematic behaviour of the service user, as well as questions around the degree of insight someone might have into their situation:

"If a situation is difficult, ... then I do stop and think.... How am I going to write the assessment so as not to offend anybody ... especially with clients who have dementia but don't recognise that they've got dementia, and they're still fully aiming to read their assessment? And ... for example, once I put on 'client has diagnosis of dementia', and the client went absolutely spare. 'Oh no I haven't.' But I've got to get it on the assessment, because that assessment goes to providers, and people who have got to know the client's needs." (interviewee 45)

The interviewees acknowledged that it was often difficult recording their professional opinion on the assessment when service users and their families might profoundly disagree with that opinion. One participant described a situation where she was asked to undertake an assessment on a young man who had a brain injury as a result of a motorbike accident. He was still in hospital and there had been concerns about his aggressive behaviour, which he and his parents did not want to acknowledge:

"And we've actually received a complaint from the person, through his parents, saying that I'd misrepresented him, because I had put that he had 'outbursts of verbal aggression', ... and his parents are just so upset that I'd put this phrase in his assessment....And it's really difficult, because he does, and because his wife has told me he's very abusive, the nurse on the ward, the OT [occupational therapist], the physio, they've all said to me he can be quite abusive; ... he can shout, he will try and throw himself out of his wheelchair, he will kick out. How do you ... deal with that when somebody doesn't want to acknowledge the fact that that's what they're doing, and the parents don't want to acknowledge the fact. And I thought that 'outbursts of verbal aggression', well, it's not the best phrase in the world, but it describes what he's doing, and it doesn't say he's abusive, or it doesn't say he's violent, it doesn't say anything like that. But ... they were quite upset by that, and ... they want it removing from the assessment. But we can't not put it in the assessment, because that is obviously part of his need, and people caring for him need to be aware ... that's part of his behaviour and that's part of his condition. So things like that are quite tricky." (interviewee 9)

This worker had struggled with the problem of how to record information which she had recognised would be potentially upsetting, and was frustrated that, despite her efforts, she had not been able to reconcile the conflict between recording relevant information and not offending the service user. Problematic behaviour was seen as particularly difficult to record:

"But I do think that sometimes on the assessments it's difficult to be totally honest if there's aggression or sexual inappropriateness." (interviewee 28)

These are very demanding situations in which to record, knowing that the information will be shared with the service user. Here the record is clearly evidence of a process of surveillance in which the service user may be presented with a picture of themselves that contradicts and possibly challenges their own sense of identity. This may be a deeply unsettling experience for anyone and especially for someone who already feels vulnerable. Service users may dispute the professional judgement of the social worker, but to contest the expert knowledge of the practitioner they are in a disadvantaged position as needy recipients of care. It is interesting to observe workers struggling with such an explicit demonstration of their professional power. The requirement to record confirms their position as expert but, by making the record available to the service user their position as expert is constantly open to challenge.

Participants described situations where family dynamics were complex and the problem of how to record that without causing undue offence:

"... sometimes you get family who are at war with each other ... and I think if that's the case I might only document that there was a difference of opinion." (interviewee 25)

There were situations where workers were concerned that the record could make a problem even worse. This was likely in vulnerable adult cases where there might be a suspicion of abuse:

"You're aware that something that you write on an assessment or a care plan may be seen, and it could make a situation an awful lot worse.... And then you get the dilemma of, well, do I just not put it on that form, and just put it on the observations, which they [service user] will never see, but then what happens if the next social worker who picks it up doesn't read the observation and only goes on what I've written on the assessment, and misses that, and it can be tricky.... It's very difficult, isn't it? I think you constantly try to be diplomatic, yet get the picture across.... Say, for example, we think that one of the service user's family members is taking their money.... On the assessment I wouldn't write, 'Mrs Smith's neighbour said that her grandson nicks her pension every week'.... I would maybe write something along the lines of: 'At the moment there seems to be some discrepancy' or 'At the moment we are investigating how Mrs Smith's pension is paid and ways of keeping that safe for her', or something like that, ... but on the observations, that they [service users] don't have access to, I would put 'The neighbour has made an allegation that it is the grandson'." (interviewee 43)

Many interviewees referred to the practice of putting information somewhere else in the file rather than include it in the assessment that is shared with the service user. This was on the assumption that, as the service user would only routinely see the assessment and the care plan, sensitive or problematic information could be more easily recorded elsewhere in the file. However, social workers do not always have time to read the file in detail, and there was the likelihood that by putting such information elsewhere in the file it might be missed or overlooked by any subsequent workers, even though it may be highly pertinent to the assessment. The next comment explicitly identifies the problem posed by shared assessments, and acknowledges that this now means that professional opinions may not always be included in the assessments for fear of upsetting the service user. Instead the professional opinion is put somewhere else in the case record:

"... sometimes situations can be quite difficult because I've worked with people with cognitive impairment.... It's trying to write an assessment that is sensitive to their needs without causing distress, which is how it should be. But sometimes there are ... discrepancies between what they are telling you and what you see. And I used to record it quite happily on the assessment, but since we're now supposed to be ... sending out these assessments I find that that's quite difficult, because if someone wants to pick up my assessment now it would be based around what the service user said and what the carer has contributed. Whereas at the end of the assessment before we sent them out, I would actually put in my view, this was the situation. So even though I do try and get it into the system how I saw the situation it doesn't form part of the assessment sent out...." (interviewee 24)

Putting important information 'somewhere else in the file' in order to maintain a particular understanding of confidentiality could result in some concerning situations. One interviewee described an occasion where she had called at a gentleman's house and not received any answer. As she later briefed her supervisor about the case, her supervisor enquired whether she had looked at the brown envelope tucked at the back of the file:

> "I said, 'No'. And she said, 'You should do, because the last person there was chased out of the house with an axe … and you shouldn't have gone on your own'. And so it was tucked there in an envelope at the back, and marked 'private and confidential'." (interviewee 26)

Another interviewee gave the example of a situation where she had recorded information in her diary rather than the case file as she did not feel confident to include it in the file record (interviewee 35). Nevertheless that information recorded in her diary was crucial evidence in an investigation following a complaint two years later.

As noted in the section on 'Communication with colleagues' and 'Communication with service providers' in Chapter Five, there was a concern to protect colleagues and care staff from perceived risks, and this was considered to be an important function of recording. However, this posed a dilemma when the service user saw that information:

> "… if somebody was likely to be violent … you wouldn't refer to their violence, but you might refer to the fact that two people should be attending, or … you would find another way of saying it, because you would be taking them [service users] into account. The fact that they would be seeing a copy of it in their home." (interviewee 41)

In addition to the question as to where information might be recorded in the file, there were constant references to the careful use of language when recording sensitive information. Over a quarter of questionnaire respondents said that they would either always or sometimes make a less explicit reference in their recording when faced with sensitive or problematic information. Implied messages relied not only on the skill of the practitioner writing the record, but also on the recognition and understanding of the implied message on the part of those reading the record. These implied messages involved the use of what was variously described as the 'careful', 'restrained' or 'veiled' use of language, which suggests a dependence on shared language codes. It raises the question as to whether these codes are peculiar to the profession, a particular local authority or a specific team:

> "It really is an art, you know." (interviewee 46)

> "I'll put it in a veiled way that the daughter would welcome a break.…
> You read between the lines. You write it as accurately as you can.…
> But there are ways of saying things." (interviewee 50)

"I'm quite good at writing things down without actually coming straight out and saying it." (interviewee 35)

"… sometimes the facts are not comfortable to read, and knowing that it is going to be read by the service user … it can make it very difficult, you then have to try and word it differently, but another professional, … they would understand what you're saying." (interviewee 2)

Here there are explicit references to the way that the recording relies on implied messages that the reader is meant to pick up from the coded language used by the writer of the record:

"… you have to bear in mind that there are some things that you want to record that are really important, that … [laughter] can be quite difficult really, to describe and to make sure that if other people are reading it, they're aware of the problem. So it's about language, and sometimes more about what you haven't said than about what you did say. It's trying to balance that, but also if you are thinking of other professionals, that they pick up the clues … you're saying things about people and trying to highlight difficulties, but not making it too obvious, because sometimes … especially people with dementia, they wouldn't acknowledge that they have that problem. It's the language you use…. It's restrained, it's restrained use of language." (interviewee 1)

An example of such restrained use of language is included in the following extract:

"You … might think that somebody is a, sounds awful, a dotty old lady, but you'd never write it down…. How would I phrase it … 'Mrs such-and-such, um, strives to be as independent as possible but isn't always aware of the risks and dangers around her'." (interviewee 20)

Sometimes the coded messages relies on the use of professional jargon:

"With dementia … people hide behind using jargon to disguise what they're writing, I suppose when they're assessing, people who put down things in jargon, so the client is not going to be able to understand." (interviewee 19)

Social workers have developed many strategies to try to overcome the tension between recording difficult or sensitive information and the requirement for their records to be available to the service users. Many of those strategies result in inconsistency in terms of where information may be recorded. They also rely on coded or implied messages as a means to avoid making the problematic nature of the recorded information accessible to the service user. The implied messages can sometimes be used to alert the reader that there is further information that the person writing the record has not felt able to include, but would be willing to pass on verbally. A third of questionnaire respondents said that they would either always or sometimes rely on passing the information verbally.

Passing on information verbally was seen to be inherently unreliable in that there was no permanent record to refer to, although that, in itself, might be an advantage where certain information was concerned:

> "But normally if I know X has been involved and X is around then I will speak to X ... because they'll tend to give me the fundamentals ... they may tell you things they haven't put in the record....So he's a pain in the arse may come up, and that's not in the record." (interviewee 39)

Sometimes it was just seen as quicker to ask for a verbal account rather than read the file:

> "... if you've got a big file and you haven't got all the pertinent information there, or sometimes it's easier under those circumstances to just find the previous worker and say 'What happened?'. Five or ten minutes can give you a better picture than trying to wade through a lot of paper really." (interviewee 41)

The greater confidence in the verbal account arose from a perception that workers felt less accountable for what they said than what they wrote:

> "We all know there are a lot of things you could say person to person to colleagues that you might not commit to writing." (interviewee 37)

> "I think sometimes we perhaps don't put it on paper: we might talk to each other about certain particular situations, but dare we say ..., 'if the parents weren't involved, then this person wouldn't have the behavioural issues that they did'. We might be sharing that with our colleagues outside of the recording, verbally...." (interviewee 48)

Participants felt that supervision (one-to-one meetings between worker and supervisor) was often a more appropriate place to discuss the issues in relation to a case. While records are made of supervision discussions, there was a belief among some workers that these were not part of the service user's file, and so could not be accessed by the service user. In point of fact this is not strictly true in legal terms, and in many authorities there is a routine procedure for any such discussion in supervision about a particular case to be recorded on the individual case file. This is in line with good practice, and is consistent with the legal interpretation that a service user's file is not just their discrete file, but any references to them in any social services departmental information systems. Nevertheless supervision was considered by some participants to be a safer place to share some of the more problematic issues in relation to a particular service user. One interviewee, when asked why she thought more reflective information was discussed in supervision rather than recorded in the case file, answered:

> " ... maybe that's because the social workers fear that people have access to the records, and they're not going to like what they read." (interviewee 36)

She continues, and highlights the difficulty of workers expressing their professional opinions in the record:

> " ... we are human beings, and we do get it wrong.... Nobody likes to know that what they've got wrong is recorded in black and white and open to the public ... and when something's uncertain, people would prefer to leave it out, even though it could be ... invaluable in doing constructive work with a person ... especially mental health." (interviewee 36)

There were concerns around insubstantial information that may depend on no more than a worker's hunch or intuition:

> "But then some places where you go in and you think hmmmm, ... and it's quite difficult to document why you didn't feel comfortable or ... and there'll be subtle things that do tell you that, but how do you evidence that and write it down. What you tend to write is that you felt very uncomfortable....Well, you see, if I went to my manager: 'I'm going to write on the files that there's a risk to workers going in and workers should go in twos because I felt really threatened but I couldn't tell why I felt really threatened'. They would take that seriously if they were worth their salt." (interviewee 29)

Despite all the difficulties in recording sensitive information there were five interviewees who felt they could work more openly with the service user, which then made the issue of recording sensitive information less problematic. Only 23.8% of the questionnaire respondents said they would always include sensitive or embarrassing information in the assessment. It requires considerable skill and confidence on the part of the practitioner, not only in their communication and recording ability, but also their capacity to anticipate the likely reaction of the service user:

> "I know if I've done quite difficult assessments on people who are constantly pressing their self-destruct button in terms of their use of alcohol, you know what they drink is ... well, I've been quite clear

within the assessment that the origin of most of their difficulties stems from their use or abuse of substance." (interviewee 3)

" … you have to put down. 'The service user believes that everything is fine and looks OK. The family's views contrast to this, and in my opinion I believe that this person doesn't have the capacity'…. I think you have to be honest with them and say, 'Well, you may think everything is all right, but well in actual fact this is what your family and what I'm seeing' … and you'd only do that if you knew, I think, that the person wasn't going to be that anxious or become upset by it; if you knew that it was going to stress people, then you wouldn't push the subject any more." (interviewee 8)

Even with this last comment there is still the qualification that the information could be included on the assessment as long as it would not make the service user more anxious or upset. That remains the dilemma for most workers. They do not always have the confidence in their own recording skills, or their ability to predict its likely impact on a vulnerable service user, and so recording sensitive information, for most workers, remains a dilemma. Lack of training in recording and inconsistent feedback from management compounds this dilemma.

Recording sensitive information highlights the tension between the record as the outcome of a process of surveillance, which is necessary to ensure relevant information is included in the record, and the increasing emphasis on openness and collaborative working with service users. Even where the issues are unproblematic the record may still underline the extent to which the service user is the subject of scrutiny, but where those issues become difficult or contentious, the record becomes the contested territory for whose definition of the situation should prevail.

Nearly half of the questionnaire respondents said that they would never use the restricted category (information not accessible to service users in the event of an access request) under which to record problematic information. It emerged during the interviews that the understanding of what was meant by 'restricted' varied somewhat between individuals. Sensitive or problematic information was being managed in a variety of ways with no particular consistency. Whether and where it might be recorded depended on the judgements of individual workers with little external guidance or direction. As a consequence, such information may or may not be readily accessible in the file.

The issue of how to record sensitive information, more than any other dilemma in recording, indicates the extent of the inconsistency and confusion surrounding recording in social services. Practitioners are concerned to record in a spirit of openness and are acutely aware of the growing emphasis on freedom of information. Yet they remain unsure how and where to record such problematic information. As a consequence, important information may not be recorded and, even if it is, it is very possible that the information will either be couched in language that is sufficiently guarded that it is misunderstood, or the information may be missed altogether, lost in the obscure recesses of the file.

It is recognised that often informal structures emerge in organisations as a response to the problems created by the formal structures (Blau, 1963). However, for those informal structures to be effective, they need to be consistently followed. In the absence of official direction and guidance on recording, informal, fundamentally inconsistent practices have developed, which then give rise to greater uncertainty and confusion among practitioners. As a consequence the record becomes an increasingly unreliable source of information, despite the considerable effort invested in its construction.

Ticking boxes

Participants' views on the impact of IT were noted in Chapter Six, and it was clear that technology could be seen as both a resource and as a constraint. Interviewees spoke of software systems being devised without any input from practitioners. The issue of tick box recording was a theme that ran through the interviews, and a third of the questionnaire respondents saw it as a concern. Recording is part of the process of providing evidence that performance indicators have been met. It was noted that the information systems being used are influencing the process of recording. Some workers felt that the software packages used for recording service user information were designed more with performance indicators in mind than gathering professionally relevant information. In this section we examine this further and consider the way that the administrative systems are seen to drive the recording process, leading to assessments becoming little more than a bureaucratic exercise.

Many felt that the forms they used, whether paper or electronic, were too prescriptive:

> "Some of us have said the new single assessment process is too restrictive, tick box. You've got to go from this sheet to that sheet, ask all sorts of questions that might not be relevant or not relevant now, it's too prescriptive, too limited. I don't like it." (interviewee 37)

This sense of ticking boxes was reinforced with the use of what were referred to as 'pick lists'. These are lists of options, or checklists, from which workers have to choose. They may form part of the assessment, and so prescribe certain needs, and they may be used again on the care plan, where only certain service responses are available:

> "You have to choose from a pick list.... And the pick list may not necessarily match your desired outcome exactly.... If everything is pick list, then why do you need qualified people doing it?" (interviewee 46)

There was a concern that increasingly prescribed procedures undermine professionalism and indeed may ultimately make professionals superfluous. One interviewee described a situation involving a gentleman with dementia who was attending a day centre. As a consequence of him becoming more agitated in the afternoons while at the day centre, the worker decided it would be better if he was taken home early, and so she needed to arrange transport to take him home as the day centre bus was only available at the end of the afternoon:

> "… the care plan is a pick list, and it says 'personal care, heat a meal, provide a frozen meal, assisted medication, shopping, pension'…. And if it isn't on that pick list you can't put it on there, and nowhere on that pick list does it say 'transport' or does it say 'escort', or even 'other'…. Because we don't usually provide unusual services, and so basically I had to just put 'personal care', and then there's a little note screen, and I put in the note screen 'pick Mr A up from the day centre and take him home'." (interviewee 9)

This underlines the extent to which the recording system is actually shaping the options that may be considered by the social worker, and so leading to not only a more prescriptive way of recording, but to more prescribed interventions. It is interesting how this again conflicts with good practice principles which exhort care managers to be more creative and innovative in their approach to care planning.

There was a sense that reliance on what were seen as overly simplistic forms led to a concentration on the more straightforward physical and functional areas of need, rather than the more complex social and emotional needs. Even when the emotional needs might be included there was a tendency to reduce them to a level that was seen as meaningless:

> " … the first part of the paperwork is tick boxes, and it's very much focused on physical ability and mental ability. So: can you wash and dress yourself; can you make a cup of tea?" (interviewee 21)

When asked about recording emotional and social needs, the same worker responded:

> "It's there, but again it's a tick box answer 'Do you feel sad or upset sometimes?'. And what does that tell you? Don't we all? [laughter] And there's a wonderful bit which is a depression score, … and I could answer negatively to all those questions on certain days, … so what does that actually tell you?" (interviewee 21)

There was a concern that during the assessment interview workers were becoming more focused on filling in the form correctly than really listening to the service user:

> " ... and then you have to cover all the tick boxes with comments ... it's a bit difficult to associate with the person because ... when you are talking you are thinking about the form you are filling in." (interviewee 42)

One participant who was responsible for training social work students felt that they were particularly vulnerable to being driven by the form:

> "... they're looking at the form and they're not looking at the person." (interviewee 40)

Some felt that the process and paraphernalia of information gathering was dominating the assessment interview:

> "One of my greatest concerns is, because there is a great emphasis on the process and on tick boxes ... the danger is doing the assessment, ie you go out with wadges of paper, you know they [service user] are looking at the machines, the [electronic] notebooks which seems totally abhorrent in terms of actually ... doing an assessment." (interviewee 39)

The 'wadges' of paper could be impressive indeed:

> "We have gone from a ... two-page assessment document to a 44-page one, ... we're struggling with it, particularly as it is supposed to be an overview." (interviewee 41)

The same interviewee complained that her large handwriting made the completion of the paper forms more difficult:

> " ... some of the forms we use ... are ... with little boxes, ... all tick boxes.... I have trouble because I have quite large handwriting and I can never fit everything I want to write into the space and I have ... less space to write the same amount of words.... So what people tend to do is go through and either do the tick boxes, if there is nothing to write at the end of that and I think unfortunately we are going more towards that, people are not writing very much inside. Other people are writing a much more descriptive bit at the end that encompasses all the ticks that they've put in the boxes." (interviewee 41)

Here there was a concern that the form was discouraging some workers from writing as much information as they judged necessary, while others were adapting their way of using the form to ensure all the information was included. One of the main concerns was that the form did not provide the space to record important information:

> "… when you put a service package on, you only have so much space to write in a care plan.… I … think you need actually more space … the care plan may say 'assistance required from two carers'; this is with personal care, and you can probably write down two or three sentences in that box, and no more. And I think in some cases there might be other relevant … like emptying the commode, helping with other tasks that can be done in that time, because the problem we have is, when the service user rings you back, 'the carer was only here for 10 minutes this morning, and they haven't made the bed, haven't pulled the curtains, and they haven't emptied the commode', or whatever. And the carer's argument will always be, 'Well, we're just doing what's written on the care plan'." (interviewee 5)

There was a clear tension between the need to work within the constraints of the form and still provide sufficient detail to specify the contractual arrangements with a care provider.

The contrast between the person-centred recording (Version A) and the case-centred recording (Version B) arises again. This time it is explained in terms of the form not providing the opportunity to record anything more than the basic functional needs:

> "There's a gap about that much on it … the social work point of view … so again, yes, you're going to be doing Version B." (interviewee 21)

> "Version A is the type of thing that you would aim to do if you had the time, and if the computer would allow you to type that amount of stuff in. We used to be able to actually word process or handwrite our running records, and it could be as long as you wanted, but with our new computer system, you've got a very small box, and unfortunately you would probably end up putting in something more like Version B." (interviewee 43)

> "… and now they're so concise I think you could take the name off the front sometimes and put another name on and you wouldn't know who it was." (interviewee 18)

Some workers found the information systems deskilling, in that the systems influenced the way practitioners actually thought about a case:

"I would definitely say that; especially with a new system, where it asks you, prompts you so many times, … what do you think about this; or what about that…. The trouble is that it also is quite deskilling as well, because it doesn't really give you the opportunity to think things through yourself." (interviewee 46)

Essentially there was a concern that the forms, instead of being seen as tools to facilitate the work of practitioners, were so prescriptive that they were becoming an end in themselves:

"… the whole of our recording process, I worry that it's becoming more of a tick box kind of culture. When I started writing assessments they were sort of virtually on a blank piece of paper, and OK when you're very new and inexperienced it's … good to have some guidelines, … which areas should we look into, … but once those areas get more and more closely defined and there's less room for, … opinion as well as factual information…. I always remember a session that we had, it wasn't particularly about forms, it was about models of behaviour in a very general way and … the lecturer was talking about, and he called it frames and cages so basically … you have a framework and … you can either build on that framework, or it can be considered to be a cage that constrains you and that's always stuck with me and … so I think the forms ought to be a framework and not a cage … I have no problem with writing in margins and making things bigger, but some people, although they may still … speak out against that would … have to adhere to what was requested of them. Those of us who are long enough in tooth don't mind." (interviewee 27)

Some workers felt that a blank page would be more useful. These were often workers who had been qualified for a number of years. Their lack of enthusiasm for current systems may be seen as the not unusual reaction of longer experienced workers to new and unwelcome systems, or it could be seen as an indication of their self-perceived greater skill and confidence, which may or may not be justified:

" … and I'm not a great advocate of ticking boxes, and partly, I suppose, because I've been at this a long time and, … would feel that I could write a professional assessment of the need which would give me far more information and would be far more useful than ticking boxes." (interviewee 25)

Some participants did find more structured forms with specific headings more useful:

"… we need certain headings, and … some consistency, so when you pick up somebody's care plan … you know the format … you can deal with it much quicker." (interviewee 28)

However, it was acknowledged that sometimes it was difficult fitting someone's story, which was often told in a narrative form, into the designated structure:

"… if we need to care for somebody we have to do what we call an X, which … goes through the background and the person's needs … we've got headings … which is useful, but I find it difficult … [fitting] the bits that are personal to the different areas." (interviewee 10)

The structure of the form may lead to unhelpful repetition:

"You go down tick, tick, tick, tick, tick, tick, tick, … the bits of text and then it says 'summary of that section', and then you might be repeating some of the stuff you've already put down." (interviewee 34)

"… it almost feels over-the-top recording, in the sense that it's more the process … there's so many forms … the information isn't over the top, it's repeated in lots of different places." (interviewee 50)

There was a perception that although less information was recorded today, much more time was spent on the task because of unnecessary duplication and administrative complexity:

"I think 30 years ago people recorded more than they record now or are encouraged to record now, but on the other hand, because we've got so many more assessment papers which we didn't have … you end up double recording." (interviewee 25)

"… the whole job has become much more bureaucratic – even in the two-and-a-half years I've been here." (interviewee 43)

The last point takes us back to the issue of performance indicators. The tick boxes are a means to gather information that can be more readily processed, and this then provides the means by which workers can be more easily monitored and held accountable. The work of social services is increasingly being regulated and monitored, and the paperwork is a reflection of that process. Whereas assessments might have once been done on a relatively blank page, with the professional making judgements about what and how to organise the information they recorded, today there is little such professional discretion allowed. The forms are being designed to ensure that there is greater consistency and standardisation of the work undertaken, where the quality of the recorded assessment will be determined as much by the form as by the worker. While such forms are being heralded as tools to enhance the quality of work, many social workers experience them as overly prescriptive and restrictive, driving social workers to produce more standardised, formulaic assessments. There was a view that the assessment process had become little more than the completion of a form, rather than an interview to explore with the service user their particular situation. Social workers believed that management was more concerned with whether the boxes had been ticked, rather than with the quality of information they produced. Instead of being encouraged to treat the recording systems as tools, social workers were being intimidated by them:

> "Much more tick boxes to make sure you've done things, and this is done and that is done, and all those kind of things." (interviewee 29)

The issue of tick box recording underlines the extent to which recording is part of the process of governance. The record must ultimately demonstrate that cases have been processed according to established procedures, and the more standardised the recording systems, the more readily that information can be gathered. The move to electronic information systems will streamline that process still further and ensure that information is instantly available at the touch of a key. As Harris (2003) noted, social workers and service users are subjects of surveillance in this concern to ensure greater efficiency and effectiveness through ever more monitoring systems. The case record is now less about information that has relevance for making professional judgements, and is now far more about providing systematic information that facilitates procedural decision making, as well as providing evidence that performance indicators have been achieved and targets met according to regulated standards. The case record is now part of the audit society (Power, 1997).

Attempts to reconcile the record

In this last section we conclude with how workers view the recording task in the light of the contradictions, tensions and constraints examined. This provides a brief summary of workers' reflections on the significance of the record in the discharge of their role responsibilities.

There was much emphasis on the record providing evidence of a job done as well as it could be in the circumstances. These comments were often couched within the idea of being realistic about what could be achieved in their role as social workers, and what the service was able to provide. The significance of the record was in documenting, almost bearing witness to the fact that a process had been correctly followed, even if the outcome was not ideal:

> "I think it's about being realistic ... you're there for a specific purpose, and you can't spend, be promising things that you know you're never going to be able to achieve.... It's about the process of negotiation

and discussion, assessing and planning, but as long as you're making sure that throughout the process you're recording that you're doing that.... Because ... even if at the end of it you're not actually providing a service, as long as you're ... recording that you've gone through a process of ... how we came to this end goal ... you've not got a magic wand.... There are going to be disappointments along the way with that." (interviewee 7)

"I think you need to record, and if you've asked for something, or if you've discussed something, ... and it's not been agreed, then it needs to be recorded that it's not been agreed, and it needs to be identified why it wasn't agreed ... you might not like it ... but it's all there, and why something isn't ... set and agreed." (interviewee 12)

This record may become significant in enabling the worker to document the extent to which they are distanced from the decision-making process. The record demonstrates that this was not the worker's decision. Someone else made that decision in spite of all the efforts made by the worker:

"If I try to get something for somebody and I hadn't been successful, you always ... record that that was the need that you assessed.... You're not the one at the end of the day that's turned it down.... And it's not kind of bending the truth; it's about being honest, isn't it. So it's the work you've done; this is how far you've got with it at the end of the day.... If the powers that be turn around and say there's not the money to do that; then that's recorded.... At the end of the day you're accountable to your team manager, if they make decisions you don't agree with, you know you're meant to kind of carry out what they said, but you record that in such a way that it's quite clear ... that you're being asked to do something, and this is exactly what you were asked to do, and this is what you've done. It's just about being, you know, it's accurate." (interviewee 47)

Sometimes the record is the means by which workers can almost console themselves. Their sense of frustration is assuaged by recording their part in the story even if the ending has not been the one they might have wished.

"It's not covering your back; it's kind of you feel better putting it down. Look, I have done this, ... so even though it's not come to anything." (interviewee 15)

There was sometimes a precisely delineated sense of role responsibility, in which the worker was very clear that they did not make decisions, they followed a process and it was up to someone else how that process was concluded:

"… if I've met the client and I've done the assessment, that's their needs – I've recorded them, and it's not up to me to decide whether the budget holders provide for those needs, it's up to the council management to decide what they can provide or not provide, and if the family make a complaint, then it's up to them to then sort it out really." (interviewee 19)

While we have already seen much evidence of the sense of frustration shared by many workers over limited resources and restricted budgets, this next participant demonstrates a pragmatic attitude which has enabled her to work within the limits of the system. It might be interesting to note that this is the same individual who earlier acknowledged that she had had to lower her standards of recording in response to the pressure of the workload (interviewee 17). While she had been reluctant to do this, she saw it as a necessary response in the situation:

"I just took a realistic understanding of what social services was like before I went into it.… I didn't have any illusions. I understood how the government … drives it from central government down. If you understand the process, then it's not so bad." (interviewee 17)

While this view suggests a very clear sense of the limits of the social work role, this was unusual and many interviewees expressed greater confusion and ambiguity. All were asked whether they saw themselves as advocates of the service user or as representatives of the department, and whether they saw any tension between these two roles. Only three individuals saw no tension between these roles, while the vast majority tried to steer a middle course. One individual described it as "walking a tightrope" (interviewee 25). Others described themselves as an:

"… advocate under pressure." (interviewee 1)

"… advocate chasing empty coffers." (interviewee 15)

Interviewees described situations in which they found themselves caught between these two roles that had implications for the way they recorded:

"We've had issues recently where the department's policy was at variance with the service user, and there was a very clear record of my … I was in the middle; I was saying to the individual, 'This is the procedure'. And then I had to record the response given by the service user … and I felt I was being neutral in that, and then a complaint went through to the director, actually … from the family. And they came back down to me, but there was this clear record on the system.… And … when the manager said to me, 'Can you show me the recording? Can you give me an account of what you've done?'

I was clearly able to say, at this meeting this was what was discussed. I gave the person some literature, which I recorded, so the manager knew they'd got the departmental literature, and they were using that in their argument.... It's just about being very open and clear about what you are doing." (interviewee 8)

The record is an important part of how this worker was able to negotiate between the roles, providing him with the means to account for how he had acted in a difficult situation. The record was used to demonstrate that he had acted professionally, while still discharging his duty of care to the service user.

These comments suggest a more considered view of the record, in which it is possible to use the record to evidence a process, which does not always allow the practitioner to meet the needs of the service user in the way that they might judge they should be met, but nevertheless conforms to agreed policy. These comments are included not because they are typical, but because they point to a way of looking at the record that has more potential for empowering workers and for more clearly evidencing the distance between the rhetoric and the reality of social care provision.

The final comment also acknowledges the power of the record to protect the individual worker in a system where they are vulnerable to blame for the shortcomings of an overly stretched service. The focus moves on to the service user and the recognition that the record is also their record, and yet for many workers there is the sense that all their efforts to engage in open recording, where information is routinely shared with service users, may seem of limited relevance when few service users show much interest in the record:

"Sadly, I think that I record some of the time to cover my own back, ... to prove that I have done everything that I'm contracted to do by my employer. And also to make sure that if I'm ever audited or questioned in any way, that I will be able to provide a good answer to the reasons why I did something, and why I took a decision, and whatever. But ... the other side of that is that I do it for the client, because they've got to have a record of their involvement with us, and it's got to be in a format that they can access if they want to do so. It's got to be as honest as possible, although really we send so much to them now, I can't imagine why they would want [to] ring up and say, 'Can I have the rest of it?' because they've already got most of it ... and people do say that: you bombard them with so much stuff that in the end it means nothing to them, – and other people will go through it with a fine tooth comb." (interviewee 46)

So again the worker is confronted with the conundrum that while most records will simply pass into social services files with little consequence, other than whether they were effective in ensuring a service or not, there is always the chance that a particular record may become the subject of a complaint or an investigation, that service users or others 'may go through it with a fine tooth comb', and so the record is still seen by many as both "essential but pointless" (interviewee 36).

EIGHT

Conclusions and implications

In this final concluding chapter we draw together the complex issues surrounding recording to present a coherent account of why recording remains such a neglected issue, and why the recording task is inherently problematic. We will look at the implications of the competing agendas, and what they might signify for future directions in policy.

We begin with a summary of the overall context within which social workers practise in contemporary adult services and, in particular, the distance between the needs-led rhetoric, which promotes service user choice, and the service-led reality. We revisit the demands of recording and look at the impact of the tensions between those different demands on recording practice. We look at the record as an organisational construct, and how practitioners struggle to reconcile the dilemmas of recording within the context of the constraints identified. This is followed by a discussion as to why recording might be seen as a conveniently neglected subject, where the record is central to a process of governance, a process more concerned with presenting the appearance of procedural compliance than the lived experience of the practitioner and the service user, which is rendered irrelevant. The chapter concludes with implications for policy in respect of recording in adult social services.

Needs-led rhetoric and service-led reality

In Chapter Two we established the extent to which social work is practised in a social and political context that is riven with contradictions. In late modernity risk is a dominant theme, and social work is charged with the management of risk in respect of particularly vulnerable groups of people. There is a constant tension between the concern to promote independence, but also to manage risk and fulfil the duty of care (Clarke, 1993). With the advent of community care, more and more vulnerable people, who had previously been cared for within residential institutions, are now living in the community. This gives rise to very difficult judgements as to what is 'safe' and how to ensure individual service users enjoy independence and a quality of life without unduly putting themselves, or others, at risk (Kemshall, 2002).

This is further complicated by recognising that individual life courses are no longer shaped to the same extent by established patterns such as kin relations. Instead, people are faced with a far greater range of options from which to reflexively make themselves and plan their lives. Social work is expected to facilitate this process, and choice has become an important principle in social care. The introduction of community care was predicated on the notion of choice as a defining feature of how provision was supposed to be managed. However, as has been shown, the rhetoric has never quite matched the reality experienced by both service users and practitioners (Postle, 2002). Choice has been undermined by ever-increasing pressure on budgets, which has restricted the options available to service users. This has put social workers in an impossible dilemma, where they are expected to work to certain principles, espoused in government policies, but without the resources to implement those policies (Powell, 2001).

This was a dominant theme in the interview data, shown in the section on 'Budgets and service provision' in Chapter Six. There was clear evidence of the frustration felt by many of the interviewees who felt caught between the increased expectations of service users and their families, and the reality of limited service provision. The interviewees also underlined the extent of the case-closing culture, identified by Webb (2006), in which workers felt they had insufficient time to properly investigate service users' needs, due to the high volume in turnover of cases and where the pressure was on meeting government targets.

Social work is seen as an impossible task, where the outcomes are often difficult to define in clear-cut terms and the methods for achieving them are variable, which leaves the social worker vulnerable to challenge (Franklin and Parton, 1991). In this context the processes by which decisions have been made are increasingly important to evidence as a means of defending professional practice. Individual social workers and social services departments rely on the record to provide an account of what, how and why certain courses of action were taken (Carson, 1995). With this they can evidence the effectiveness, or otherwise, of their strategies in managing the risky and messy business of providing social care to vulnerable people, in a situation where the expectations often exceed the means to meet them.

Competing agendas

The functional agenda

The functional agenda is dominated by a preoccupation with assessing and managing risk according to the technical-rational approach that now dominates social work. That approach assumes that responding to service users' needs involves a linear process in which risk can be calculated in terms of particular factors, which have been identified empirically (Webb, 2006.) The neoliberal political agenda has underlined the targeting of resources according to prioritised need. Need has been subsumed under risk, and risk is now the basis on which eligibility for services is determined. The degree of risk in relation to a potential service user is determined by the extent to which they exhibit the risk factors already identified (Castel, 1991).

Practitioners described the main function of the record as presenting the relevant risk factors that would demonstrate a service user's eligibility, or otherwise, for services. Their experience of writing assessments confirmed the view that those making resource allocation decisions were focused exclusively on risks. It was widely believed that there was little interest, when the criteria were being applied, in a service user's strengths or details about their past. The preoccupation was exclusively with the present circumstances and the information relevant to establishing the priority of risk among the numerous potential service users being assessed.

All communications made by practitioners in respect of service users become focused on what is considered relevant information, that is, what are their problems/risks? The categorisation or labelling of service users as at risk can be self-fulfilling, so that only information confirming the problematic nature of the service user is seen as relevant. This process has a long history in social care.

Goffman (1968 [1961]) described the way in which mental health patients' behaviour was understood and explained by professionals solely in terms of the disorder with which the patients had been diagnosed. The diagnosis served as a label. All behaviour exhibited by the patients only became meaningful in terms of the label, and so the diagnosis was continually confirmed in the observations of professionals, and the record they made of those observations. The record then provides the evidence of the correctness of the professional judgement and legitimates the subsequent 'treatment' administered.

This long-established tendency to view patients, clients or service users in terms of the deficit they present is then compounded by the pressure on service demand. With more cases to process, and more exacting expectations in relation to the time taken to assess and process cases, practitioners are concerned to concentrate on what their experience demonstrates is necessary to successfully manage a case. The functional demands, driven by establishing eligibility, then become dominated by a distorted version of the service user, which emphasises a negative description in accordance with the concern with risk. This leads to a predominance of the negative (Version B) descriptions in the record, which focus exclusively on the problems and weaknesses presented by the service user, and the employment of the 'worst-case scenario' strategy, which relies on describing the service user in the worst possible terms in the assessment in order to make an effective case for resources.

Recorded communications with colleagues emphasise the risks and problems identified in respect of a service user because that is what practitioners see as the purpose of their professional involvement. This is the information that is then relevant to pass on to colleagues; there is no time to consider anything else. Workers described the intense and unrelenting pressure under which they worked. Their time was constantly interrupted, and the unpredictable nature of the work made it impossible to plan work in any real sense. The demand to process cases as quickly as possible, and still produce a coherent record of the work undertaken, inevitably led to an exclusive focus on the minimal information that was necessary to process and close the case. The holistic, balanced description of the service user, while it might be considered 'nicer', is seen as superfluous in the overriding focus on prioritising on the basis of risk.

Social work is increasingly organised around short-term work with service users, where the assessment and setting up of the care package are the principal objectives. In this situation the record assumes greater significance in being the source of information on which successive practitioners depend, to learn what has happened and what is currently happening with a case. The record is expected to provide a readily accessible account of the issues of concern in a case and the work undertaken. In this way continuity is ensured, although it was evident from many workers' experience that even a minimal account of the risks and problems in a case did not always feature in the record.

The technical-rational approach in social work has been justified in terms of ensuring a more focused, equitable and transparent approach, but this underlines the extent to which attention has shifted from the delivery of the service to the process of deciding who should have the service. This returns us to the debate over the role of social worker operating in the context of community care, where the practitioner is no longer expected to deliver a service, but simply assesses the level of need for a service. Their function is to follow a prescribed procedure in prioritising risk, which the recording tools themselves were designed to emphasise. The focus on systems of decision making is perhaps an attempt to address the challenge to 'expert' knowledge, where decisions are increasingly made on the basis of following an explicit process, rather than the exercise of individual judgement. As such decision making is seen to be more systematic, and as a consequence more defensible. In this way it can be argued that the functional agenda does, to a certain extent, anticipate some of the issues that arise with the accountability agenda. It is the values agenda that is most in conflict with, and vulnerable to, the pressures exerted by the other two agendas.

The values agenda

The values agenda underlines person-centred, holistic, balanced recording, emphasising strengths as well as areas of need. Service user choice and promoting independence are also emphasised. Community care was introduced in 1991 as an opportunity to extend service user choice, and it is interesting to note that many practitioners welcomed it on that basis (Lewis and Glennerster, 1996). The agenda to reduce public spending was made much less evident in the attempt to sell community care to professionals. Policy initiatives since then have continued to advocate person-centred practice as well as person-centred recording (HMSO, 1991, p 29). Assessments are supposed to include service users' strengths as well as their areas of need. This is to ensure an accurate picture of a service user and their situation, on which appropriate decisions could then be based.

The overwhelming majority of practitioners involved in the research endorsed the person-centred description of the service user as more consistent with professional values. It was recognised that information about someone's history might be relevant in understanding their current behaviour and circumstances, and assist in devising a more appropriate intervention that would promote independence and not undermine it.

However, in an increasingly competitive situation, where practitioners are competing with each other for all too scarce resources, the assessment has become a rationing mechanism. Workers recognise that in order to obtain the services they deem necessary for their service users, they cannot afford to employ the values agenda, with the likely result that their assessment will be afforded a lower priority. Instead, they yield to an inflationary pressure to emphasise the negatives in their service user's situation in order to make an effective case for the services they judge should be provided. Workers see the skill they exercise in the recording of assessments as the means by which they either succeed or fail in the competition for those services.

For many practitioners, the value agenda is understood in terms of doing what is necessary to serve the best interests of the service user. If that requires writing negative assessments in order to obtain those services, then that is seen as part of advocating on behalf of a service user. The difficulty arises in that, because of the commitment to more open sharing of information, those same service users will then see the negative description of themselves, which would do little for their self-image or self-esteem.

Open recording and the introduction of 'freedom of information' can also be seen as part of the values agenda. This is an attempt to make the recording process more transparent and thus render the surveillance process, inherent in recording, more acceptable. Open recording is an attempt to shift the balance in power between service user and professional, and to make the professional and their practice more accountable to the service user. Practitioners see this as an important and desirable development in how they work with service users, but it has left them with some uncomfortable dilemmas. It has made the reflexive process of surveillance more explicit. Service users are made more aware of the extent to which practitioners are observing them. Practitioners are then anticipating, as they record, how service users will respond to the recorded account of those observations. This has had a considerable impact on what practitioners feel they can and cannot now record, and has introduced a degree of discomfort and unease in the recording task. The issue of recording sensitive information highlighted this most starkly, and has demonstrated the uncertainty and confusion among practitioners in how to reconcile the value of open recording with the functional agenda of communicating relevant information to colleagues.

Essentially, the values agenda in recording, which promotes person-centred and open recording, can be seen as a legitimating process, on the part of policy makers, which attempts to perpetuate the rhetoric of a user-led approach to social care. The policy rhetoric is necessary to distract from the service-led reality, and can be seen as an attempt to square the circle of good practice principles that are actually impossible to implement. Good practice principles in recording are constantly undermined by the functional agenda, which is driven by the relentless struggle to meet ever-increasing demand within a given level of resources.

The accountability agenda

The values agenda is further complicated by the accountability agenda, which includes both legal accountability and the process of regulation, as typified in the widespread reliance on performance indicators as measures of efficiency and effectiveness of service delivery. These two aspects of the accountability agenda interact with the values agenda in somewhat different ways.

Regulation can be seen as the attempt both to control market distortions and failure, and to make the neoliberal reliance on the market more acceptable. Performance is monitored and regulated through the audit of recorded information. Information systems are concerned with giving an account of both organisational and individual efficiency and effectiveness. Quantifiable information dominates; quality of service is meaningful only to the extent it can be counted. The need for standardised information increases and so recording becomes ever more prescribed in its format. Recording is restricted to a 'tick box' exercise where complex information is reduced and simplified to facilitate more consistent and explicit decision making. This is clearly in tension with person–centred recording.

Recording tools are designed to ensure greater consistency in order to reduce the scope for individual professional judgement. Whereas assessments might have been undertaken with a blank form at one time, now the concern is to ensure that standardised information is gathered so that cases can be reliably compared when resource allocation decisions are being made. While such forms are introduced as tools to improve the quality of work, many practitioners experience them as overly restrictive. On the one hand, this can be seen as an example of professional discretion becoming more constrained.

On the other hand, it can be argued that while increasingly prescribed tools suggest more precise direction in how assessments should be recorded, the actual experience of workers is that recorded assessments demonstrate considerable inconsistency. Even very detailed forms have to be interpreted and applied in the practical work situation, which provides much scope for individual discretion. So as the forms and guidance procedures become more elaborate and tightly drawn in their attempts to ensure consistency of practice, the opposite is achieved in creating more opportunity for infinite possibilities in how they are interpreted (Evans and Harris, 2004). Despite the efforts to ensure greater consistency, the record becomes less consistent and more unreliable, where workers feel unable to record the information that they see as meaningful because the form does not permit them to do so, but are still constructing their own versions of what they think the form does require.

While the functional agenda is concerned with prioritising and managing risk, the accountability agenda is concerned with producing an account that adequately documents, for legal and audit purposes, that both the individual practitioner and the organisation have properly discharged their duties and responsibilities. Legal accountability demands that the record be sufficiently robust in situations of challenge. The extent to which service users are challenging departments requires the record to demonstrate that decisions have been made appropriately, following procedural directives. Those directives are concerned, as we have seen with the functional agenda, to present a technical–rational process of risk management, dependent on the exercise of expert knowledge.

Risk is assessed as the calculation of a number of identified factors rather than a holistic evaluation of the individual. However, expert knowledge is an area that is increasingly contested, and so the concern to successfully manage risk becomes more problematic. With more knowledge there is an expectation that risk might be more precisely measured and anticipated. Greater knowledge encourages a greater preoccupation with risk and provides the basis for the recognition of additional risk, as well as raising concern over who is responsible for creating or managing the risk (Giddens, 1991). Risk calculations in the field of social care are fraught with the difficult, complicated and unpredictable business of trying to deal with human behaviour. Professional decision making in social care has become an increasingly problematic area, as well as one that is more likely to be contested.

Legal accountability demands more detailed recording in order to comply with the expectation that recorded information complies with the 'rules of evidence'. While practitioners acknowledged that they discriminated between cases in terms of the level of detail recorded, based on their judgement of the anticipated complexity or contentiousness of the case, they admitted that this was difficult, when even the most seemingly straightforward cases can prove unpredictable. Some might record in greater detail after having their file subjected to legal scrutiny, but this conflicted with the functional demand to process cases as quickly and efficiently as possible. Practitioners described the dilemma of being under pressure from managers to reduce the time they spent on recording and record in less detail, in order to keep up with the demand to process referrals within the time scales laid down by government targets. This resulted in an uneasy compromise, where workers accepted it was not possible to record in the detail required to meet the demands of legal accountability in every case. They relied on trying to distinguish between the potentially difficult cases that might be the subject of legal dispute and the rest, only recording in more careful detail with the former. There was a sense that this was a pragmatic accommodation to an irreconcilable dilemma, in which bad luck rather than bad judgement might be their professional undoing, given the level of risk involved in many of the cases they dealt with.

Accountability has triumphed, but not in the form of legal accountability. That continues to lurk as a spectre that threatens to cause havoc, should the record be found wanting in a situation where things have gone wrong, as so many inquiries have demonstrated. Instead, accountability has triumphed in the form of the social care record being dominated by the requirements of audit. The record is designed to provide information in order to demonstrate efficient and effective working. Performance indicators are the mechanism by which departments are able to monitor and report on the extent to which they are meeting nationally set targets. Meeting those targets is not optional. Departmental funding is crucially dependent on successfully achieving central government targets; such targets represent both sanction and incentive to ensure departmental compliance.

Funding is at the root of the matter. Just as recording systems are being driven by the requirement to produce management information in order to maximise budgets, so individual assessments are being driven by the need to demonstrate risk in order to make a successful case for the allocation of scarce resources. Person-centred, holistic and balanced recording of assessments, while encouraged in government policy, and supported by social work values, is losing out to the formula-driven approach to recording, which is derived from the need to compete for resources.

An impossible task?

The limited literature on recording has revealed it as a neglected issue. Despite the awareness of the potential significance of recording in terms of legal accountability, and the catalogue of inquiries that have criticised the recording process in social services, the focus remains on exhorting practitioners to just do better, without any clear or practical guidance on what 'better' might entail. Many departmental policy documents urge workers to record relevant information accurately, concisely and appropriately, without any meaningful explanation of how to interpret those terms in the messy world of social work, where workers are routinely faced with complex recording dilemmas.

As we saw, social workers have very ambivalent and contradictory attitudes towards the task. They realised its importance, with 94.7% of respondents agreeing that it was important in 'covering your back', while 95.8% saw it as a professional task and 87.2% said they took pride in their recording. Nevertheless, 79% regarded it as a chore and 70.7% believed that it reinforced their sense of feeling like they were administrators. We return to the previously quoted interviewee who caught the essence of the recording dilemma, when she described recording as "pointless" but "essential" (interviewee 36).

The competing agendas inherent in the recording task leave workers trying to reconcile the demands to produce a record that can be shared with the service user, even though it might include problematic information, and at the same time to make an effective case for scarce resources, while using recording systems which are increasingly being designed to produce management information, preoccupied with performance indicators. In addition, they also have to be alert to the possibility that their record may one day be legally scrutinised as to how far it conforms to the rules of evidence.

As Kinnibrugh (1984) acknowledged, the fundamental ambiguity in the recording task may be seen as a reflection of the fundamental ambiguity of the social work role itself. The interviewees identified a very real tension between their roles as advocates of the service user and representatives of the department. The record required them to devise a coherent account, which presented an acceptable professional negotiation of those two roles. Recording is at the heart of the distance between the rhetoric and reality of social care today.

In the quagmire of contradictions created by the competing demands on the recording task, workers may try to exercise discretion in the way that Lipsky (1980) suggested. We have already identified the exercise of discretion in how workers variously interpret the increasingly prescribed recording tools that they are required to use. Recording, however, is an individual task that workers usually undertake in isolation. They may share busy office space, but the actual writing of the record is something that is done by the workers with little reference to colleagues in terms of asking advice on how to write this or that. Nevertheless, workers do read other colleagues' recordings and so, while ideas and opinions in respect of recording may not be openly shared, workers are constantly presented with examples of how other people have decided to write about certain information. These examples only serve to reinforce the idea that there is no consistency in how the recording dilemmas might or should be addressed. As we have seen, that creates even more uncertainty and confusion but, because recording remains such a submerged issue, which people rarely discuss, there is little opportunity to develop a more collective or shared approach in how to address the dilemmas. Discretion is individually exercised and inconsistency is perpetuated. Inconsistency in recording then renders the file unreliable as a source of meaningful information. All too often the inconsistency, particularly in respect of sensitive information, makes the record not only unreliable but inaccessible.

It is perhaps not surprising that recording remains neglected. It does not seem to excite much enthusiasm. The 'paperwork burden' is something that is seen to take valuable time away from the 'real' work. It gives rise to so many seemingly intractable dilemmas, which arise from fundamentally competing agendas for which there are no simple answers or solutions, and so it continues to be ignored. Nevertheless, social workers struggle with this task, and perhaps it is time that there was more frankness on the part of policy makers and those responsible for social worker education and training in acknowledging its problematic nature and providing more explicit guidance.

The 'good enough' record: a problematic concept

The record forms such an important and pivotal object in managing social care, and yet the overwhelming majority of both interviewees and respondents said that they had received little or no training on how to record, either during or subsequent to their professional qualifying course. Many interviewees referred to training on using specific recording systems rather than actual recording practice, although even this was limited. Some said that they drew on training from other occupations, such as nursing.

Among respondents, 95.9% said that they learned from doing the job, and 61.5% thought that reading other people's recordings had been an important influence. The interviewees described a similar process of learning on the job, which included reading existing files. However, the inconsistency in recording, in terms of both level of detail and how information should be presented, led to confusion and uncertainty. It also became evident that, although recording skills were developed on the job, more experience did not necessarily result in a greater sense of confidence about what and how to record. Indeed, the sense of confusion over the problematic nature of recording seemed to increase with experience.

Management guidance and feedback was, for the most part, considered unhelpful, with a few notable exceptions. Many interviewees complained of managers preoccupied with stylistic considerations, which usually translated into directives to follow the style of the manager. The overriding management priority, however, was with the completion of information that would contribute to achievement of the performance indicators.

It is astonishing that an activity that now takes up more than half of most practitioners' time and is central to their work is not usually addressed in professional training. It may be argued that social workers will find themselves working with very different recording systems in different social services departments, and any training is therefore better locally organised. This misses the point that recording practice includes professional issues about how, and what information, to record, rather than the simple mechanical process of entering information into a particular system. Such a view reinforces the perception that recording is no more than an administrative process. As we have seen throughout this research, recording is an extremely complex activity, and it is the very dilemmas that are central to the task that need to be directly addressed in any training.

It is acknowledged that those dilemmas will raise uncomfortable questions and point to unresolved, and perhaps, insoluble issues. The neglect of this issue of recording is a convenient way of ignoring those issues. Instead of confronting them and attempting to address them, professional training has preferred to regard recording as a purely administrative activity, and so avoid its powerful implications. As a consequence, generations of practitioners have been left to grapple with those dilemmas in their individual daily practice.

A direct consequence of the lack of training, and the reliance on workers learning to record on the job, is the widespread inconsistency in recording, exacerbated by the lack of time to record and the pressure to process an ever-greater volume of cases as quickly as possible. Social workers are constantly torn between judging what constitutes sufficient recording, and still managing to achieve that standard in the time available. The emphasis in policies on accuracy and conciseness is particularly unhelpful, as those standards are often in tension with one another. How much should be recorded to achieve accuracy, but still maintain conciseness? How are those standards reconciled with the pressure to complete assessments within the time limits set by government, regardless of the supply of practitioners relative to the demand for assessments?

There was a sense of confusion and frustration over practitioners' wish to record according to person-centred principles, and their experience of the day-to-day reality of the workplace, where the pace of work made that seem impossible to achieve. Policy directives to produce balanced, holistic assessments seem removed from that reality, and only add weight to the argument that such directives are about creating an illusion of ideal practice, which the constant constraints on resources make it impossible to achieve.

The considerable ingenuity displayed by practitioners in devising the numerous ways in which to record sensitive information also underlines the inconsistency of the record. Such information may be recorded openly in the assessment, submerged in the ongoing 'contact' or 'observation' record, or even in a brown envelope at the back of the file! A significant proportion of social workers engage in the practice of negative recording, which puts an inflationary pressure on the neediness and level of risk necessary to ensure a service. This is not meant as a criticism of those workers. The strategy is entirely understandable, and represents the workers' attempts to protect the interests of the service user in what is perceived to be an unreliable system of rationing. As a result, the record itself is made increasingly unreliable as a source of meaningful information about the service user. This view was underlined by the number of interviewees who expressed doubts about the value of reading the record. This was in part due to pressure on time, but also because the record was seen as the product of a previous worker's subjective perception at a particular point in time, which may or may not accord with the current worker's view, and which will reflect the dilemmas and conflicts currently inherent in the recording.

Inconsistency in recording perpetuates the sense of confusion among practitioners as to what constitutes a 'good enough' record, and reinforces their feeling of vulnerability. If there is no clear standard of what the record should include, nor efforts to monitor and maintain a standard, then it is very easy to blame the individual worker for any shortcomings identified at some future point.

Recording: a conveniently neglected issue

This research was prompted by the issues surrounding recording that seemed to go beyond the training scenario to resolve. The findings suggest that those issues lie at the heart of many of the problems facing social care today. The expectations are ever increasing and the resources are inadequate to meet the escalating demand. The dissonance between the rhetoric and reality of community care is matched by the dissonance between the principles of recording practice and the reality of the organisational record. Just as the reality of limited community care provision undermines the principles of service user choice, so recording is similarly constrained by the pressure on time and resources. The dissonance cannot be fully acknowledged without admitting the extent to which the system does not deliver what it claims to deliver, and so the attention shifts to demonstrating good governance. Effectiveness is determined by compliance with regulation. The aspiration to balanced, holistic assessments gives way to the procedural requirements, concerned with documenting transparent, equitable and consistent decision making.

While the emphasis on procedural imperatives suggests an objective process of risk assessment and calculation, it would seem that the reality is often dependent on subjectively interpreted procedures, which give rise to inconsistent decisions. Social services are caught between the expectation that they will successfully calculate and manage the risks to and from service users, and the expectation that they will do that within a given level of resources. In the event that the latter are insufficient to achieve the former, the responsibility for reconciling them remains not with the government, but with local authorities charged with running social services. The record is required to try and square the circle by presenting an account that demonstrates that the exercise of prioritising and rationing provision has been undertaken according to due process. The main objective, it would seem, is not to deliver services, but to substantiate that agreed procedures have been followed.

Social services are not alone in the public sector in this respect. Healthcare, education and the police have been subject to the same pressure from central government. The essential impossibility of reconciling the dilemma cannot be openly acknowledged without admitting to a failure in management, and so the appearance of squaring the circle becomes the priority. Central government discharges its responsibility by establishing regulatory mechanisms and setting performance targets to monitor the process of compliance by public services. The management of those services is then concerned to demonstrate compliance by providing evidence of good governance through the adherence to procedures and the meeting of targets. Departments are challenged, not on their failure to provide care, but on their failure to comply with the regulations. The record is the lasting evidence of how far they have succeeded. The service users' experience of services becomes secondary in this process of creating the semblance of efficiency and effectiveness. The record is the means to demonstrate such good governance. The record is not expected to engage with the issue of insufficient resources. It is required, instead, to document that procedures have been correctly followed. It is only the failure to follow established procedures for which the agency is liable. The record is also used to demonstrate that targets have been achieved and, as we have seen, the focus on such performance indicators is increasingly shaping the information-gathering process in the case record.

Much depends on the record and yet, as this research has shown, the recording task is inherently problematic, subject to numerous tensions, conflicts and contradictions. Yet these issues remain submerged, only acknowledged when practitioners are afforded the opportunity to talk about their frustrations. The competing agendas entangle practitioners in a struggle with trying to reconcile the functional and accountability demands, which are driven by the governance agenda, while at the same time conforming to the values and principles contained in the good practice agenda. The rhetoric is there, ready to be held up as the principle by which they should be working. The impossibility of realising the rhetoric is avoided. Neither the competing agendas nor the low priority given to the recording task in terms of time available has been recognised. The conundrum has been left for practitioners to resolve without any meaningful help or guidance in the form of training or feedback.

The reliance on procedural propriety enables local authority departments and the government to avoid awkward questions over the adequacy of resources; it also enables them to avoid the problematic nature of recording. Practitioners are required to follow procedures and at the same time urged to follow good practice. The contradictions between them are not admitted. This leaves practitioners confused, uncertain and potentially vulnerable. Lack of training enables the issues to go on being ignored, with yet more social workers left to their own devices in trying to figure out the expectations in relation to recording. As a consequence departments can more easily distance themselves from practitioners when investigations into individual cases highlight recording practice as an area of concern. The procedures are there; social workers are required to follow them. As long as social workers can provide evidence, through the record, that they have followed the procedures, they can be seen to have discharged their responsibility. The record has become a procedural formality. The fact that many practitioners struggle to always fully document their adherence to procedures because of the sheer volume and pace of work, necessitated by the functional demands relative to the supply of practitioner time, is ignored. It is tempting to see the neglect of recording as a convenient response to an inconvenient subject.

The issues go beyond training, and yet without training in recording, social workers do not have the opportunity to engage with these issues and to explore the options available to them. As we saw, some workers recognise the power of the record to bear witness to the difficult process they are required to follow when departmental decisions seem contrary to the interests of the service users they are working with. Frustrated in their ability to act as effective advocates for the service user, and expected to position themselves as departmental representatives, the record becomes the means by which they can provide an account which, instead of obscuring the distance between the rhetoric and the reality, actually brings it into focus.

We have examined the conflicting demands that result in competing agendas in recording. We have identified the constraints that make the reconciling of those agendas difficult, if not impossible, to achieve. We have also seen how the fundamental contradictions that beset social workers in trying to construct a coherent record continue to be avoided, ignored and even denied in the rhetoric of policy makers. It is unlikely that the resource constraints that ultimately influence the way in which social care is managed and delivered will see any significant improvement in the foreseeable future. Yet social workers demonstrate a remarkable resilience and resourcefulness in their approach to their role and the recording task. It is clear, nevertheless, that the intractable tensions they face in respect of both often leave them frustrated and confused. More meaningful and practical guidance in the recording task would not make those tensions disappear, but it would help practitioners to develop a more explicit understanding of those tensions, which would then enable them to see the potential power of the record to document the dilemmas they struggle with on a daily basis.

The business of social work is still about meeting the needs of service users, albeit within limited resources. As we have seen, the record has considerable power to define the service user and their situation. Person-centred recording is curiously in the interests of both service users and those delivering services. It is the means by which we can better understand the service user and their needs, and so ensure the most appropriate response. Social workers recognise the significance of the person-centred record in this respect, and regret that it seems difficult to implement. We need to address how we can ensure that records more accurately reflect the individuals they describe. This has implications for the priority given to recording, as well as the confidence practitioners have in those making resource decisions.

Recording is a neglected activity, but it is one that takes up much time and it is one on which much depends. We need to recognise its importance and see it as more than a regrettable administrative necessity, something that has considerable potential to influence people's lives. Recording raises issues about practitioners' skills but, as we have found, the issues go beyond the individual's capacity to write a coherent account. If we continue to ignore those issues, a considerable amount of time will continue to be spent producing records of questionable validity or value in meeting the needs of the people who look to social services for support.

The way forward

While the dilemmas may seem intractable and the dissonance between the rhetoric and reality difficult to reconcile, there would be little practical worth in this research if it did not address how to go forward with specific recommendations. These are discussed at two levels. First, there are the implications for professional practice and management, and second, there are investment and policy issues.

Practice and management issues

Training on recording should be included as part of basic qualifying training for every social worker and should also be extended to all care managers. That training should include clear and consistent guidance on what constitutes good practice, with practical and concrete examples. It should address fundamental questions such as distinguishing fact from opinion, establishing relevance and avoiding assumptions, as well as acknowledging the impact of selective perception on how we interpret and then record information. The training should also help practitioners explore the conflicting agendas in recording, underlining the importance of both person-centred recording and the need to conform to the rules of evidence.

Recording should be seen as something that is inextricably entwined with professional practice, not simply an administrative task that relies solely on competent writing skills or familiarity with a particular IT system or set of forms. Practitioners must be encouraged to see the systems for recording information as *tools* and not *drivers* of the process. The specific dilemmas around recording sensitive information must be recognised and openly debated. Practitioners again need clear guidance in terms of the issues they need to consider in how and where to record such information, with practical examples to illustrate how the principles and guidance translate into actual practice.

Recording is a complex activity and it is not suggested that a 'how to' approach is desirable; nevertheless, any training must go beyond a vague discussion of principles. The dilemmas are more effectively addressed in the form of scenarios, which can be used to generate debate as to what an effective record of that particular situation might include. The purpose of different features of the case record would also need to be clarified, ensuring greater consistency in the case file. Consistency has been assumed to follow from the use of increasingly standardised forms. This has led to a 'reductionist' tendency in recording, but it has not, in itself, led to consistency. Consistency depends on practitioners having shared understandings of what is required in the recording process. Consistency will not be achieved until recording is a subject that is openly discussed among practitioners and managers, instead of being left to individuals to construct their own interpretation of what is expected.

Whatever principles and guidance are established in recording training, managers must also reinforce them. Managers need to recognise that effective guidance is not synonymous with insisting on certain stylistic forms. Recording must also be a respected activity that is given priority. Recording is an essential part of the social work/care management task, and there needs to be an acknowledgement that dedicated time is needed to produce a coherent, reasoned report. This will inevitably have implications for resources as practitioner time is at a premium, and much of the pressure experienced by workers was the excessive demands on often too little time. Nevertheless, recording may actually be accomplished more efficiently if it is not done as a continually interrupted activity, as most time management advice will endorse.

Those making funding decisions also need to engage in a much closer and more meaningful dialogue with practitioners about what is required in the record. There needs to be a clearer and more explicit understanding on both sides as to the criteria on which decisions are made, and how that translates into the record. While the eligibility criteria are held as the reference point, like the standardised forms, they too are open to different interpretations that then lead to inconsistency in decisions and increase practitioners' confusion. It was evident from the research that where practitioners had confidence in the funding panel members to make their decisions consistently and appropriately, they did not feel obliged to engage in the 'worst-case scenario' strategy. Person-centred recording is in the best interests of the service user, and management must recognise its own part in encouraging negative recording rather than simply blaming practitioners.

Investment and policy implications

As stated previously, significant per capita increases in the social care budget are unlikely. The consequences of an ageing population may increase the overall budget but the effects are likely to lead to even more being squeezed out of available resources. This will result in even greater pressure to work more efficiently and effectively.

IT is part of the efficiency agenda, and yet it is apparent that much could be done to improve the chaotic and somewhat anarchic situation that was often described in the research. It is a basic prerequisite of a computerised system that everyone has access to a computer terminal when they need one, and that they have the skills to operate the system. Workers not only require familiarisation with a particular software system, but basic competence in operating a computer, including keyboard skills. Leaving workers to acquire these skills on the job results in them taking even longer to achieve any degree of efficiency. There should be effective technical and support structures in place so that practitioners can speedily call on expert help rather than waste valuable professional time trying to address problems they do not, and should not, be expected to have the expertise to solve. In addition the systems need to be more user-friendly, less complex and cumbersome, and designed to produce meaningful professional information that encourages a person-centred record. Information systems must also be designed to avoid unnecessary duplication of information and to ensure efficient retrieval of information. Recording systems need to be developed so that they can produce both professional and management information. The former should not inevitably have to bow to the latter. Information to demonstrate that targets have been met and regulatory requirements complied with is a prerequisite in public services, accountable to government, and ultimately the tax payer. We may question the validity of some of that information, but it should be possible to develop recording systems that are sufficiently sophisticated that the person-centred record is not incompatible with required management information.

It is acknowledged that the development of such systems would be an ambitious, and initially, resource-intensive undertaking. This would be more readily achieved if less effort went into devising and implementing the plethora of information systems that now populate the social care world. Developing one unified system would also reduce the time it takes for workers to acclimatise when they move from one authority to another, wasting valuable practitioner time as they have to familiarise themselves with yet another system.

In order to achieve these transformations in the effectiveness and efficiency of recording systems, practitioners must be more closely involved in their design. Too often such systems have been devised by administrative and IT experts with little reference to the people who have to work with them on a daily basis, resulting in unnecessary time wasting, frustration and despondency. Social workers are not opposed to computer technology. As the research revealed, many participants recognised its many advantages, but there was also a sense that its potential was not being realised, that practitioners were often bogged down by technical problems, unreliable systems, with a helpless sense that the computer was more in control than they were.

Further considerations

It is not within the scope of this research to make recommendations in respect of the role of care management in adult social services today. While the research has certainly confirmed the widespread frustration felt by qualified social workers regarding the limitations of the role in comparison with their level of skill, it was not the intention of the study to explore the issue in any wider context. Nevertheless, it is relevant to the research to question the value of the case-closing culture that necessitates repeated assessments of the same service users, often within relatively short periods of time. Much of the time spent on recording was concerned with the assessment process and it is a direct consequence of the pressure to close cases that when circumstance change, as they frequently do with many service users, the assessment process has to begin all over again with a new worker, and so the recording process proliferates. Without the pressure to close cases so quickly, changes in circumstances could prompt a review rather than a full assessment, which would be more rational in terms of practitioner time and more sensitive to service users, who fundamentally want help in meeting their needs rather than collecting more and more assessment documents. This is perhaps an area for further research and consideration. It could have important implications for the considerable time that is presently spent on the recording of assessments.

Conclusion

These recommendations are intended as practical suggestions for improving a situation that has many complex dimensions. The scope of this research has been necessarily broad. It was only by examining those complex dimensions together that the recording task could be fully understood. Recording has been neglected because successive generations of policy makers and social work educators have preferred to avoid and ignore the implications of these competing agendas. It has been convenient to suggest that recording is a straightforward administrative task that practitioners do not relish and therefore it is a subject undeserving of attention. This research has demonstrated that recording is far from routine or straightforward. It is a challenging task that practitioners would welcome clearer guidance and support in undertaking. It is acknowledged, however, that once responsibility for recording practice is no longer just left to individual workers, it will not be so easy to lay the finger of blame on them when recording practice is criticised in the future.

Appendix 1: The interview

Appendix 1a: Interview schedule

'On record': case recording in social work (adult services) – schedule for semi-structured interviews with social workers

Language

Show copy of vignette 'Being positively objective – Miss Vera Miles'. Ask interviewee to compare the two descriptions of Miss Miles in terms of the effectiveness of the recordings.

Discuss the extent to which Version A or Version B has featured in their own experience of recording.

Experience

1. How long have you been qualified?
2. In what setting do you work, for example, service user group, short- or long-term team?
3. How many hours per week do you work?
4. How long have you worked in your present post?
5. What training, if any, have you received in recording skills?

Attitudes to recording

6. How confident do you feel about recording?
7. How do you view the recording task?
8. Why do you describe it like that?

Who is the record for?

9. When writing the record, who are you thinking about and in what ways do they influence how you record:
   - service users/carers?
   - your manager?
   - those making resource allocation decisions, for example, resource allocation panels?
   - colleagues within the department?
   - professionals outside the department?

        – service providers?
        – lawyers?
        – any others?

10.   How much do you discuss the recording process with your service users?
11.   How much use of the 'restricted access' category do you make in your recording?
11a. In what circumstances would you use it?

Purpose of recording

12.   Here is a list of possible reasons for recording (Appendix 1b). How would you rate their importance?

Recording task

13.   How do you record:
        – using a manual system, if so, which?
        – using a computerised system, if so, which?
        – a combination of both
14.   How would you describe your experience of recording in this authority?
15.   Has your experience of recording changed over the period of your career?
15a. If so, how?
16.   How many hours per week do you think you spend on recording?
17.   How many hours per week do you think you spend on reading information in case files?
18.   How long after a visit do you usually manage to make a record of the visit?
19.   To what extent do you prioritise your recording of different cases?
20.   What feedback do you receive from your manager on your recording?

Transcript recording

I am now going to show you a short video sequence of a home visit. I would like you to watch it, make any notes you feel necessary while the sequence is being played. After it is finished I would like you to imagine you are the worker and decide what you should record from this visit. The object is not to evaluate your intervention, only to identify what information needs to be recorded. This is not concerned with testing your skills, rather it is designed to explore how you record, to understand how you decide what is relevant and the way you choose to describe that in the record.

21.   How did you decide what was relevant to record?
22.   Were there any particular considerations you thought about in terms of how you described what had been discussed between Gerry and David?

Standards of recording

23. How would you rate the standard of record keeping in case files in this department?
24. Here is a list of concerns that have been identified about standards of recording in various inspections of different departments across the country. How far do you think they apply to your own recording and that of others in this department?
25. What do you think are the reasons for these problems?

The social work role in care management

26. How much do you think the role of the social worker has changed since the introduction of care management?
26a. And how do you feel about that?
27. How do you think other professionals see the role of social workers?
28. To what extent do you see yourself as an advocate of the service user and/or a representative of the department?
28a. How comfortable do you feel with those two roles?
29. How would you compare your priorities in the care management process with those of the department?
29a. If there are differences in priorities how does that affect you?
30. How do you think issues around what is your professional role and the priorities of care management influence the way you record?

Having come to the end of the interview, are there any other issues you would like to raise?

Appendix 1b: Purpose of recording (interview prompt material)

How would you evaluate the importance of the following items in relation to the purpose of recording, on a scale of high, medium or low, according to your own view? Can you indicate if you think there would be a difference between your view and your agency's view?

1   Up-to-date information on service user's needs and eligibility for services
2   Statement of purpose and plan of work
3   Aid to worker understanding, for example, reflective practice
4   Continuity of case work
5   Communication with other agencies
6   Assist others, for example, service providers in carrying out social services purposes
7   Legal accountability
8   Service planning and development

9   Information for statistical returns to government
10   Staff supervision and practice development
11   Evaluation of worker performance
12   Documentary record for service user

Are there any other reasons for recording?

Appendix 1c: Identified problems with case recording (interview prompt material)

1   The case record cannot be easily followed
2   No evidence for decisions is provided
3   Assessments are service-led rather than needs-led
4   The service user's voice is not heard
5   Assessments are not focused on outcomes
6   Analysis of information is insufficient
7   Facts and opinions are not always distinguished
8   Relevant information is buried in irrelevant detail
9   Inappropriate language, including jargon, is used
10   Inaccurate information
11   Judgemental language
12   Assumptions and speculation
13   Distortions and exaggerations

Any other

Appendix 2: Questionnaire: Experiences of recording in social work

Are you a qualified social worker?
Do you work in adult services?
Do you carry a case load?

If you answered no to any of these questions please pass this questionnaire to someone who can answer yes to all of them.

If you answered yes to all three of these questions please continue.

Please read the following descriptions of a service user.

Version A

Miss Vera Miles, aged 81, is a quiet lady who has recently moved from sheltered accommodation into residential care. Although very reluctant to leave her flat, her increasing confusion was putting her at considerable risk. She was diagnosed with Alzheimer's disease eight years ago. Miss Miles has no family, although she does frequently ask for her mother, who died when she was 12. She worked as a librarian for many years and was an active member of the Ramblers' Association. If prompted, she enjoys talking about the past.

Miss Miles has suffered from arthritis for over 15 years, which has particularly affected her fingers and hands. She is still otherwise very mobile and spends a lot of time walking around the building. Despite her confusion, she seems to be settling in to her new home, smiling at staff and other residents, and relating well to her keyworker, who she now appears to recognise. Miss Miles responds positively to one-to-one social contact, but can become anxious in larger groups or in more noisy environments.

Miss Miles needs help with personal care, but likes to choose her clothes if given the opportunity. She needs some assistance when using the toilet, but occasionally does not always give sufficient warning to get there in time.

Version B

Miss Miles is aged 81, single with no family. She suffers from Alzheimer's disease, arthritis and a degree of incontinence. She recently moved from sheltered accommodation where she posed too serious a risk to herself and others. She spends long periods aimlessly wandering around the building, frequently calls for her dead mother, has poor short-term memory and lacks orientation to time and place. She requires personal care and toileting. She has been assigned a keyworker. Miss Miles becomes very agitated with large groups of people, sometimes shouting and shrieking during social activities.

1. **Which version would you prefer to read in the record?** *(Tick one box)*
   a.   Version A ☐
   b.   Version B ☐
   c.   Depends on the context of the recording ☐

2. **Which version do you tend to see most in your experience of reading other people's records?** *(Tick one box)*
   a.   Version A ☐
   b.   Version B ☐
   c.   Depends on the context of the recording ☐

3. **How long have you been qualified?**
   (Tick one box)
   a.   Less than a year ☐
   b.   1-5 years ☐
   c.   6-10 years ☐
   d.   11-15 years ☐
   e.   16-20 years ☐
   f.   More than 20 years ☐

4. **In what setting do you primarily work?**
   (Tick one box)
   a. Older people/physical disability ☐
   b. Learning disability ☐
   c. Mental health ☐
   d. Sensory impairment ☐
   e. Hospital ☐

5. **Do you work:**
   (Tick one box)
   a. Full time ☐
   b. Part time ☐

6. **Do you have management or supervisory responsibilities?**
   (Tick one box)
   a. Yes ☐
   b. No ☐

7. **Have you worked for more than one local authority as a care manager/ social worker?** *(Tick one box)*
   a.   Yes ☐
   b.   No ☐

8. Please can you rate the significance of each of the following in the development of your recording skills. *(Please include recording assessments, care plans, reports for funding applications as well as the ongoing case record)*
  (Tick one box for each line)
  My recording skills were developed from:

	Very significant	Quite significant	Some significant	Little significance	No significance
a. Formal teaching on qualifying training	☐	☐	☐	☐	☐
b. Learning during practice placements	☐	☐	☐	☐	☐
c. Guidance and feedback from supervisor	☐	☐	☐	☐	☐
d. Experience of doing the job	☐	☐	☐	☐	☐
e. Reading other workers' recording	☐	☐	☐	☐	☐
f. Formal training since qualifying	☐	☐	☐	☐	☐
g. Clear policies and procedures	☐	☐	☐	☐	☐
h. From other work role, please specify	☐	☐	☐	☐	☐
i. Other influences, please specify	☐	☐	☐	☐	☐

9. How do you record sensitive information about a service user? For example, you observe their behaviour is more confused than they are able or willing to acknowledge. Assuming you routinely send a copy of your assessment to the service user, would you: *(Tick one box for each line)*

	Always	Sometimes	Often	Never
a. Make an explicit reference to the confused behaviour in the assessment?	☐	☐	☐	☐
b. Make a less explicit reference to the confused behaviour in the assessment, and make a more explicit reference elsewhere in the case file?	☐	☐	☐	☐
c. Make a less explicit reference to the confused behaviour in all of your recording?	☐	☐	☐	☐
d. Make a less explicit reference to the confused behaviour in all of your recording, and pass on the information verbally?	☐	☐	☐	☐
e. Make a less explicit reference to the confused behaviour in the assessment, and make an explicit reference elsewhere in the case file, marking that information confidential or 'restricted', that is, not to be shared with the service user?	☐	☐	☐	☐

10. Which of the following statements do you agree with? *(Tick one box for each line)*

When writing reports to request funding for care packages for your service users you need to present:

	Agree	Disagree
a. A person-centred, holistic account of the service user?	☐	☐
b. An account that focuses on needs and risks only?	☐	☐
c. A picture of the service user on their 'worst day'?	☐	☐

11. What systems do you use for recording (including assessments, care plans and ongoing case recording)? *(Tick one box)*

a. Completely computerised   ☐
b. Completely manual   ☐
c. Combination of both   ☐

12. How would you describe your experience of using those systems on a score of 1-5? *(Circle appropriate score)*

Positive				Negative
1	2	3	4	5

13. How much of your time would you estimate you spend recording on and reading information in case files? *(Tick one box)*

a. Less than 50%   ☐
b. 50% or more, but less than 75%   ☐
c. 75% or more   ☐

14. How far do you agree with the following statements? *(Tick one box for each line)*

The recording system I use:

	Strongly agree	Agree	Disagree	Strongly disagree
a. Enables me to record all the information which I consider important	☐	☐	☐	☐
b. Enables me to find the relevant information quickly and efficiently	☐	☐	☐	☐
c. Involves unnecessary duplication	☐	☐	☐	☐
d. Has become little more than a tick box exercise which sometimes overlooks important information	☐	☐	☐	☐
e. Is overly complicated to use, either in terms of recording or retrieving information	☐	☐	☐	☐
f. Is designed more to produce management information rather than be a professional tool	☐	☐	☐	☐

15. How far do you agree with the following statements? *(Tick one box for each line)*

	Strongly agree	Agree	Disagree	Strongly disagree
I find recording a:				
a. Straightforward task that relies on the application of professional skills and principles	☐	☐	☐	☐
b. Complicated task because I have to record for a number of different readerships who have different concerns	☐	☐	☐	☐
c. Difficult task to judge what is relevant to record	☐	☐	☐	☐
d. Difficult task to describe objectively someone else and their situation	☐	☐	☐	☐
e. Frustrating task when the volume of work means I do not always have the time to record in as much detail as I think is required	☐	☐	☐	☐
f. Confusing task when people record in such different ways and there seems to be no consistent standard maintained	☐	☐	☐	☐

16. How far do you agree with the following statements? *(Tick one box for each line)*

	Strongly agree	Agree	Disagree	Strongly disagree
a. Recording is important to cover your back	☐	☐	☐	☐
b. Recording is a professional task	☐	☐	☐	☐
c. Recording is a necessary chore	☐	☐	☐	☐
d. I take pride in my recording	☐	☐	☐	☐
e. I resent the time I spend recording	☐	☐	☐	☐
f. I feel more like an administrator than a social worker	☐	☐	☐	☐

If there are any further comments you would like to make please continue on this
sheet and overleaf.

....

....

....

....

....

....

....

....

....

....

....

....

Bibliography

American Hospital Association (2001) *Patients or paperwork: The regulatory burden facing American hospitals*, New York, NY: PricewaterhouseCoopers.

Ames, N. (1999) 'Social work recording: a new look at an old issue', *Journal of Social Work Education*, vol 35, no 2, pp 227-38.

Balloch, S., McLean, J. and Fisher, M. (1999) *Social services: Working under pressure*, Bristol: The Policy Press.

Barrett, M. (1991) *The politics of truth: From Marx to Foucault*, Cambridge: Polity Press.

BASW (British Association of Social Workers) (1983) *Effective and ethical recording: Report of the BASW Case Recording Project Group*, London: BASW.

Baudrillard, J. (1981 [1988]) 'Simulcra and simulations', *Jean Baudrillard: Selected writings* (translated by M. Poster), Oxford: Polity Press.

Bauman, Z. (2000) 'Am I my brother's keeper?', *European Journal of Social Work*, vol 3, no 1, pp 5-11.

Beck, U. (1992) *Risk society: Towards a new modernity*, London: Sage Publications.

Beck, U. (1995) *Ecological politics in an age of risk*, Cambridge: Polity.

Beck, U. and Beck-Gernsheim, E. (1996) 'Individaulisation and "precarious freedoms": perspectives and controversies of a subject-orinted sociology', in P. Heelas, S. Lash and P. Morris (eds) *Detraditionalization: Critical treflections on authority and identity*, Oxford: Blackwell.

Berger, P.L. and Luckman, T. (1966) *The social construction of reality*, New York, NY: Doubleday.

Beveridge, W.H.B. (1948) *Voluntary action: A report on methods of social advance*, London: Allen and Unwin.

Bichard, M. (2004) *Bichard Inquiry – Report*, London: The Stationery Office.

Blau, P. (1963) *The dynamics of bureaucracy*, Chicago, IL: University of Chicago Press.

Bourdieu, P. (1977) *Outline of a theory of practice*, Cambridge: Cambridge University Press.

Bourdieu, P. (1990) *In other words*, Cambridge: Polity Press.

Bourdieu, P. (1991) *Language and symbolic power* (edited by J.B. Thompson), Cambridge: Polity Press.

Bourdieu, P. (1998) *Acts of resistance*, Cambridge: Polity Press.

Braithwaite, J. (1984) *Corporate crime in the pharmaceutical industry*, London: Routledge and Kegan Paul.

Brannen, J. (ed) (1992) *Mixing methods: Qualitative and quantitative research*, Aldershot: Ashgate.

Brayne, H., Martin, G. and Carr, H. (2001) *Law for social workers*, Oxford: Oxford University Press.

Brewer, J. and Hunter, A. (1989) *Multimethod research: A synthesis of styles*, London: Sage Publications.

Bristol, M. (1936) *Handbook on social case recording*, Chicago, IL: University of Chicago Press.

Broadie, A. (1978) 'Authority and social casework', in N. Timms and D. Watson (eds) *Philosophy in social work*, London: Routledge and Kegan Paul.

Brown, H. (2001) *Making records work! Recording with care in services to adults with learning disabilities*, Salomons, Canterbury: Canterbury Christ Church University.

Bryman, A. (1988) *Quantity and quality in social research*, London: Unwin Hyman Ltd [reprinted by Routledge in 2005].

Bryman, A. (1992) 'Quantitative and qualitative research: further reflections on their integration', in J. Brannen (ed) *Mixing methods: Qualitative and quantitative research*, Aldershot: Ashgate.

Bryman, A. and Cramer, B. (1990) *Quantitative data analysis for social scientists*, London: Routledge.

Burnham, J. (1989) 'The misinformation era: the fall of the medical record', *Annals of Internal Medicine*, vol 110, no 6, pp 482-4.

Bury, M. (1994) 'Ageing and sociological theory: a critique', Paper presented at the 'Ageing and Gender' Conference, Guildford, University of Surrey, July.

Calhoun, C., Gerteis, J., Moody, J. and Indermohan, V. (eds) (2002) *Contemporary sociological theory*, Oxford: Blackwell.

Camilleri, P. (1996) *(Re)constructing social work*, Aldershot: Avebury.

Carson, D. (1995) 'Calculated risk', *Community Care*, 26 October-1 November, pp 26-7.

Castel, R. (1991) 'From dangerousness to risk', in G. Burchell, C. Gordon and P. Miller (eds) *The Foucault effect: Studies in governmentality*, Hemel Hempstead: Harvester Wheatsheaf.

Cicourel, A. V. (1964) *Method and measurement in sociology*, New York, NY: Free Press.

Cicourel, A. V. (1968) 'Police practices and official records', in A. V. Cicourel, *The social organisation of juvenile justice*, London: John Wiley and Sons, pp 112-23.

Cicourel, A. V. (1983) 'Hearing is not believing: language and the structure of belief in medical communication', in S. Fisher and A. Todd (eds) *The social organisation of doctor and patient communication*, Washington, DC: Centre for Applied Linguistics.

Clarke, J. (1993) 'The comfort of strangers: social work in context', in J. Clarke (ed) *A crisis in care: Challenges to social work*, London: Sage Publications, pp 5-23.

Clarke, J. (1996) 'After social work', in N. Parton (ed) *Social theory, social change and social work*, London: Routledge.

Cochrane, A. (1993) 'Challenges from the centre', in J. Clarke (ed) *A crisis in care: Challenges to social work*, London: Sage Publications, pp 69-97.

Cowan, J. (2003) 'Risk management, records and the Laming Report', *Clinical Governance: An International Journal*, vol 8, no 3, pp 271-7.

Cowan, J. (2004) 'The new GMS contract, risk and clinical information', *Clinical Governance: An International Journal*, vol 9, no 1, pp 73-7.

Davies, M. (1991) *The sociology of social work*, London: Routledge.

de Sola Pool, I. (1957) 'A critique of the twentieth anniversary issue', *Public Opinion Quarterly*, vol 21, pp 190-8.

Derrida. J. (1978) *Writing and difference* (translated by Alan Bass), London: Routledge and Kegan Paul.

DH (Department of Health) (1997) *The Caldicott Report: Report on the Review of Patient Identifiable Information*, London: The Stationery Office.

DH (2000) *Information for social care: A framework for improving quality in social care through better use of information and information technology*, London: The Stationery Office.

DH (2002a) *Guidance on the single assessment process for older people*, LAC 1, London: DH.

DH (2002b) *Fair access to care services: Guidance on eligibility criteria for adult social care*, LAC 13, London: DH.

DH (2004) *The electronic social care record*, London: DH.

DH (2007) *Independence, choice and risk: A guide to best practice in supported decision making*, London: The Stationery Office.

DHSS (Department of Health and Social Security) (1988) *Community care: Agenda for action: A report to the Secretary of State for Social Services* (the Griffiths Report), London: DHSS.

Douglas, M. (ed) (1973) *Rules and meanings*, Harmondsworth: Penguin.

Douglas, M. (1992) *Risk and blame: Essays in cultural theory*, London: Routledge.

Ericson, R.V. (1993) *Making crime: A study of detective work* (2nd edn), Toronto: University of Toronto Press.

Ericson, R.V. and Haggerty, K.D. (1997) *Policing the risk society*, Oxford: Oxford University Press.

Evans, T. and Harris, J. (2004) 'Street-level bureaucracy, social work and the (exaggerated) death of discretion', *British Journal of Social Work*, vol 34, pp 871-95.

Ewald, F. (1991) 'Insurance and risks', in G. Burchell, C. Gordon and P. Miller (eds) *The Foucault effect: Studies in governmentality*, Hemel Hempstead: Harvester Wheatsheaf, pp 197-210.

Ferguson, H. (2001) 'Social work, individualisation and life politics', *British Journal of Sociology*, vol 31, no 1, pp 41-55.

Ferguson, H. (2005) 'Trust, risk and expert systems: child protection, modernity and the (changing) management of life and death', in S. Watson and A. Moran (eds) *Trust, risk and uncertainty*, Basingstoke: Palgrave Macmillan.

Finch, J. (1986) *Research and policy: The uses of qualitative methods in social and educational research*, Lewes: Falmer Press.

Foddy, W. (1993) *Constructing questions for interviews and questionnaires: Theory and practice in social research*, Cambridge: Cambridge University Press.

Foucault, M. (1975) *Discipline and punish: The birth of the prison* (translated by Alan Sheridan), London: Allen Lane.

Foucault, M. (1977) *The archaeology of knowledge*, London: Tavistock.

Foucault, M. (1991) 'Governmentality', in G. Burchill, C. Gordon and M. Miller (eds) *The Foucault effect: Studies in governmentality*, Hemel Hempstead: Harvester Wheatsheaf.

Foucault, M., Martin, L., Gutman, H. and Hutton, P. (eds) (1988) *Technologies of the self*, Amherst, MA: University of Massachusetts Press.

Franklin, B. and Parton, N. (1991) 'Media reporting of social work', in B. Franklin and N. Parton (eds) *Social work, the media and public relations*, London: Routledge.

Froggett, L. and Sapey, B. (1997) 'Communication, culture and competence in social work education', *Social Work Education*, vol 16, no 1, pp 41-53.

Gabe, J. (1995) 'Health, medicine and risk: the need for a sociological approach', in J. Gabe, *Medicine, health and risk: Sociological approaches*, Oxford: Blackwell.

Garfinkel, H. (1967) 'Good organisational reasons for bad clinic records', in R. Turner (ed) *Ethnomethodology*, Harmondsworth: Penguin Books.

Giddens, A. (1976) *New rules of sociological method: A positive critique of interpretive sociologies*, London: Hutchinson.

Giddens, A. (1979) *Central problems in social theory: Action, structure and contradiction in social analysis*, Basingstoke: Macmillan Press.

Giddens, A. (1990) *The consequences of modernity*, Oxford: Polity Press.

Giddens, A. (1991) *Modernity and self identity: Self and society in the late modern age*, Cambridge: Polity Press.

Giddens, A. (1992) *The transformation of intimacy*, Cambridge: Polity Press.

Giddens, A. (1994) 'Risk, trust and reflexivity', in U. Beck, S. Lash and A. Giddens (eds) *Reflexive modernization*, Cambridge: Polity Press.

Giglioli, P. (1972) *Language in social context*, Harmondsworth: Penguin.

Gillen, S. (2008) 'Warnings of database flaws buried', *Community Care*, April, pp 4-5.

Glastonbury, B. (2001) 'Calling the tune in social care information', *New Technology in Human Services*, vol 13, nos 3 and 4, pp 1-10.

Goffman, E. (1968 [1961]) *Asylums: Essays on the social situation of mental patients and other inmates*, Harmondsworth: Penguin.

Goldsmith, L. and Beaver, R. (1999a) *Recording with care – Inspection of case recording in social services departments*, London: The Stationery Office.

Goldsmith, L. and Beaver, R. (1999b) *Recording with care – Summary report: Inspection of case recording in social services departments*, London: The Stationery Office.

Gould, N. (2003) 'The caring professions and information technology – in search of a theory', in E. Harlow and S.A. Webb (eds) *Information and communication technologies in the welfare services*, London: Jessica Kingsley Publishers.

Grint, K. and Woolgar, S. (1997) *The machine at work: Technology, work and organisation*, Oxford: Polity Press.

Grinyer, A. (1995) 'Risk, the real world and naïve sociology', in J. Gage (ed) *Medicine, health and risk: Sociological approaches*, Oxford: Blackwell.

Hadley, R. and Clough, R. (1996) *Care in chaos: Frustration and challenge in community care*, London: Cassell.

Hall, C., Slembrouck, S. and Sarangi, S. (2006) *Language practices in social work: Categorisation and accountability in child welfare*, London: Routledge.

Hamilton, G. (1946) *Principles of social case recording*, New York, NY: Columbia University Press.

Hammersley, M. (1992) 'Deconstructing the qualitative and quantitative divide', in J. Brannen (ed) *Mixing methods: Qualitative and quantitative research*, Aldershot: Ashgate.

Harris, J. (2003) *The social work business*, London: Routledge.

Harris, N. (1987) 'Defensive social work', *British Journal of Social Work*, vol 17, no 1, pp 61-9.

Harrison, S. (1999) 'Clinical autonomy and health policy: past and futures', in M. Exworthy and S. Halford (eds) *Professionals and new managerialism in the public sector*, Buckingham: Open University Press.

Hayes, D. (2007) 'Staff pressured to deny services', *Community Care*, November, pp 10-11.

Heywood, J. (1964) *An introduction to teaching casework skills*, London: Routledge and Kegan Paul

Hill, M.J. (1978) 'Social workers' attitudes to information systems', *BURISA Newsletter*, issue 33, March.

HMSO (Her Majesty's Stationery Office) (1946) *Report of the Care of Children Committee* (the Curtis Report), London: HMSO.

HMSO (1968) *Report of the Committee on local authority and allied personal social services* (the Seebohm Report), London: HMSO.

HMSO (1974) *Report of the Committee of Inquiry into the Care and Supervision Provided in Relation to Maria Colwell*, London: HMSO.

HMSO (1977) *Records in social services departments*, London: DHSS Development Group Social Work Service.

HMSO (1991) *Care management and assessment: Practitioners' guide*, London: HMSO.

Holstein, J. and Gubrium, J.F. (2000) *The self we live by: A narrative identity in a post modern world*, Oxford: Oxford University Press.

Hopkins, J. (1996) 'Social work through the looking glass', in N. Parton (ed) *Social theory, social change and social work*, London: Routledge.

Horlicks-Jones, T. (2005) 'On "risk-work" – professional discourse, accountability and everyday action', *Health, Risk and Society*, vol 7, no 3, pp 293-307.

House of Commons (2003) *The Victoria Climbié Inquiry*, London: The Stationery Office.

House of Commons (2009) *The Protection of Children in England: A progress report*, London: The Stationery Office.

Howe, D. (1991) 'The family and the therapist: towards a sociology of social work method', in M. Davies (ed) *The sociology of social work*, London: Routledge, pp 146-62.

Hughes, E.C. (1984 [1942]) *The sociological eye: Selected papers*, Chicago, IL: Aldine.

Huntingdon, A. (2000) 'Differing perceptions of legislative and policy change in children and families services: a vertical analysis', PhD thesis, University of Central Lancashire.

Huntingdon, A. and Sapey, B. (2003) 'Real records, virtual lives', in E. Harlow and S.A. Webb (eds) *Information and communication technologies in the welfare services*, London: Jessica Kingsley Publishers.

Jenkins, R. (1992) *Pierre Bourdieu*, London: Routledge.

Jones, C. (1999) 'Social work – regulation and managerialism', in M. Exworthy and S. Halford (eds) *Professionals and the new managerialism in the public sector*, Buckingham: Open University Press.

Jones, C. (2001) 'Voices from the front line: state social workers and New Labour', *British Journal of Social Work*, vol 31, pp 547-62.

Jordan, B. (1997) 'Social work and society', in M. Davies (ed) *The Blackwell companion to social work*, Oxford: Blackwell.

Kagle, J.D. (1991) *Social work records*, Prospect Heights, IL: Waveland Press Inc.

Kagle, J.D. (1993) 'Record keeping: directions for the 1990s', *Social Work*, vol 38, pp 190-6.

Kelly, A. (1998) 'Concepts of professions and professionalism', in A. Symonds and A. Kelly (eds) *The social construction of community care*, Basingstoke: Macmillan.

Kemshall, H. (2000) 'Conflicting knowledges on risk: the case of risk knowledge in the Probation Service', *Health, Risk and Society*, vol 2, no 2, pp 143-58.

Kemshall, H. (2002) *Risk, social policy and welfare*, Buckingham: Open University Press.

Kemshall, H., Parton, N., Walsh, M. and Waterson, J. (1997) 'Concepts of risk in relation to organisational structure and functioning within the Personal Social Services', *Social Policy and Administration*, vol 31, no 3, pp 213-32.

Kinnibrugh, A. (1984) *Social work case recording and the client's right to privacy*, Bristol: SAUS Publications, University of Bristol.

Kitwood, T. (1998) 'Improving dementia care – a resource for training and professional development', *Journal of Dementia Care*, training manual.

Kitwood, T. and Bredin, K. (1991) *Person to person: A guide to the care of those with failing mental powers*, Loughton: Gale Centre Publications.

Kuhn, T.S. (1962) *The structure of scientific revolutions*, Chicago, IL: University of Chicago.

Lash, S. (1994) 'Reflexivity and its doubles: structure, aesthetics, community', in U. Beck, A. Gidddens and S. Lash (eds) *Reflexive modernization: Politics, tradition and aesthetics in the modern social order*, Cambridge: Polity Press.

Laslett, P. (1994) 'The third age, the fourth age and the future', *Ageing and Society*, vol 14, no 3, pp 436-47.

Lawson, J. (1996) 'A framework of risk assessment and management for older people', in H. Kemshall and J. Pritchard (eds) *Good practice in risk assessment and risk management*, London: Sage Publications.

Lewis, J. and Glennerster, H. (1996) *Implementing the new community care*, Buckingham: Open University Press.

Lipsky, M. (1980) *Street-level bureaucracy: The dilemma of individuals in public service*, New York, NY: Russell Sage Foundation.

Lupton, D. (1999) *Risk*, London: Routledge.

MacIntyre, A. (1981) *After virtue*, Notre Dame, IN: University of Notre Dame Press.

Marsland, D. (1996) *Welfare or welfare state?*, London: Macmillan.

Mead, G.H. (1934) *Mind, self and society*, Chicago, IL: University of Chicago Press.

Merquior, J.G. (1985) *Foucault*, London: Fontana.

Middleton, L. (1999) 'Could do better', *Professional Social Work*, November, pp 8-9.

Miller, J. (2001) *One of the guys: Girls, gangs and gender*, New York, NY: Oxford University Press.

Miller, P. and O'Leary, T. (1987) 'Accounting – the construction of the governable person', *Accounting, Organisations and Society*, vol 12, no 3, pp 235-65.

Morrison, A. (2001) 'Improving the quality of written assessments – a participative approach', in V. White and J. Harris (eds) *Developing good practice in community care: Partnership and participation*, London: Jessica Kingsley Publishers.

Mouzelis, N. (1995) *Sociological theory: What went wrong? Diagnosis and remedies*, London: Routledge.

O'Rourke, E. (2002) *For the record*, Lyme Regis: Russell House Publishing.

O'Rourke, E. and Grant, H. (2005) *It's all in the record – Meeting the challenge of open recording*, Lyme Regis: Russell House Publishing.

Øvretveit, J. (1986) *Improving social work records and practice*, BASW/BIOSS Action Research.

Owen, T. and Powell, J. (2006) '"Trust". Professional power and social theory, lessons from a post-Foucauldian framework', *International Journal of Sociology and Social Policy*, vol 26, nos 3/4, pp 110-20.

Parton, N. (1996) 'Social work, risk and the blaming system', in N. Parton (ed) *Social theory, social change and social work*, London: Routledge.

Parton, N. (1998) 'Risk, advanced liberalism and child welfare: the need to rediscover uncertainty and ambiguity', *British Journal of Social Work*, vol 28, no 1, pp 5-27.

Phillips, J. (1996) 'The future of social work with older people in a changing world', in N. Parton (ed) *Social theory, social change and social work*, London: Routledge.

Pinkus, H. (1977) 'Recording in social work' in *Encyclopaedia of Social Work*, 17th issue, vol 2, New York, NY: National Association of Social Workers.

Pithouse, A. (1998) *Social work: The social organisation of an invisible trade*, Aldershot: Ashgate.

Polkinghorne, D. (1988) *Narrative knowing and the human sciences*, New York, NY: State University of New York Press.

Poster, M. (1990) *The mode of information*, Cambridge: Polity Press.

Postle, K. (2002) 'Working between the idea and the reality: ambiguities and tensions in care managers' work', *British Journal of Social Work*, vol 32, no 3, pp 335-51.

Powell, F. (2001) *The politics of social work*, London: Sage Publications.

Powell, J. and Gilbert, T. (2007) 'Performativity and helping professions: social theory, power and practice', *International Journal of Social Welfare*, vol 16, no 3, pp 193-210.

Power, M. (1997) *The audit society: Rituals in verification*, Oxford: Oxford University Press.

Prince, K. (1996) *Boring records: Communication, speech and writing in social work*, London: Jessica Kingsley Publishers.

Prior, L. (2003) *Using documents in social research*, London: Sage.

Pugh, R. (1996) *Effective language in health and social work*, London: Chapman and Hall.

RCCJ (Royal Commission on Criminal Justice) (1993) *Report*, Cm 2263, London: HMSO.

Rea, D. (1998) 'The myth of the market in the organisation of community care', in A. Symonds and A. Kelly (eds) *The social construction of community care*, Basingstoke: Macmillan.

Regan, S. (2003) 'Technology and system referral taking in social services – from narrative to code', in E. Harlow and S.A. Webb (eds) *Information and communication technologies in the welfare services*, London: Jessica Kingsley Publishers.

Rennison, G. (1962) *Man on his own: Social work and industrial society*, Melbourne: Melbourne University Press.

Revans, L. (2007) 'Finding the time', *Community Care*, April, pp 18-19.

Richards, S. (2000) 'Bridging the divide: elders and the assessment process', *British Journal of Social Work*, vol 30, no 1, pp 37-49.

Richardson, L. (1990) *Writing strategies: Reaching diverse audiences*, Newbury Park, CA: Sage Publications.

Richmond, M. (1917) *Social diagnosis*, New York, NY: Russell Sage Foundation.

Ritchie, J. and Lewis, J. (2003) *Qualitative research practice: A guide for social science students and researchers*, London: Sage Publications.

Ritzer, G. (2003) *Contemporary sociological theory and its classical roots: The basics*, New York, NY: McGraw Hill.

Ritzer, G. and Goodman, D. (2004) *Modern sociological theory*, New York, NY: McGraw Hill.

Rule, J.B. (1974) *Private lives and public surveillance: Social control in the computer age*, New York, NY: Schocken.

Schutz, A. (1962) *Collected papers 1. The problem of social reality*, The Hague: Martinus Nijhoff.

Seed, P. (1973) *The expansion of social work in Great Britain*, London: Routledge and Kegan Paul.

Sermeus, W. (2003) 'Information technology and the organisation of patient care', in E. Harlow and S. Webb *Information and communication technologies in the welfare services*, London: Jessica Kingsley Publishers.

Sheffield, A. (1920) *The social case history: Its content and construction*, New York, NY: Russell Sage.

Shepherd, E. (2006) 'Why are records in the public sector organisational assets?', *Records Management Journal*, vol 16, no 1, pp 6-12.

Silverman, D. (1985) *Qualitative methodology and sociology: Describing the social world*, Aldershot: Gower.

Silverman, D. (2001) *Interpreting qualitative data: Methods for analysing talk, text and interaction*, London: Sage Publications.

Simpson, L.C. (1995) *Technology, time and the conversations of modernity*, London: Routledge.

Smart, B. (1985) *Michael Foucault*, London: Routledge.

Smith, C. (2001) 'Trust and confidence: possibilities for social work in "high modernity"', *British Journal of Social Work*, vol 31, no 2, pp 287-305.

Stainton, T. (1998) 'Rights and rhetoric of practice: contradictions for practitioners', in A. Symonds and A. Kelly (eds) *The social construction of community care*, Basingstoke: Macmillan.

Stalker, K. (2003) 'Managing risk and uncertainty in social work: a literature review', *British Journal of Social Work*, vol 3, no 2, pp 211-33.

Steele, L. (1998) 'Keeping a precarious balance', *Community Care*, 9 September, pp 10-16.

Strauss, A.L. (1987) *Qualitative analysis for social scientists*, Cambridge: Cambridge University Press.

Szerszynski, B., Lash, S. and Wynne, B. (1996) 'Introduction: ecology, realism and the social sciences', in S. Lash, B. Szerszynski and B. Wynne (eds) *Risk, environment and modernity: Towards a new ecology*, London: Sage Publications.

Taylor, G. (1993) 'Challenges from the margins', in J. Clarke (ed) *A crisis in care*, London: Sage Publications.

Taylor, J.M., Gilligan, C. and Sullivan, A.M. (1995) *Between voice and silence: Women and girls, race and relationships*, Cambridge, MA: Harvard University Press.

Timms, N. (1968) *The language of social casework*, London: Routledge and Kegan Paul.

Timms, N. (1972) *Recording in social work*, London: Routledge.

Topss England (2004) *The national occupational standards for social work*, London: Topss England.

Turner, B.S. (1997) 'Foreword', in A. Petersen and R. Bunton, *Foucault, health and medicine*, London: Routledge.

Turner, B.S. (1992) 'The interdisciplinary curriculum for social medicine to postmodernism', in B.S. Turner (ed) *Regulating bodies: Essays in medical sociology*, London: Routledge.

Turner, R. (1974) *Ethnomethodology*, Harmondsworth: Penguin.

Walker, S. (2003) 'Information technology and the organisation of patient care', in E. Harlow and S.A. Webb (eds) *Information and communication technologies in the welfare services*, London: Jessica Kingsley Publishers.

Walker, S. and Beckett, C. (2003) *Social work assessment and intervention*, Lyme Regis: Russell House Publishing.

Walker, S., Shemmings, D. and Cleaver, H. (2005) 'Write enough: Pitfalls of practitioners (4)', available online at www.writeenough.org.uk/pitfalls_for_practitioners_4.htm, accessed 19 April 2005.

Weber, M. (1949) '"Objectivity" in social science and social policy', in M. Weber, *The methodology of the social sciences*, New York, NY: The Free Press.

Webb, B. (1926 [1980]) *My apprenticeship*, Cambridge: Cambridge University Press.

Webb, S.A. (2003) 'Technologies in care', in E. Harlow and S.A. Webb (eds) *Information and communication technologies in the welfare services*, London: Jessica Kingsley Publishers.

Webb, S.A. (2006) *Social work in a risk society: Social and political perspectives*, Basingstoke: Palgrave Macmillan.

Wheeler, S. (ed) *On record*, New York, NY: Russell Sage Foundation.

Woodroofe, K. (1966) *From charity to social work*, London: Routledge and Kegan Paul.

Younghusband, E.L. (1959) *Report of the Working Party on Social Workers in the Local Authority, Health and Welfare Services*, London: HMSO.

Zimmerman, D. (1969) 'Record-keeping and the intake process in a public welfare agency', in S. Wheeler (ed) *On record: Files and dossiers in American life*, New York, NY: Russell Sage Foundation.

Index